MW00710033

THE
LAWYER'S
GUIDE TO
FINDING
SUCCESS
IN ANY
JOB
MARKET

THE
LAWYER'S
GUIDE TO
FINDING
SUCCESS
IN ANY
JOB
MARKET

RICHARD L. HERMANN

KAPLAN

PUBLISHING

New York

This publication is designed to provide accurate and authoritative information in regard to the subject matter covered. It is sold with the understanding that the publisher is not engaged in rendering legal, accounting, or other professional service. If legal advice or other expert assistance is required, the services of a competent professional should be sought.

Copyright © 2009 Richard L. Hermann

Published by Kaplan Publishing, a division of Kaplan, Inc.
1 Liberty Plaza, 24th Floor
New York, NY 10006

All rights reserved. The text of this publication, or any part thereof, may not be reproduced in any manner whatsoever without written permission from the publisher.

The Library of Congress-in-Publication Data has been applied for.

Printed in the United States of America

10 9 8 7 6 5 4 3 2 1

ISBN-13: 978-1-60714-521-9

Kaplan Publishing books are available at special quantity discounts to use for sales promotions, employee premiums, or educational purposes. Please email our Special Sales Department to order or for more information at *kaplanpublishing@kaplan.com,* or write to Kaplan Publishing, 1 Liberty Plaza, 24th Floor, New York, NY 10006.

To Anne, for always showing me how to find success.

Contents

Chapter 3
Countercyclical Opportunities

Chapter 4
Hot Practice Areas During the Great Recession

Chapter 5
Using Your Law Degree Outside the Mainstream: Law-Related Careers

Part III
Job-Hunting Tactics for Tough Times

Introduction

THE PAST SEVERAL YEARS have been dark times for everyone, including attorneys. The economy tanked, and the causes of the economic collapse are still being sorted out and understood, even by the so-called experts. When I watched former Federal Reserve Chairman Alan Greenspan, the "Maestro," testify before Congress that he had erred on the side of too much deregulation of the financial markets, I felt that it was probably time to take to the hills with provisions.

Layoffs are sweeping through American lawyerdom like a tsunami. Moreover, they go way beyond law firms. Corporate in-house counsel offices are also feeling the pain, and not just in the financial sector. Before this catastrophe is over, tens of thousands of attorneys will be out of work. State and local governments, especially those constitutionally required to balance their annual budgets, are laying off lawyers. Nonprofits, particularly those that rely on donations or endowments, have also been affected by the need to cut jobs, including legal staff positions. The federal government has been spared thus far. In fact, federal legal hiring is experiencing a resurgence. Massive bailout and stimulus legislation and the return of Keynesian economic theory to prominence all call for spending our way out of the Great Recession (my shorthand term for the deepest economic downturn since the Great Depression).. As a result, what I call Hermann's Corollary to Newton's Third Law of Motion—*For every government action, there is an equal and often greater private sector reaction*—comes into play and creates opportunities for attorneys throughout society.

The attorney job market has been intensely competitive now for a generation. The massive number of layoffs from law firms, corporate in-house counsel offices, nonprofits, and state and local governments in 2008 and 2009 has created a buyer's market unlike any we have

experienced since the Great Depression, when new law graduates had to
pay employers for the privilege of working for them.

Consequently, today's attorney job seeker and career changer has to
be more sophisticated about what to pursue and how to pursue it. *The
Lawyer's Guide to Finding Success in Any Job Market* is designed to teach you
how to accomplish both.

This book is directed at (1) attorneys who have lost their jobs and
want to return to work and (2) attorneys who want to move into practice
areas that have an upside and can protect you against the inevitable
ups and downs of the economy. However, it is more than that: It shows
you where and how to return to work or transition into a psychologi-
cally rewarding, financially satisfying job where you can both achieve
work/life balance and maximize your job security—to the extent that is
possible in the volatile employment environment of the 21st century.

The Lawyer's Guide to Finding Success in Any Job Market is a distillation of
the information and advice I have provided to my legal career transition
counseling clients over the years about recovering from a job loss, viewing
job loss as an opportunity, and doing what is necessary to get back in the
game and enjoy what you spend most of your waking hours doing.

This book is divided into three parts:

Part I presents eleventh-hour strategies to salvage a desperate situation.
It describes four innovative techniques that some of my clients have
employed with success when job loss appeared imminent.

Part II discusses 25 mainstream and law-related "recession-proof" practice areas. Each section is organized as follows:

- Introduction to the Practice Area
- What Is It?
- Who Does It?
- What Does It Pay?
- What Are Its Future Prospects?
- How Do You Break In?
- Where to Go for More Information

Furthermore, part II distinguishes among the following categories of recession-proof practices:

- Mainstream law practice areas that thrive regardless of the economy
- "Countercyclical" opportunities (i.e., practices that do well in a down economy)
- Hot practice areas during the current Great Recession
- Law-related practice areas that are also impervious to economic fluctuations

Part III recommends ten job-hunting strategies that will boost your job prospects and give you an edge in tough economic times (and in good times, for that matter).

Three phenomena that account for my selection of many of the recession-proof practice areas are referenced frequently throughout this book:

1. Science and technology outpacing regulation, forcing government and society to play catch-up
2. A major demographic upheaval—in this case, the mass movement of the Baby Boom generation into senior status
3. Crises that reach the point of critical mass and can no longer be ignored, such as energy policy and healthcare reform

Any one of these upheavals causes opportunity to knock loudly for attorneys. The practice areas detailed in this book largely result from one or more of these paradigm shifts.

If you want additional information about any of these recession-proof practice opportunities, you will find hundreds of references to websites and other resources that you can consult for further elaboration.

Richard Hermann
Arlington, Virginia
July, 2009

Part I

Eleventh-Hour Job Preservation Strategies

Chapter 1

Staying Where You Are

I F YOU ARE THREATENED with job loss (by an employer who is not going out of business), you do not just have to roll over and accept it. There are four job-saving strategies that you can attempt. There is no guarantee they will be successful (they have worked for some, but certainly not all, of my clients), yet they are worth making the effort.

MAKE SURE IT'S *REALLY* OVER

You should, of course, have been preparing for possible job loss your entire career. But if, like most of us, you practiced denial (despite surveys that show that the average attorney who graduates from law school in the first part of the 21st century will hold eight jobs during a career), you probably did not do very much to insulate yourself or develop possible fallback positions.

While the vast majority of my legal career transition counseling clients delude themselves into thinking that their jobs are secure, even after they have been informed otherwise, a few have rushed headlong into incorrect assumptions about their job fate, only to take some rash action they soon regretted.

If you have not been informed that your job security is at risk or the negative signals are just not there, do not assume that the end is near and act on that assumption. Doing so is the opposite of denial and may be just as destructive.

It is also vitally important to have a good sense of where you stand in the organization's esteem. A mass decimation of the workforce does not mean that everyone is out the door. Employers are not that dumb. They will take a number of factors into account in determining who is going to be a victim and who gets to remain. If you were a fly on the wall during a discussion of which attorneys a firm would cut as part of a mass layoff, you would see that these decisions are made with a scalpel, not a broadsword. If you examine who goes and who stays, you will see that the top performers (those who stay) are the last ones to leave and turn out the lights.

Knowing where you fall in the organizational success spectrum can tell you a lot about your jeopardy, if any.

Sometimes it's possible to keep your job even if you have been given notice. The stars have to be perfectly aligned for the following tactic—which I call "keep on keeping on"—to work. They were for one of my clients.

A large national law firm sent me a candidate who was told she was being terminated. From everything I was able to discover, she had a stellar background and achievements as a securities litigator. She specialized in several rather exotic practice subspecialties and speculated that her firm just did not want to build out this particular practice.

She was not only highly intelligent but extremely personable and friendly and very presentable. In short, she had it all.

She did not at all fit the "template" of terminated attorneys from this particular firm with whom I had dealt in the past. I was befuddled by the firm's wanting to let her go after having invested seven years in her career and could not determine what the "hidden" problem might be.

As we proceeded down the counseling road, she often complained that her workload at the firm was such that she had no time to engage in a job search. As our professional relationship grew longer, her workload grew more intense.

The time came when she found herself in her last week at the firm without having made much progress toward a new job. When she came to see me on a Friday—her official last day at the firm—her first comment was that she was in the middle of preparing for a major litigation and that no one at the firm had bothered to assume responsibility for the case or client.

I suggested to her that she report to work on the following Monday morning as if nothing had happened and continue to forge ahead on her trial preparation. She was skeptical, to say the least, but I made the case to her that she had nothing to lose by trying my approach. She said she would think about it over the weekend.

On Monday evening, she called me to report that she had, in fact, gone to work that morning and had spent most of the day developing her case, when her practice area leader walked into her office and assigned her a new project!

Two years later, she made partner in her same firm. No one ever mentioned her "termination" in the intervening period.

Go figure.

Even if you believe that a job loss is imminent, it may be much better if you stick it out in the event that you have not yet found a new position. *It is more difficult to get a new job if you are unemployed than if you are currently working.* Unemployment leaves a "mark of Cain" on your forehead, and while that mark is fainter today than it has been in the past, it is still there.

Besides, you never know what might happen to save the situation in the eleventh hour. For example, sometimes, a "white knight" comes along at the last minute to save a takeover candidate company or a firm about to go belly-up from being absorbed or disappearing. The examples of Goldman Sachs (Warren Buffet and the government), Merrill Lynch (Bank of America), Wachovia (Wells Fargo), and the many other outfits that recklessly invested in or insured toxic mortgage securities—and then were rescued—are instructive. These rescues saved many more jobs than would have been the case had the firms gone down the well-deserved toilet.

SUGGEST AN ALTERNATIVE WORK ARRANGEMENT

If you know or have strong evidence that being let go may be imminent, consider proposing an *outsourcing* arrangement to your employer. Outsourcing for an individual means moving from being an employee to becoming an independent contractor. Technically, you would be performing the same job, but your employment relationship would be altered.

Several years ago, the U.S. government was about to deep-six several hundred employees who performed background investigations of prospective federal employees. Instead, the affected employees proposed that they form a company and provide the services from outside, at favorable rates to the government. This proved quite successful, especially because the new private company was also able to promote its services to other private sector government contractors who needed to vet new hires who required security clearances. The private contractors established a firm that knew the government investigation and clearance process inside out. The government saved a lot of money. The new firm's employees kept their jobs. It was a win-win situation for all concerned.

The economics of outsourcing are often very favorable to employers. If the employer does not have to pay benefits, it may well be interested in your proposal. Certainly, you would be earning less compensation than you do as a full-time employee, but consider the alternative. Moreover, outsourcing is a means of securing financing (the ongoing "paycheck") for your entrepreneurial spirit.

Try to recognize outsourcing opportunities before they mature. A strong indicator of outsourcing potential is if the work is periodic and the staff handling the function is not consistently busy. Another is if your analysis clearly shows that you can save your employer money by going off the payroll.

You may, of course, propose other compensation or flexible work arrangements to your employer: hourly, fixed-fee, project-based, percentage of savings, telecommuting, part-time; etc.

If you think the axe might soon fall, this is the best time to wax creative when it comes to proposing alternative work arrangements.

TRANSFER YOUR SKILLS TO ANOTHER PRACTICE AREA IN THE ORGANIZATION

My standard opening to almost every candidate being laid off is to pose the following questions:

- Are there any practice areas to which you could transfer your skills and experience?
- Is there anything else that you could do to remain with the organization (assuming you so desire)?

Every attorney develops multiple skills during both law school and practice. Often, these are skills the attorney does not even know he or she possesses.

As an example, litigators only try a small handful of their cases. The overwhelming majority settle before trial. Consequently, litigators develop in-depth experience negotiating settlements. Negotiating a case settlement is very much akin to negotiating a transaction. That means that a typical litigator is also an accomplished transactional lawyer, something very few litigators realize and, as a result, omit from their résumés and from their sights.

In addition, many attorneys and law students have developed the following skill sets that might be transferable within many legal organizations:

- Project management skills
- Interpersonal skills
- Teaching and training skills
- Oral communication skills
- Writing, drafting, and editing skills
- Analytical and strategic skills
- Research skills
- Legal document preparation and management skills
- Investigative skills
- Organizational skills
- Risk management skills

What you need to do is (1) identify your transferable skills, (2) determine where in your organization these skills are valued, and then (3) make the case for a transfer by doing the following:

- Draft a document that includes the following:
  1. Your transferable skill sets
  2. How, where, and when you developed these skill sets (give examples)
  3. Where else they could be employed within your organization
  4. Your value to the transferee entity
- Craft a 30–60 second transferable skills "sales pitch," which you can deliver verbally to your organization's decision makers.

Before severing—or getting severed—from your employer, carefully investigate whether roles exist within the organization where the skills you have developed might be valuable. Do not expect your employer to delve into your background to figure this out. It is up to you.

MOVE WITHIN THE ORGANIZATION, BUT OUTSIDE THE MAINSTREAM

Law Firm Subsidiaries

As more and more law firms realize that they are businesses just like any other, they desire to expand their offerings to existing clients and to attract new clients by launching subsidiary businesses. Another factor prompting law firms to go this route is competition, not only from other law firms but also from other non–legal professional services firms. Law firms have seen that accounting firms, consulting firms, real estate organizations, and others have begun offering their clients legal and law-related services, labeling them as something else to avoid the impact of Unauthorized Practice of Law regulations.

To date, several hundred law firms—primarily large ones—have adopted this subsidiary business model. A number of law firms have launched more than one subsidiary. The services most often offered by these subsidiaries include the following:

- Online training in such areas as human resources and compliance
- Business counseling on entry into foreign countries
- Crisis management
- Insurance-related services
- Government relations and lobbying
- Sports and talent representation
- Wealth management and financial advising

When confronted with likely job loss, you need to examine your law firm's subsidiary businesses to determine if you can make a compelling case for transferring to one of them as an alternative to being laid off.

Law Firm Support Positions

One of my clients, a law firm litigator, was notified that he was being terminated. He had developed a reputation among his colleagues for his computer prowess. I suggested that he approach the firm about transferring from his litigation role to one in which he would have formal responsibility for the firm's technology. We crafted a document making the pitch, and he was able to persuade the firm that this was worth a try.

I am not suggesting that this approach works all of the time. But with the transformation of law firms from professional services partnerships to bottom-line businesses, the number of law firm management and support positions is growing and now includes the following: firm administration, knowledge management, client development and marketing, technology, recruitment, professional development, practice area support, and more. A law degree is advantageous and preferred by some firms for these positions.

Part II

Legal Careers That Thrive in Any Economy

Chapter 2

The Dynamic Dozen: Twelve Mainstream Opportunities

WHILE WHAT GOES ON in the general economy is of utmost importance to your legal career, some modern-day law practice areas are assured of thriving despite economic conditions. The principal reason why these practice areas are destined to be solid is that they are much more heavily impacted by noneconomic factors, such as demographics, political and policy considerations, and commodity scarcity and corresponding pricing, to name a few, than by economic factors.

The 12 mainstream practice areas described below all fall within this paradigm.

These selected practice areas are not presented in any kind of order of significance or opportunity. The only organizing principle in this section is that areas that bear a relationship to one another are presented sequentially.

Before beginning a discussion of the practice areas, it's important to be able to answer the following question:

How can you tell if a practice area is growing? Here are three very good indicators:

1. The practice area spawns a large number of seminars, conferences, and webcasts. Classic recent examples of this phenomenon include homeland security law, corporate governance, climate change, and e-discovery. Another indicator is how much is being charged for the seminar. The higher the cost, the hotter the topic.
2. A survey of law firm websites gauges that firms are writing about the practice area in their newsletters, blogs, white papers, etc. In late 2007, the top five issues for law firms were corporate governance, health law, food and drug law, international business, and intellectual property. In late 2008, the emphasis had changed to financial services, health law, securities law, environmental law, and intellectual property.
3. Umbrella organization membership is increasing. Membership in the National Employment Lawyers Association, for example, increased substantially in the last decade.

HEALTH LAW

Introduction

Health law opportunities for attorneys in both mainstream law and nontraditional law-related arenas are expanding rapidly. Hospitals and other healthcare providers confront the same array of problems that other corporations face, such as governance, employee relations, and transactional matters, plus additional issues that are often more acute and time-sensitive, with shorter windows for favorable resolution.

As federal and state governments attempt to respond to growing public pressure to do something about a U.S. healthcare system that is much too expensive (healthcare expenditures are rising at three times the rate of [pre–Great Recession] inflation), broken (my own physician says so), and in need of massive overhaul (the World Health Organization ranks the U.S. healthcare system 37th, behind even some developing world countries), the number of both mainstream attorney and law-related positions is growing in the public sector as well as in the private sector, which must respond to public sector regulatory initiatives.

In addition to profitability, four metrics underscore the health law practices as a major expansion arena for law firms, healthcare provider organizations, healthcare regulators, and a variety of other entities:

1. The dramatic growth of health law professional organizations, such as the American Health Lawyers Association; American College of Legal Medicine; American Society of Law, Medicine and Ethics; American Society for Healthcare Risk Management; and the Health Care Compliance Association, all of which have increased their membership rolls substantially in recent years, a sure sign of a strong and expanding practice area

2. The large number of health law seminars, Continuing Legal Education programs, conferences, and such and the premium price charged for many of these programs

3. The inevitability of at least some healthcare reform, restructuring, and increased regulation—an overhaul likely during the Obama administration. A great deal of positioning and repositioning is going on within the health law community in an attempt to take advantage of the opportunities resulting from healthcare reform

4. New technologies, such as telemedicine and e-prescribing, plus treatment breakthroughs, new drugs, etc., which arrive fraught with cutting-edge legal, regulatory, ethical, business, and other issues yet to be resolved.

Law firm, corporate, nonprofit, and government health law practices are booming. Health law has become one of the most profitable law firm practice areas. Many firms are now rushing to add food and drug regulatory practices to their health law mix in anticipation of stepped-up Food and Drug Administration (FDA) regulation (see section on Food and Drug law). Health law practice will only continue to grow.

What Is It?

Health law is among the most dynamic and wide-ranging legal careers and is changing constantly, usually by accretion—adding new issues to the mix that compel lawmakers to scramble to keep pace. The practice is incredibly diverse, replete with numerous subspecialties.

Law Firm Practice. A law firm healthcare practice involves one or all of the following issues and subspecialties:

- Accreditation
- Acquisitions
- Affiliations
- Antitrust
- Bioethics advice
- Business planning
- Certificates of Need
- Civil and administrative defense
- Compliance
- Corporate governance
- Corporate structure and organization
- Credentialing
- Data privacy
- Divestitures of health facilities and businesses
- Food and drug matters
- Finance
- Government relations
- Guardianships
- Healthcare fraud
- Healthcare technology matters
- Hospital/physician contractual relationships
- Insurance regulation
- Internal and government investigations
- Joint ventures
- Labor, employment, and employee benefits
- Legal audits for healthcare organizations
- Licensing of facilities and medical staff
- Managed care contracting
- Managed care defense
- Medical staff matters
- Medicare/Medicaid/ private insurance
- Mental health law
- Patient consent
- Peer review
- Physician contracting and recruitment
- Practitioner defense (medical malpractice)
- Real estate
- Regulatory counseling
- Restructuring
- Representing healthcare providers
- Risk management
- Tax-exempt status
- Telemedicine
- Transactions

The potential client pool is enormous; it includes academic medical centers, ambulatory care facilities, assisted living facilities, clinical laboratories, continuing care retirement communities, diagnostic facilities, dialysis companies, insurers, e-health companies, HMOs, health plans, healthcare systems, home healthcare agencies, hospices, hospitals, imaging services providers, long-term care facilities, medical equipment companies, nursing homes, PPOs, physician-based entities, physician practice management companies, physician practices, pharmaceutical firms, pharmacists, benefits managers, and trade and professional associations.

Healthcare Provider Practices. Healthcare provider organizations deal with many of the same legal issues that concern their outside counsel. While they outsource many legal matters to law firms, certain core issues are commonly handled in-house, at least in the first instance:

- Intellectual property matters
- Technology transfer
- Contract negotiations and drafting
- Staff licensing and credentialing
- Transactions
- Labor and employee relations
- Grants and procurement
- Regulatory compliance
- Interaction with regulators
- Accreditation
- Clinical risk assessment
- Management and staff training
- Claims against the provider
- Some administrative and trial litigation
- Employee benefits
- Medicare, Medicaid and insurance
- Litigation management
- Healthcare fraud and abuse
- HIPAA and privacy
- Stark I, II and III (physician self-referral)
- Product offerings

Healthcare Regulators and Other Government Agencies' Practices. Federal and state agency health law practice is another growing field spurred by many factors such as the advent of HIPAA (Health Insurance Portability and Accountability Act), primarily its privacy mandates, and the efforts at Medicare, Medicaid, and private health insurance fraud recovery by the Departments of Health and Human Services (HHS) and Justice (DOJ) and by Medicaid Fraud Control Bureaus and other state government agencies. Government health law practices are also fueled by the growth of Medicare and Medicaid programs, including Medicare Part D—the Medicare Prescription Drug, Improvement, and Modernization Act (Pub.L. 108-173); the Stark Laws (42 U.S.C. §1395nn), dealing with physician self-referral; tobacco regulation; skyrocketing Social Security Disability Income dockets; stem cell research regulations; nursing home quality of care enforcement; veterans' health problems; organ donation regulation; and others. Government health law practice will grow even more during the Obama administration, because healthcare reform is such a high policy priority.

Who Does It?

Private Practice. Private practice encompasses large national law firms; smaller firms; and boutique firms, focus their entire practice on health law. Sole practitioners are also in this mix.

Not all law firms that tout their healthcare practices are created equal. Just visiting their websites will not tell you whether they actually do all of the things they proclaim or just *aspire* to do them. Also, keep in mind that health law covers an awful lot of ground and that some firms will emphasize certain aspects of the practice over others.

As for other healthcare employers, it's more straightforward. For the most part, healthcare providers and regulators pretty much are who they say they are on their websites and in their brochures.

Healthcare Providers. Hospitals and other healthcare providers are the major employers of health law attorneys. Most legal positions in the provider community are found in hospital general counsel offices.

However, not every hospital or healthcare provider has an in-house legal staff. As a rough rule of thumb, hospitals with 200 or more beds (more than 1,600 such hospitals in the United States) are the most likely to have their own in-house legal offices. Hospitals of this size may also employ attorneys in their Risk Management Office, Compliance Department, Contract and Procurement Office, Ethics Office, Ombudsman Office, and/or a Patient Rights and Advocacy Office.

See the American Hospital Directory (*www.ahd.com/freesearch.php3*).

HMOs are the largest employer of health law professionals after hospitals. See *www.the-health-pages.com/directory/hmo.html.*

Federal Government. The U.S. government has more than 200 legal and law-related offices that have a health law practice employing several thousand attorneys, a number certain to increase in the near term. Government healthcare employers with the most substantial health law practices are these:

- U.S. Department of Health and Human Services (49 offices) (*www.hhs.gov*)
- Social Security Administration (24 offices, plus 147 Hearing Offices nationwide) (*www.ssa.gov*)
- Occupational Safety and Health Review Commission (3 offices in Headquarters & Regional Offices in Atlanta and Denver) (*www.oshrc.gov*)
- U.S. Department of Defense (5 offices) (*www.defenselink.mil*)
- U.S. Department of Veterans Affairs (29 offices) (*www.va.gov*)
- U.S. Department of Labor (43 offices) (*www.dol.gov*)
- U.S. Department of Agriculture (2 offices) (*www.usda.gov*)
- U.S. Department of Energy—Office of Laboratory Counsel, Los Alamos, NM (*www.energy.gov*)
- Federal Mine Safety and Health Review Commission (3 offices) (*www.fmshrc.gov*)
- Federal Trade Commission Bureau of Competition— Health Care Division (*www.ftc.gov*)
- U.S. Agency for International Development—Bureau for Global Health (*www.usaid.gov*)
- U.S. Department of Justice—Civil Division, Office of Consumer Litigation; Criminal Division, Fraud Section; U.S. Attorneys' Offices nationwide (*www.usdoj.gov*)
- Government Accountability Office—Office of General Counsel (*www.gao.gov*)
- Congress—19 Senate and House Committees and Subcommittees, plus 26 Congressional Caucuses*

  **Note:* Caucuses sometimes have a limited life span. Also, their names tend to change often.

State and Local Government. While the primary governmental organization administering and regulating healthcare programs in each state is typically the State Department of Health (or comparable nomenclature), ever-increasing health-related concerns have prompted a division of labor and of powers among more than one agency in most states. This means expanded job opportunities and career options for attorneys. Separate state agencies might include organizations responsible for aging, alcohol and drug programs, children's health, children's health insurance, emergency medical services, health insurance generally, health planning, healthcare fraud (usually a section within the Attorney General's office), managed care, mental health, occupational safety and health, rehabilitation, and veterans affairs.

Health agencies in different states do not necessarily share the same priorities at the same time. Hawaii, for example, focuses attention on the health effects of volcanic ash emissions, a nonissue almost everywhere else. However, all states generally share the following regulatory concerns:

- Licensing and regulating healthcare providers, suppliers, and clinical laboratories
- Certificate of Need regulation, requiring certain providers to obtain state approval before offering new or expanded services or making major capital expenditures
- Registering homemaker companion agencies and health-care services pools
- Certifying home health agencies and hospices for Medicare and Medicaid

Following are the places to look for in health-related law jobs in state and local government:

- *State health departments* are the first place to turn for overall health regulatory and administrative responsibilities. Virtually all state health departments have job and career pages on their websites. In addition, many permit you to search for the entities they regulate, making these websites a good source of targeted, private sector employer information.

The Centers for Disease Control and Prevention links to each state health department at *www.cdc.gov/mmwr/ international/relres.html.*

- *State healthcare professional licensing boards* increasingly hire attorneys because they have become more and more embroiled in disputes with licensees. This is especially true of physician licensing boards but is also spreading to boards that license nurses, therapists, and other healthcare professionals.

  How different states execute licensing and disciplinary functions is not uniform. Some have separate boards for each healthcare profession. Others perform the functions under one roof for all or a number of healthcare professions.

  The American Medical Association's website links to each state's medical licensing board (*www.ama-assn.org/ama/ pub/education-careers/becoming-physician/medical-licensure/state-medical-boards.shtml*).

- *State insurance fraud bureaus,* found in 42 states, have insurance fraud bureaus, often with law enforcement powers. Some states require insurers to establish Special Investigations Units (SIUs) and to file antifraud plans with the state insurance department. Increasingly, fraud bureaus focus on health insurance fraud.

  Link to state insurance fraud bureaus at *www.insurance fraud.org/links.htm#fraud_bureaus.*

- *State Medicaid Fraud Control Units* (MFCUs) investigate and prosecute healthcare providers that defraud the Medicaid program. MFCUs also review complaints of abuse or neglect of nursing home residents, among other responsibilities.

  The National Association of Medicaid Fraud Control Units links to state Medicaid Fraud Control Units at *www. namfcu.net/states.*

- *State and local long-term care ombudsman programs* address complaints and advocate improvements in the long-term care (LTC) system. There are 53 state LTC ombudsman programs with networks of almost 600 regional (local) programs

  Approximately 1,300 paid ombudsmen are responsible for oversight of 16,750 nursing facilities with 1.8 million beds and 47,000 other residential care facilities with 1.1 million beds, according to the National Health Policy Forum.

You can link to LTC ombudsman programs at the National Association of State Long-Term Care Ombudsman Programs website (*www.nasop.org*).

- *State Medicaid agencies* administer the Medicaid program in the states. You can link to each state's Medicaid agency at *www.nasmd.org.*
- *State Medicare Quality Improvement Organizations* (QIOs) are physician-directed organizations that share information about best practices with physicians, hospitals, and nursing homes. QIOs are paid by Medicare to resolve appeals by Medicare enrollees protesting early discharge from a hospital stay and to investigate complaints by Medicare enrollees regarding the quality of care, among other duties.

  Go to QualityNet.org (*www.qualitynet.org*) to link to state QIOs.

Insurance Companies. Health and/or disability insurers are the primary legal and law-related employers in the industry. Virtually every insurance company has, at a minimum, an in-house counsel office, a litigation management unit, and a regulatory compliance office. Most insurance companies have also established SIUs, while some insurance companies outsource the SIU function to other insurers.

Complex cases involving large-scale criminal operations or individuals that repeatedly stage accidents may be turned over to the National Insurance Crime Bureau (*www.nicb.org*), an industry-sponsored organization with special expertise in preparing fraud cases for trial.

Other Companies. Many companies in industries other than healthcare nevertheless have healthcare law practices; for example, the American Red Cross, Marriott, and GE Healthcare Finance and companies in the pharmaceutical industry (which is rapidly consolidating), to name just a few.

Other Nonprofit Healthcare Provider Organizations. There is a large and growing number of healthcare law, policy, and advocacy organizations, research entities, think tanks, foundations, universities, etc. that employ attorneys (see below). Healthcare nonprofits are also subject to increased government regulatory oversight and examination, which has necessitated the hiring of in-house attorneys.

Nonprofit healthcare policy and research organizations that employ attorneys include the following:

- Alliance for Health Reform (*www.allhealth.org*)
- American Society of Law, Medicine & Ethics (*www.aslme.org*)
- Center for Healthcare Strategies (*www.chcs.org*)
- Center for Studying Health System Change (*www.hschange.com*)
- The Centers for Law and the Public's Health (*www.public healthlaw.net*)
- Georgetown University Institute for Health Care Research & Policy (*www.georgetown.edu/research/ihcrp*)
- Institute for Health Policy Solutions (*www.ihps.org*)
- Kaiser Permanente Center for Health Research (*www.kpchr.org*)
- Leaders' Project on the State of American Health Care (*www.bipartisanpolicy.org*)
- National Health Policy Forum (*www.nhpf.org*)
- Public Citizen Health Research Group (*www.citizen.org/hrg*)

Healthcare trade and professional associations have a powerful presence in Washington, D.C., in major state capitals, and in the larger cities (e.g., New York, Philadelphia, Baltimore, Chicago, Cleveland, Kansas City, Los Angeles, San Francisco, Seattle). Many of them have a General Counsel office, all of them have Government Affairs/Relations offices, and some of them have Ethics offices that advise members with respect to professional responsibility questions.

Representative healthcare trade and professional associations include these:

- America's Health Insurance Plans (*www.ahip.org*)
- American Academy of Nurse Practitioners (*www.aanp.org*)
- American Bar Association Health Law Section (*www.abanet.org/health*)
- American Health Lawyers Association (*www.healthlawyers.org*)

- American Hospital Association (*www.aha.org*)
- American Medical Association (*www.ama.org*)
- American Nurses Association (*www.nursingworld.org*)
- American Psychological Association (*www.apa.org*)
- American Society for Healthcare Risk Management (*www.ashrm.org*)
- American Telemedicine Association (*www.americantelemed.org*)
- Blue Cross and Blue Shield Association (*www.bcbs.com*)
- International Association of Special Investigation Units (*www.iasiu.org*)
- National Association of Health Data Organizations (*www.nahdo.org*)
- Pharmaceutical Research and Manufacturers of America (*www.phrma.org*)

Healthcare advocacy organizations are typically organized around specific healthcare issues on which they lobby legislators and regulators; file lawsuits; and represent individuals, interest groups, and/or businesses in healthcare disputes.

- Alliance for Healthcare Reform (*www.allhealth.org*)
- American Association of Retired Persons (*www.aarp.org*)
- Bazelon Center for Mental Health Law (*www.bazelon.org*)
- Center for Health Transformation (*www.healthtransformation.net*)
- Council for Affordable Health Insurance (*www.cahi.org*)
- National Association for Healthcare Quality (*www.nahq.org*)
- National Committee for Quality Assurance (*www.ncqa.org*)
- National Health Care Anti-Fraud Association (*www.nhcaa.org*)

Legal services organizations such as the following also employ attorneys:

- National Health Law Program (NheLP) (*www.healthlaw.org*)
- Children's Law Center Health Access Project (*www.childrenslawcenter.org*)

Healthcare foundations that employ attorneys include the following:

- Commonwealth Fund (*www.cmwf.org*)
- Grantmakers in Health (*www.gih.org*)
- Kaiser Family Foundation (*www.kff.org*)
- Medical Outcomes Trust (*www.outcomes-trust.org*)

Other healthcare-related nonprofits that do not fit neatly into one of the categories listed above include the following:

- California Telemedicine and eHealth Center (*www.cteconline.org*)
- Center for Practical Bioethics (*www.practicalbioethics.org*)
- Joint Commission on the Accreditation of Healthcare Organizations (*www.jcaho.org*)
- Kaiser Permanente (*www.kaiserpermanente.org*)
- National Institute for Health Care Management (*www.nihcm.org*)
- New York Alliance Against Insurance Fraud (*www.fraudny.com*)

Law Firm Subsidiaries. Law firms that want to compete effectively with management consulting firms and maximize revenues from existing clients have launched a broad array of subsidiary businesses, a number of which deal with healthcare matters. Because the parent organizations are law firms, there is a hiring preference for attorneys who also bring healthcare expertise to the table.

Selected law firms with health-related subsidiaries are listed below:

- Bingham Consulting Group (Bingham McCutchen) (*www.binghamconsulting.com*)
- Concord Health Partners (DKW Law Group) (*www.dkwlaw.com/website/dkwlaw.nsf/ancillary?OpenForm*)
- Dorsey Health Strategies (Dorsey & Whitney) (*www.dorseyhealthstrategies.com*)
- Implant Purchasing Solutions (Duane Morris) (*www.implantpurchasing.com*)
- ML Strategies (Mintz Levin) (*www.mlstrategies.com*)

Consulting Firms. Healthcare consulting firms have proliferated in recent years, with no end in sight, thanks to the large number of difficult emerging issues that healthcare providers must address. Healthcare is such a dynamic, fast-changing industry that their growth prospects are very positive. A great deal of their attention is on health law and law-related areas, including the following:

- Anti-kickbacks
- Certificate of Need Issues
- Development and financing of facilities
- Employment agreements
- Ethics
- Governance and regulatory compliance
- Fraud and abuse prevention
- Litigation management
- Privacy
- Insurance reimbursement
- Licensing and credentialing
- Legislative and public policy issues
- Physician-hospital transactions
- Practice management
- Staff privileges
- Stark rules
- Telemedicine counseling

International Organizations. Several international organizations that hire U.S. citizens have healthcare legal and/or law-related practices and functions:

- World Health Organization Geneva, Switzerland (2 offices) (*www.who.int*)
- Pan American Health Organization, Washington, D.C., and Santiago, Chile (3 offices) (*www.paho.org*)
- International Committee of the Red Cross, Geneva, Switzerland (*www.icrc.org*)

Research Integrity Offices. Research integrity is a growing area of health law concern. It is broadly defined as covering research misconduct, protection of human subjects, welfare of laboratory animals, conflicts of interest, data management practices, mentor and trainee responsibilities, collaborative research, authorship and publication, peer review, policies, and codes and guidelines.

Research integrity offices can be found in government, colleges and universities, and healthcare provider organizations. A representative list follows:

- U.S. Department of HHS, Office of Research Integrity (*www.ori.hhs.gov*)
- National Science Foundation, Office of Inspector General (*www.nsf.gov/oig*)
- Cornell University, Office of Research Integrity and Assurance (*www.oria.cornell.edu*)
- Duke University School of Medicine, Research Integrity Office (*http://medschool.duke.edu/modules/som_conflict/index. php?id=1*)
- University of California, Office of Ethics, Compliance and Audit Services (*www.universityofcalifornia. edu/compaudit/researchcomp*)
- University of Louisville Hospital, Office of Research Integrity (*www.uoflhealthcare.org/Default.aspx?tabid=523*)
- Children's Mercy Hospital, Office for Research Integrity, Kansas City, MO (*www.childrensmercy.org/Content/view. aspx?id=2792*)

Law-Related Healthcare Careers. In addition to mainstream practice, a growing array of law-related healthcare careers are open to attorneys. Following are the principal ones:

- Healthcare regulatory compliance
- Healthcare privacy
- Healthcare risk management
- Healthcare ethics
- Health policy
- Government/legislative affairs/lobbying
- Legal nurse consulting
- Research integrity
- Health technology transfer
- Insurance product consulting
- Patient rights advocacy
- Healthcare and disability claims
- Healthcare consulting
- Healthcare contracting and procurement

What Does It Pay?

The healthcare industry is full of providers with both money and survival interests at stake, a combination that drives up the price of legal services.

Health law attorney salaries vary widely, depending on location, industry, employment sector, experience, and the nature of the work. Private practitioners in major law firms are at the high end of the health law salary scale, with starting salaries around $160,000 and median salaries in the $300,000+ range. Smaller law firms pay substantially less, the exception being health law boutique firms that are highly specialized. Their compensation regimes can approach those of major law firms.

Corporate compensation for attorneys is comparable to general counsel office compensation across the board, subject to geography, employer size, and the nature of the practice. Corporate compliance lawyers earn the most, with median salaries in the $200,000–$250,000 range. In-house health law transactional lawyers with midlevel experience generally earn between $110,000 and $160,000. Interestingly, geographic variances for transactional attorneys are minimal. In-house litigators earn less, with median salaries ranging from around $80,000 to $140,000, depending on location (large cities in the Northeast and California being at the high end).

General government pay scales also apply to attorneys engaged in a health law practice. Federal salaries are usually higher than state salaries for comparable positions and range between $50,000 for entry-level lawyers to $150,000 for senior attorneys.

Salaries at healthcare nonprofits are substantially lower than in other sectors.

Attorneys working in law-related positions in the health industry generally earn less than their attorney colleagues. However, certain fields are advancing their pay scales faster than the overall rise in attorney pay, especially compliance and risk management. Compliance salaries for attorneys with very little or no experience range from around $44,000 in rural states to $75,000 in New York City and San Francisco. Risk management professional salaries for less experienced individuals are very similar to compliance compensation, ranging from around $47,000 in rural areas to $80,000 in the Northeast and California.

Future Prospects

One of the factors making health law such a vibrant field is its rapidly changing technological, scientific, and ethical environment, which makes it extremely fast moving and cutting-edge.

In addition to the huge challenges that will be addressed by the major healthcare reform initiatives being proposed and vigorously debated, a spate of emerging issues will keep the legal community busy for years to come.

Skyrocketing Healthcare Costs. Americans spend more than $24 trillion a year on healthcare—twice as much as any other nation in terms of the percentage of gross domestic product (17 percent). In return, we rank 45th in life expectancy and 37th in a World Health Organization study on the performance of national health systems. Seventy-five cents of every healthcare dollar are spent on chronic disease treatment, while only 5 cents are spent on prevention (four out of every five chronic diseases could be prevented).

For more information:

- National Conference of State Legislatures (*www.ncsl.org/ programs/health/healthcostsrpt.htm*)
- Brookings Institution Engelberg Center for Healthcare Reform (*www.brookings.edu/health.aspx*)
- Center for Health Transformation (*www.healthtransformation.net*)

Telemedicine Licensing and Credentialing. The rapid and accelerating development of new information technologies is rendering healthcare geographic boundaries anachronistic. "Telemedicine" is the use of electronic information and telecommunications technologies to support long-distance clinical healthcare, patient and professional health education, public health, and health administration. The practice of medicine across state lines includes any medical act that occurs when the patient is physically located within a state and the physician is located outside the state.

Telemedicine technologies typically include videoconferencing, the Internet, store-and-forward imaging, streaming media, and land and wireless communications. The potential of telemedicine exponentially increases access to health information and expands opportunities for practice across state and even national borders.

However, telemedicine remains severely constrained by a state-based licensure system. The current state-specific medical licensing regimes are inadequate to keep up with medical delivery technology.

Eleven states (Alabama, Minnesota, Montana, Nevada, New Mexico, Ohio, Oregon, South Dakota, Tennessee, Texas, and Utah) permit out-of-state physicians to provide telemedicine services to their in-state residents, provided the physicians obtain a special telemedicine license or register with the state medical board. In all other states, physicians must obtain a full state medical license to deliver telemedicine care across state lines. Getting a license in each state is expensive and time consuming.

The gradual liberalization of state telemedicine licensing require-ments and the ethical issues associated with telemedicine, along with the regulation of healthcare provider services via telemedicine by healthcare professionals other than physicians, will generate a great deal of legal work now and in the future.

For more information:

- Office for the Advancement of Telehealth (*www.hrsa.gov/ telehealth*)
- Center for Telehealth and E-Health Law (*www.ctel.org*)
- American Telemedicine Association (*www.americantelemed.org*)

"Right of Conscience" Issues. The typical right of conscience situation arises in the pro-life versus pro-choice debate when healthcare workers who are pro-life refuse to perform abortions or when pharmacists refuse to dispense contraceptives, especially the "morning-after pill."

One of the Bush administration's last regulatory moves expanded protections for healthcare workers who invoked right of conscience to refuse to offer or participate in certain procedures due to moral objec-tions. The new rule took effect January 18, 2009.

The Obama administration announced in February 2009 that it would rescind the rule.

Forty-seven states have adopted "conscience clauses," which give pri-vate hospitals, nurses, and physicians the right to conscientiously object to participating in abortion. Right of conscience advocates are lobbying for laws that recognize an affirmative civil right for all healthcare providers—both individuals and institutions—to refuse to participate in the provision of any healthcare service to which they conscientiously object. To date, only Mississippi has such a sweeping law.

For more information:

- 73 *Federal Register* 78071–78101 (December 19, 2008)
- Center for Bioethics and Human Dignity (*www.cbhd.org*)
- Americans United for Life (*www.aul.org/Rights_of_Conscience*)
- Planned Parenthood Federation of America (*www.planned parenthood.org*)

Healthcare Privacy. This is a big issue with many nuances, made even bigger by virtue of the call for healthcare reform. Almost every American has heard about the HIPAA privacy provisions, and healthcare providers and millions of healthcare consumers have been frustrated and confused by them. This situation is about to get worse.

A centerpiece of the Obama administration's healthcare reform proposals is digitizing healthcare record keeping. E-health privacy concerns focus on the potential for inadvertent disclosure of patient healthcare information, as well as medical identity theft. Both concerns will create numerous opportunities for health law attorneys in every employment sector—law firms, corporations, nonprofit hospitals, and government.

For more information:

- Health Privacy Project (*www.healthprivacy.org*)
- U.S. Department of Health and Human Services—
  Office of the National Coordinator for Health Information
  Technology (http://*healthhit.hbs.gov*)
- Workgroup for Electronic Data Interchange (*www.wedi.org*)

Healthcare Transparency. You can find a great deal of information about your attorney, broker, CPA and many other professionals—but not about physicians.

The National Practitioner Data Bank (NPDB) was created by Congress and implemented by the Department of Health and Human

Services (HHS). The NPDB is designed to facilitate access to healthcare practitioners' professional credentials by prospective employers and out-of-state licensing and disciplinary agencies. NPDB information is not available to the general public.

The parallel Healthcare Integrity and Protection Data Bank (HIPDB) was established pursuant to HIPAA to combat fraud and abuse in health insurance and healthcare delivery. HIPDB information is also unavailable to the general public.

A few states make some practitioner information available to the public. However, the majority keep this information from the consumer.

Another transparency issue concerns hospital quality data, which is largely the province of the private accreditation agency and not even the government.

For more information:

- National Organization for State Medical and Osteopathic Board Executive Directors (*www.docboard.org*)
- AboutHealthTransparency.org (*www.abouthealthtransparency.org*)

Blurring the Lines of Professional Practice. Nonphysician healthcare professionals are assuming more responsibilities for patient interaction and care. This recent development has healthcare delivery, economic, and credentialing implications. Payment issues arise for the obvious reason that physicians are paid much more than other healthcare deliverers. Nevertheless, physician practices that employ auxiliary healthcare professionals often bill patients and third-party payers the same as if a physician were providing the service.

Economic pressures drive this issue in two other ways: (1) Many physicians feel that their livelihood is threatened by other "competing" healthcare professionals, and (2) other healthcare professionals feel underpaid when providing the same service as a physician. Another matter of concern is the denial of hospital privileges to nonphysician healthcare professionals.

A related set of issues arises from new and creative partnering arrangements between physicians and hospitals, including hospital acquisitions of physician practices, hospital syndications, and joint ownership arrangements between nonprofits and for-profit entities.

For more information:

- American Academy of Physician Assistants (*www.aapa.org*)
- American Academy of Nurse Practitioners (*www.aanp.org*)
- American Association of Nurse Anesthetists (*www.aana.com*)

Bioethics. The ethical implications of interaction between healthcare providers (e.g., hospitals and physicians) and vendors (e.g., pharmaceutical and medical device companies) give rise to some of the thorniest issues in healthcare today. Stem cell research, end-of-life care, reproductive technologies, cloning, biomedical research, gene therapies, genetic testing, human subject research, human specimen repositories, "neuroethics," laboratory animal use, and clinical trial ethical considerations are some of the issues currently on the bioethics agenda. An increasing number of attorneys are being sought throughout the healthcare community to help identify and resolve these vexing issues.

For more information:

- National Institutes of Health (*http://bioethics.od.nih.gov*)
- American Society of Law, Medicine & Ethics (*www.aslme.org*)
- Bioethics Portal, National Library of Medicine (*www.nlm.nih. gov/bsd/bioethics.html*)
- Bioethics.com (*http://bioethics.com*)

Expedited Partner Therapy. The Centers for Disease Control and Prevention (CDC) defines Expedited Partner Therapy (EPT) as the clinical practice of treating the sex partners of patients diagnosed with a sexually transmitted disease (STD) by providing prescriptions or medications to the patient to take to his or her partner without the healthcare provider first examining the partner.

Assuring treatment of the sex partners of persons with STDs has been a healthcare focus for decades. "Partner management," the older, traditional means of informing, evaluating, and treating sex partners of infected persons, relies upon either patients or healthcare providers to notify partners of their exposure to an STD. The problem is that partner management is rarely assured, while patient referral has had limited success.

Under EPT, clinicians provide patients with medications directly or via prescription for both them and their partners. Numerous studies have demonstrated EPT's effectiveness.

EPT's legal status is uncertain. EPT is legal in 15 states; prohibited in 11 states; and potentially available in the remaining 24 states, the District of Columbia, and Puerto Rico.

EPT raises important issues about informed consent, confidentiality, insurance payments, and patient safety due to the absence of the traditional physician-patient relationship.

For more information:

- Centers for Disease Control and Prevention (*www.cdc.gov*)
- The Centers for Law and the Public's Health (*www.publichealthlaw.net*)
- American Public Health Association (*www.apha.org*)

Retail-Based Clinics. Retail-based clinics are an emerging healthcare delivery model operating through drug stores, supermarkets, and "big-box" retailers. The number of retail clinics grew from about 60 in 18 states at the end of 2005 to more than 900 in 30 states by the end of 2007. The Convenient Care Association (CCA) predicts there will be 5,000 by the end of 2010. Traditional primary care providers consider such clinics a threat.

The uninsured are avid users of retail clinics. Low cost, convenient hours and locations and the ability to obtain care without an appointment are major draws.

However, retail-based healthcare brings with it a number of legal and policy issues, including scope of practice, collaborative practice arrangement requirements, information privacy, referral relationships, commercial payer contracts, Medicare and Medicaid reimbursement, patient safety, the potential for increased medical malpractice litigation (the corporations behind retail clinics have very deep pockets), and the current absence of regulation.

For more information:

- Convenient Care Association (*www.ccaclinics.org*)
- Center for Studying Health System Change (*www.hschange.com*)

Clinical Research Trials. Clinical research trials are expanding and becoming increasingly entrepreneurial. Nearly 3 million Americans volunteer annually to be subjects in clinical research projects.

A growing number of reported deaths and research violations, however, have caused the closing of several research institutions and raised critical questions about how to protect human subjects. Recalls of medications and medical devices, plus nondisclosure of clinical trial data and subsequent patient harm, have spawned litigation and increasing legislative and regulatory scrutiny.

Lawsuits against clinical trial researchers generally fall into three categories: breach of the standard of care, lack of informed consent, and conflicts of interest.

Additional legal concerns include the following:

- The new FDA Amendments Act of 2007 (Pub. L. 110-85) contains a clinical trial certification requirement, which is causing major confusion among clinical research organizations.
- The FDA has new enforcement authority over postmarketing trials.
- The FDA cannot meet its expanded legal and regulatory obligations without more resources.
- Clinical trial registration and resultant disclosure requirements differ from state to state.
- Proper management of protocols, contracts, consents, and other documents, including negotiation of the applicable agreement documents, raises important issues.
- Management of clinical trials, from recruiting incentives and overcoming key Medicare issues to avoiding data privacy and security pitfalls, increases liability exposure.
- Legal risks inherent in tailored therapies are now emerging.
- The recently approved heart failure drug BiDil® is the first drug targeted exclusively to a specific racial group, African Americans, thereby designating race a biological category.
- NIH has increased its focus on its Eliminating Disparities in Clinical Trials initiative, a program intended to assess minority participation in clinical trials.

- Demand for more clinical research transparency has increased.
- Overseas regulation is expanding. The FDA recently opened three offices in China and plans to open similar offices in Europe, Latin America, and India.
- Fake products sneak by medical review boards (the Government Accountability Office tested the system in March 2009 and successfully hoodwinked several boards).

For more information:

- Association for the Accreditation of Human Research Protection Programs (*www.aahrpp.org*)
- Association of Clinical Research Organizations (*www.acrohealth.org*)
- National Institutes of Health (*www.clinicaltrials.gov*)

New IRS Form 990. Charities and other tax-exempt organizations file Form 990 annually. The IRS released a redesigned Form 990 in December 2007, effective for tax year 2008.

The new form provides more opportunities for the organization to explain its activities, including executive compensation, related organizations, foreign activities, hospitals, noncash contributions, and tax-exempt bonds. The new form requires tax-exempt hospitals to report on governance, community benefit, charity care, and bad debt policies, among other things.

For more information:

- Internal Revenue Service (*www.irs.gov*)
- American Hospital Association (*www.aha.org*)

New Joint Commission 2009 Hospital Accreditation Standard. The Joint Commission accredits and certifies almost 19,000 U.S. healthcare organizations and programs. The Joint Commission has issued a new 2009 standard, which requires hospitals to evaluate safety and quality regularly and to have a code of conduct that defines acceptable, disruptive, and inappropriate behavior of healthcare professionals.

The new standard, much resisted by hospitals and their medical staffs, may be an attempt to stave off the increasing clamor for a federal government hospital overseer and regulator rather than the hodgepodge of state and Joint Commission oversight that now exists.

For more information:

- Joint Commission (*www.jointcommission.org*)
- American Hospital Association (*www.aha.org*)
- American Medical Association (*www.ama.org*)

New Stark Physician Self-Referral Rules. The physician referral law (Social Security Act, §1877, 42 U.S.C. 1395) generally prohibits a physician from referring patients to an entity for certain health services if the physician or a member of his or her immediate family has a financial relationship with the entity. The law also prohibits an entity from presenting a claim for such services provided under a prohibited referral. Civil money penalties and other remedies may apply.

Stark is one of the most confusing and complicated medical/healthcare laws and regulatory schemes extant, and its meaning and nuances are the topic of constant debate among healthcare professionals and their legal advisors. The new Stark rules do little to clarify the situation.

Compounding the Stark problem is the Centers for Medicare and Medicaid Services' (CMS) intent to audit hospitals for Stark Law compliance, including examining financial relationships between hospitals and referring physicians. This has enormous financial and liability exposure implications.

For more information:

- Centers for Medicare and Medicaid Services (*www.cms.hhs.gov*)
- American Health Lawyers Association (*www.ahla.org*)

Stepped-up Fraud and Abuse Enforcement. Healthcare fraud and abuse is an enormous problem that contributes mightily to the high costs of healthcare in the United States, as evidenced by the following facts:

- Drug diversion costs health insurers up to an estimated $72.5 billion a year in bogus claims involving opioid abuse alone.

- At least 3 percent of U.S. healthcare spending—or $72 billion—is lost to fraud each year, according to the National Health Care Anti-Fraud Association (NHCAFA). The NHCAFA says that every $2 million invested in fighting healthcare fraud returns $17.3 million in recoveries and other antifraud savings.
- The U.S. government recovers $15 for every $1 invested in False Claims Act (31 U.S.C. §§ 3729–3733) healthcare investigations and prosecutions (Taxpayers Against Fraud, 2008). To date, 21 of the top 22 recoveries under the Act have been in healthcare-related cases. The top six settlements in 2008 all involved healthcare cases. Look for these trends to continue as the incentives that encourage individuals to invoke the False Claims Act become more widely known.
- Every $1 spent on Medicare fraud prevention would stop $10 in fraud, according to HHS. Yet Medicare spends less than two cents of every $1 of its budget combating fraud.
- Medicare paid deceased physicians for 478,500 claims ($92 million) from 2000 to 2007.
- Nearly one of three claims (29 percent) Medicare paid for durable medical equipment was erroneous in fiscal year 2006 (HHS Inspector General [IG]).
- State Medicaid Fraud Control Units obtained a collective 1,205 convictions and claimed total recoveries of more than $1.1 billion in court-ordered restitution, fines, civil settlements, and penalties in fiscal year 2007, according to the HHS IG.
- More than 61 percent of medical providers banned from state Medicaid programs in 2004 and 2005 did not show up in the National Practitioner Database, making it easier for banned providers to set up shop in other states (HHS IG).
- The Federal Trade Commission says more than 250,000 Americans have been victims of medical identity theft in recent years.

In response to these problems, government enforcement activities are growing. In 2007, the U.S. Department of Justice (DOJ) and HHS launched a Medicare Fraud Strike Force in Miami to combat certain improper billing. The Miami Strike Force proved very successful and has now been expanded to Los Angeles. In seven months, 74 Miami cases returned indictments involving charges filed against 120 defendants who collectively billed the Medicare program more than $400 million; 35 guilty pleas were negotiated and four jury trials litigated, winning guilty verdicts on all counts charged. During the same period, a 50 percent reduction was seen in billing and payments for Medicare Part B.

Certain HIPAA funds are, by law, set aside for Medicare and Medicaid activities of the HHS IG. In fiscal year 2007, this amounted to $165.9 million. This amount is almost certain to increase in future years, if only because these activities bring in money for the government. In addition, DOJ and HHS IG, working with their other law enforcement partners, are likely to step up their investigations and prosecutions, including fraud by pharmaceutical firms, pharmacies, hospitals, HMOs, home healthcare agencies, and physicians, among others.

Also, look for an increase in the following government initiatives, which could provide health law subspecialty opportunities:

- *Corporate and other integrity agreements with healthcare providers that settle False Claims Act cases.* At the close of fiscal year 2007, HHS IG was monitoring compliance with more than 380 such agreements. The number of such agreements is increasing each year.
- *Program Exclusions.* In fiscal year 2007, the HHS IG excluded 3,308 individuals and entities from participating in federal and state healthcare programs. In addition, HHS collected approximately $185.7 million in disallowances of improperly paid healthcare funds.
- *Civil monetary penalties (CMPs).* HHS imposes CMPs against providers and suppliers who knowingly submit false claims to the government, participate in unlawful patient referral or kickback schemes, fail to treat appropriately or refer patients at hospital emergency rooms, or engage in other proscribed activities.
- *Program integrity activities.* The HHS Office of General Counsel (OGC) is increasingly focusing on these activities.

OGC also provides litigation support to DOJ in actions relating to Medicare or Medicaid fraud under the False Claims Act.

- *Nursing home enforcement.* The HHS Centers for Medicare & Medicaid Services (CMS) is using advanced technology to detect and prevent fraud and abuse and to ensure that the right providers get the right amount for the right service to the right beneficiary. CMS administers numerous CMP provisions to enforce program compliance and payment integrity. For example, such provisions enforce compliance with respect to nursing homes that do not meet certification standards. An aging population means an increase in such efforts.
- *OGC assists CMS to assure high-quality care,* particularly with respect to "special focus facilities," nursing homes habitually out of compliance with certification requirements.
- *Bankruptcy litigation.* OGC asserts CMS's recoupment rights in bankruptcy proceedings, an extensive and complex workload that is growing significantly.
- *Medicaid integrity.* CMS has a new Medicaid Integrity Program responsible for federal audits of Medicaid providers and increased support for state program integrity efforts.
- *Review of regulations and manual provisions.* CMS is developing a compliance program for Medicare Part D sponsors and Medicare Advantage plans, including identifying enforcement options against noncompliant sponsors.
- *HIPAA enforcement.* The CMS Office of e-Health Standards and Services investigates security incidents. HHS recently established a Personally Identifiable Information Breach Response Team. Additionally, CMS has launched an effort to educate and assist covered entities within the healthcare industry to prepare to comply with the provisions of the HIPAA National Provider Identifier Rule (45 CFR Part 162).
- *Medical identity theft project.* The HHS Office of the National Coordinator for Health Information Technology is developing a knowledge base for medical identity theft and a report and on roadmap for actions to help prevent, detect, and remedy medical identity theft.

- *U.S. Attorney Offices'* healthcare fraud and abuse litigation is increasing. Each of the 94 offices has a designated Criminal Health Care Fraud Coordinator and a Civil Health Care Fraud Coordinator. Civil cases also arise from *qui tam* complaints.
- *DOJ Civil Division Elder Justice and Nursing Home Initiative.* This initiative supports prosecution and coordination to fight abuse, neglect, and financial exploitation of the nation's senior and infirm population. The DOJ also makes grants to promote prevention, detection, intervention, investigation, and prosecution of elder abuse and neglect.
- The *DOJ Criminal Division Fraud Section* undertakes complex healthcare fraud litigation. Most of its recent litigation involved Medicare Fraud Strike Force cases.
- *Enforcement of the Civil Rights of Institutionalized Persons Act (42 U.S.C. §§ 1997 et seq.).* The DOJ's Civil Rights Division pursues relief in cases related to public residential health-care facilities. The Division has established an initiative to eliminate abuse and grossly substandard care in public Medicare -and Medicaid-funded nursing homes and other long-term care facilities.
- *Internet Pharmacy Fraud Initiative.* This FBI program focuses on websites and individuals selling illegal prescription drugs and controlled substances, identifying fraudulent Internet pharmacies and targeting physicians who write prescriptions for financial gain outside of the doctor/ patient relationship and with no legitimate medical purpose. The initiative also focuses on the online sale of counterfeit and diverted drugs.
- *DoD Instruction 5505.12.* This recent directive establishes an antifraud program at each military treatment facility. The Defense Department's TRICARE Program Integrity Office oversees the programs and all Defense Health Program antifraud activities worldwide.
- *Federal Tax Interdiction Program.* The increasing use of tax fraud violations to combat healthcare fraud is based on a successful Los Angeles County program.

For more information:

- The False Claims Act Legal Center (*www.taf.org*)
- National Health Care Anti-Fraud Association (*www.nhcaa.org*)
- International Association of Insurance Fraud Agencies (*www.iaifa.org*)
- National Insurance Crime Bureau (*www.nicb.org*)
- TRICARE's Fraud and Abuse Web Page (*www.tricare.mil/fraud*)

Breaking In

Health law, as this section demonstrates, is far-flung, wide-ranging, and changing rapidly. There is a dearth of legal experts and specialists for many of the new areas and emerging issues discussed above. The demand that this creates translates into fewer barriers to entry than might be found in other practice areas.

It helps to have taken a number of health law courses in law school. Law schools are adding to their health law curricula, prompted by both the growing complexity of the field and growing interest from students and prospective employers. A growing number of law schools offer students the opportunity to write for health law publications, which is an excellent way to gain some experience and build a credible résumé. Networking organizations, such as the American Health Lawyers Association (*www.ahla.org*) and its state chapters, provide another means for attorneys to educate themselves about health law, keep up with fast-changing developments in the field, and position themselves for career opportunities and advancement.

Enhancing Your Credentials. Numerous credential enhancements are available that can make you a stronger candidate. Health law has become a very popular law school LLM offering.

The following law schools offer LLMs and/or certificates in Health Law and/or related topics: Albany, Chicago, Concord Law School (online), DePaul, George Washington, Georgetown, Harvard, Houston, Indiana University—Indianapolis, Loyola, Saint Louis University, San Diego, Seton Hall, Southern Illinois, and Widener.

The following universities and other organizations offer certificates in Health Law and/or related areas: Association of Health Care Compliance

Professionals (*www.hcca-info.org*), University of Washington Extension (*www.extension.washington.edu*), National Board of Trial Advocacy (*www. nbtanet.org*), University of Illinois—Chicago (*www.uic.edu*), University of New Mexico (*www.unm.edu*), University of Florida (*www.ufl.edu*), Kaplan University (*www.kaplan.edu*), Florida International University Legal Studies Institute (*www.fiu.edu*), American College of Healthcare Executives (*www.ache.org*), American Association of Legal Nurse Consultants (*www. aalnc.org*), American Hospital Association Certification Center (*www. aha.org*), Healthcare Quality Certification Board (*www.cphq.org*), Johns Hopkins University (*http://commprojects.jhsph.edu/academics/Certificate.cfm*), American Society for Healthcare Risk Management (*www.ashrm.org*), Northeastern University (*www.spcs.neu.edu*), and American Board of Professional Liability Attorneys (*www.abpla.org*)

Making Good Contacts. There is no shortage of health-related legal and other membership organizations you can join (if qualified) to develop a health law network:

- American Bar Association Health Law Section (*www.abanet. org/health*)
- American Health Lawyers Association (*www.healthlawyers.org*)
- American Association of Nurse Attorneys (*www.taana.org*)
- American College of Legal Medicine (*www.aclm.org*)
- American Society for Healthcare Risk Management (*www.ashrm.org*)
- American Society for Pharmacy Law (*www.aspl.org*)
- American Society of Law, Medicine and Ethics (*www.aslme.org*)
- Association of Corporate Counsel Environmental, Health, and Safety Committee (*www.acc.com*)
- Center for Telehealth and E-Health Law (*www.ctel.org*)
- Ethics and Compliance Officers Association (*www.theecoa.org*)
- Federation of Defense and Corporate Counsel Healthcare Practice Section; Drug, Device and Biotechnology Section; and Life, Health and Disability Section (*www.thefederation.org*)
- Federation of Regulatory Counsel (*www.forc.org*)
- Federal Bar Association Health Law Section (*www.fedbar.org/ healthlaw_section.html*)

- Food and Drug Law Institute (*www.fdli.org*)
- Health Care Compliance Association (*www.hcca-info.org*)
- International Association of Privacy Professionals (*www.privacyassociation.org*)
- National Bar Association Health Law Section (*www.nationalbar.org*)
- National Organization of Social Security Claimants' Representatives (*www.nosscr.org*)
- National Organization of Veterans Advocates (*www.vetadvocates.com*)

For More Information

In addition to the many organizations and information resources already cited in this section, see the following for detailed information about healthcare law, reform initiatives, and job leads:

- American Hospital Directory (*www.ahd.com*)
- California Office of the Patient Advocate (*www.opa.ca.gov*)
- National Center for Complementary and Alternative Medicine (*http://nccam.nih.gov*)
- The Health Law Resource (*www.netreach.net/~wmanning*)
- Center for Health Law Studies (*http://law.slu.edu/healthlaw/index.html*)
- Health Law News (*www.blawgrepublic.com/cat/Health-Law*)
- Health Law Week (*www.straffordpub.com/products/health-law-week*)
- Healthcare Administration (*www.healthcareernet.com*)
- Healthcare Industry Organizations (*www.hospitalmanagement.net/industry/united_states.html*)
- Duke Health Policy Gateway (*www.hpolicy.duke.edu/cyberexchange*)
- Massachusetts Health Connector (*www.mahealthconnector.org*)

ENERGY LAW

Introduction

I worked at the then new U.S. Department of Energy 1978–79 during the Second Oil Shock (the first was 1973–74), when Ayatollah Khomeini turned off the Iranian spigot and caused both gas station lines to lengthen and the price of oil to skyrocket. My first assignment was to draft regulations to govern the U.S. geothermal steam industry, sure to thrive when the price of oil hit $100 a barrel, which Department economists assured me would happen within a year. It never came close, and my regulations have been collecting dust at the Department for 30 years.

One of President Jimmy Carter's few triumphs was a sane energy policy based on tax incentives for energy conservation and strict automobile fuel economy standards. When President Ronald Reagan succeeded him, the tax incentives vanished, and the fuel economy standards policy was put on hold.

This era of total neglect is over. The "Third Oil Shock" of 2008 demonstrated the harsh reality of what dwindling supply and increased demand does to oil prices. The United States and every other country can no longer continue their oil addiction. The era of purely political oil shocks is also over. The ones henceforward will be real. This is very good news for energy law practitioners. The number of energy attorneys in the United States increased by 14 percent from 2007 to 2008. The more attention is paid to energy independence and climate change initiatives, the more job opportunities there will be for attorneys. And energy independence initiatives are coming at us from all directions—government, corporations, think tanks, and international organizations. Because these initiatives will take a long time to bear fruit, energy law is likely to be a hot practice area for decades.

What Is It?

Energy law practice developed in response to U.S. government regulatory involvement in the creation, usage, sale, transmission, transportation, disposal, and conservation of energy in all forms. Energy law deals with everything involved with exploration, development, distribution, and pricing of energy resources. There is a heavy emphasis on transactions, followed closely by regulation and litigation. Energy law encompasses many practice areas, often with a unique twist. For example, acquiring land for oil and gas exploration and development might mean securing surface rights and/or subsurface rights and competing for oil and gas tracts in government Outer Continental Shelf Lease Sale auctions.

Our political leaders have now concluded, in a rare bipartisan consensus, that waiting for oil prices to make an alternative energy resource economically preferable will not achieve energy independence. We need to act now, regardless of oil prices, because more than economics is at stake. We subsidize many things that the government believes are essential to national security, like defense and transportation, for example. If we left it to the market to decide when to build next-generation jet fighters, navy ships, or nuclear warheads, they would never get built because they are very expensive and no investor could ever envision a return on the investment. When it comes to energy, subsidizing now is likely to pay great rewards on several levels.

Energy practice is changing dramatically in an attempt to keep pace with massive policy changes because of our dependence on foreign oil and our need for energy independence, Nothing is likely to be overlooked in constructing a national energy independence plan. Every possible energy alternative and technology will likely be pursued, which is good news for attorneys interested in this practice area.

Who Does It?

Private practice is the province primarily of large law firms and energy companies, and law firms are leaping aboard the energy bandwagon with alacrity. Almost every major U.S. law firm now has an energy law practice. Most claim to be all things to all energy clients; others focus their attention on specific energy resources, providers, or industries.

Law firms of all sizes are finding an energy practice increasingly attractive. The number of boutique firms that focus on energy law is growing rapidly. One reason is that energy law is becoming so diversified that it is possible to concentrate a practice in niche areas differentiated by type of feedstock—oil, gas, coal, nuclear, wind, solar, biofuels, geothermal, waves, hydrogen, etc.—and/or by type of legal expertise—transaction, litigation, or regulatory.

Public sector energy practice is weighted toward regulation. Government energy practice is not limited to the U.S. Department of Energy's General Counsel's Office. In fact, there are more than 80 U.S. government law offices with energy law practices, 19 separate ones in the Energy Department alone. Other agencies with multiple offices practicing energy law include the Federal Energy Regulatory Commission, Nuclear Regulatory Commission, and the Departments of Interior and Justice.

Every state government has at least one regulatory agency overseeing aspects of the energy industry. State agencies work on a wide range of energy issues, including the following:

- Energy efficiency in homes, buildings, industry, and agriculture
- Renewable energy (e.g., solar, wind, geothermal, biomass
- Residential, commercial, and institutional energy building codes)
- Transportation and heating fuel supplies, pricing, and distribution
- Oil, natural gas, electricity, and other forms of energy production and distribution
- Energy–environment integration (such as conservation to reduce air emissions)
- New and emerging high-efficiency transportation fuels and technologies
- Energy security and emergency preparedness

Traditional energy-producing states have several such agencies. For example, Texas has the following: Railroad Commission, Attorney General Natural Resources Division, Coastal Coordination Council, General Land Office, Board of Professional Geoscientists, Lower Colorado River Authority, Public Utility Commission, and Office of Public Utility Counsel.

The energy industry has spawned a large number of trade associations and advocacy and public interest organizations, many with law departments. This group includes the American Petroleum Institute, American Coal Council, American Gas Association, Edison Electric Institute, Interstate Natural Gas Association of America, National Association of Royalty Owners, National Association of State Energy Officials, Clean Energy States Alliance, National Petrochemical & Refiners Association, Solar Energy Industries Association, Association of Oil Pipe Lines, Geothermal Energy Association, American Council on Renewable Energy, and the American Hydrogen Association, to name just a few. The prominence of energy issues means that these offices are growing their attorney staffs. Venture capital firms are making significant energy industry investments, prompted by government and private interest in renewable fuels and energy efficiency technologies.

The nature of energy resources and their utilization makes this an international practice, too. Many major law firms have both a domestic and international practice, as do multinational energy companies. There are also many international agencies with an energy law practice, including the International Energy Agency, International Gas Union, World Energy Council, World Trade Organization, International Geothermal Association, International Centre for Settlement of Investment Disputes, International Atomic Energy Agency, World LP Gas Association, and the European Bank for Reconstruction and Development.

What Does It Pay?

Private sector energy practice compensation is roughly comparable to other law firm and corporate practices. Large law firm compensation ranges from approximately $150,000 for entry-level attorneys to very high six figures for full-equity partners. Average salaries for corporate in-house energy attorneys range from around $80,000 in rural and less-populated areas to $125,000 in Washington, D.C. Corporate regulatory and transactional attorneys are at the high end of corporate salary scales. These figures do not include annual bonuses.

Public sector agencies pay energy lawyers according to the standard government pay scales that apply to other federal and state workers, with the U.S. government at the top level (up to approximately $150,000 plus locality pay).

Nonprofit pay ranges widely, with oil, gas, and coal trade associations paying significantly more than newer associations representing alternative energy resources, such as wind, solar, and biofuels. Other nonprofits that employ energy attorneys pay quite poorly. It is not uncommon to see salaries under $50,000.

The two primary international energy agencies are the International Energy Agency (IEA) in Paris and the International Atomic Energy Agency (IAEA) in Vienna. The 2009 IEA pay scale begins at $65,040 and ranges to $178,548 at the highest level. The 2009 IAEA pay scale begins at $35,570 for an entry-level professional without dependents and goes to $194,820 for senior-level professionals with dependents. International agency pay scales generally apply across the board to all professional-level agency employees and, if the job is located outside the United States, often include an additional amount based on location and/or number of dependents. It should also be noted that international agency salaries are generally U.S.-tax-free.

As with all industries, practice areas, and economic sectors, compensation also depends very much on the size and location of the employer.

Future Prospects

Historically, energy law has had its ups and downs due to the politicization of energy supplies. When the Saudis in 1973–74 and the Iranians in 1979 cut off the West's oil supplies because they did not like Israel and hated America, energy practices grew rapidly. When the political crises ended, the practices retreated.

This time is different. Energy practices are here to stay. The Third Oil Shock saw to that.

The ultimate goal of the new U.S. energy policy is energy independence. In addition to the revival of liberal energy conservation tax incentives for homeowners and industry, look for the following new policy elements, each of which will create numerous job opportunities and career paths for attorneys.

Drill, Baby, Drill. Drilling for oil will benefit us a little bit in the medium term. A carbon-based, supply-side strategy will only result in finding a smidgen more oil here and there. That's not a long-term policy, just a finger in the dike. Nevertheless, it is a useful finger.

Offshore drilling has been going on for 110 years, more than 50 years in the Gulf of Mexico, without appreciable damage to the environment. Look for it to expand to other coastal and oceanic regions, both domestic and abroad.

Oil exploration and development requires teams of attorneys to help bring new oil sources onstream, such as "landmen" to negotiate oil leases with private land and mineral rights owners; transactional lawyers to draw up contracts for government-run onshore and outer continental shelf lease sales; negotiators to effect agreements with drilling equipment vendors, pipeline owners, and others; regulatory attorneys to monitor, explain, and comply with government regulations; and many more.

A Boon to T. Boone. T. Boone Pickens's TV ads about the need to cultivate our immense natural gas resources and switch from using oil to using natural gas have a good point (plus a strong self-interest because he owns immense gas reserves). Some buses and cabs already run on natural gas. The problem is that there are only a handful of natural gas filling stations.

Flaring off natural gas from oil wells will stop. Natural gas is an extraordinarily valuable resource and a linchpin of any energy independence effort.

The United States has enough proven natural gas reserves (211 trillion cubic feet) to last us approximately 120 years. The volume of proven reserves is actually growing from year to year, thanks to new discoveries—a sharp contrast to shrinking global oil reserves.

We need the infrastructure to (1) retool the auto industry to permit the building of natural gas guzzlers, (2) encourage retrofitting of cars to run on natural gas, and (3) provide incentives to the private sector to pepper the map with natural gas filling stations.

Attorneys who focus on the natural gas industry mirror oil lawyers' duties to a great extent. For example, they negotiate and document deals, which for natural gas are very complex and eventuate in hundreds of transactions that contribute to bringing gas from its source to consuming homes and businesses. In addition, natural gas lawyers must also be concerned with the complexities of pricing and an array of complex government price regulations.

Going Nuclear. We will be compelled to unleash nuclear power. The overreaction to Three Mile Island in 1979 was to slap a total freeze on building and licensing new reactors. Meanwhile, France now gets more than 75 percent of its electricity from nuclear energy (the United States, 19 percent). You don't see French President Nicholas Sarkozy glow in the dark, and you don't need to run a dosimeter over the wine aisle at the supermarket before you buy your bottle of 1982 Chateau Lafitte Rothschild.

The problem at Three Mile Island Reactor Unit 2 was not that the unit was unsafe. A minor pump failure caused Unit 2 to overheat and close two feedwater lines from the Susquehanna River designed to cool the overheating reactor. This prompted two warning lights to go on in the control room, but the poorly designed control room panel—I am not making this up—had the warning lights *positioned on the back of the panel.* Consequently, the control room staff did not notice that the feedwater lines had closed and a meltdown was in progress. Instead of blaming the panel contractor and the Three Mile Island operating company who accepted such abysmal design work, we took it out on the entire nuclear energy concept.

Chernobyl should also be discounted. The Chernobyl reactor was highly unsafe, lacking a lead containment structure. Unlike the Soviets, the United States has never built a reactor without a lead containment shield surrounding the reactor itself, which minimizes the possible leakage of radioactive material into the atmosphere.

Final argument: Fewer people have suffered injury or death from nuclear power than from coal mining or oil drilling.

The revival of nuclear power will require the services of a large number of lawyers. They will be needed by the companies that build reactors; their outside law firms which will advise and assist them with the highly complex and lengthy reactor licensing process; states and localities, which will be designated as reactor sites or nuclear waste repositories; and government (principally the U.S. Department of Energy and the Nuclear Regulatory Commission).

Café au Lait. A centerpiece of the new energy policy will be to increase the CAFE (Corporate Average Fuel Economy—pronounced *café*) standards; that is, the fleet average gas mileage mandates that automakers must achieve by law. President Gerald Ford pushed the first CAFE standards through Congress in 1975 (they were implemented by the Carter Administration). Blame for doing nothing about this since then falls equally on Ronald Reagan, George H. W. Bush, Bill Clinton, and George W. Bush, as well as Congress. In 2008, prompted by people having to pay more than $100 each time they filled up their Hummers, Congress reluctantly addressed the issue for the first time in 33 years and marginally increased the CAFE requirements.

Look for even more stringent CAFE standards as part of the new energy policy and, as such, new opportunities in this niche for attorneys, principally in government to enforce the standards and in the automobile industry in a regulatory and compliance role.

Alternative Energy Sources

- *Biofuels.* Ethanol is nice, but what it (predictably) did to food prices is not. There is a lot of feedstock out there other than corn that can produce ethanol, and this element of the energy independence policy will be redirected there. Agricultural residue, sawdust, dead trees, municipal solid waste, etc., are capable substitutes for corn and will not affect food prices.

- *Wind.* We will construct transmission and distribution systems to get the electricity that wind farms produce to the power grid and, in turn, to consumers. The American Recovery and Reinvestment Act, Pub. L. 111-5 (aka the Stimulus Bill) is spurring this development. Much more is coming.

  Also, watch for offshore wind farm development in shallow ocean and Great Lakes regions, where there is always a lot more wind than onshore. Michigan produces more wind than any other state and is pinning its economic diversification hopes in large part on wind energy.

- *Clean coal.* The United States has enough coal reserves to fuel our economy for 800 years. However, the human and environmental costs are huge obstacles.

  "Clean coal" is, to date, a myth. Scrubbers are not effective at minimizing air pollution, and coal gasification is too expensive at present (the price of a barrel of East Texas light crude would have to be around $300 a barrel for it to become economically viable). Companies know this, and as a result, there is now a grand total of one small coal conversion plant in the United States. Moreover, one of the tradeoffs of "going coal" is generating more carbon emissions.

  Like the tale of "The Emperor's New Clothes," the myth about clean coal has been accepted by both political parties, meaning there will be significant activity here., with companies and utilities receiving government incentives to build so-called clean coal plants.

- *Wave energy.* Many years ago, I hitched a ride to Miami from a conference in Ft. Lauderdale with a gentleman who was on his way to Florida Power and Light to pitch the utility on his wave energy device. I pored over his blueprints during the ride and concluded that both he and his invention were certifiable (underscored by his passing slower vehicles on the right shoulder). Not anymore.

Wave energy technology has tested as viable in recent experiments. The U.S. Navy recently awarded a contract that, indirectly, will test the concept further. The company—Ocean Power Technologies of Pennington, New Jersey—also recently won a contract from the Energy Department to test its "Power Buoy."

These efforts will expand under the new energy policy. There are a lot of waves out there. Harnessing them might tick off some bronzed guys named Biff surfing on the Kona Coast, but so what?

- *The hydrogen economy.* Hydrogen is the "wave" of the future. The universe is loaded with it. The sun burns 11 billion pounds of hydrogen *every second.*
- It is by far the most abundant element on earth. If we can convert to hydrogen power, we can replace fossil fuels altogether.

Hydrogen plants do nothing more complicated than split water molecules into hydrogen and oxygen. The problem is that, at current costs, hydrogen cannot compete with oil. Currently, it is too expensive in electricity costs to produce a gallon of hydrogen. But that does not mean we will not be pouring research dollars into making hydrogen more efficient and safe. If successful, we can kiss Middle Eastern oil goodbye.

- *Solar power.* Solar power R&D was essentially put on the shelf on January 21, 1981. At the time, the federal government had been doling out a small amount of money ($30 million) to General Electric and a few other companies to experiment with solar technologies. Then ideology got in the way, and the research came to a screeching halt. U.S. solar power development has basically been stalled ever since. The Obama administration wants to get it moving again.
- *Shale oil, tar sands, and trapped natural gas.* A lot of oil gets trapped in shale and tar sands. Wyoming has more shale

oil than the world's current conventional oil reserves. The
Alberta tar sands contain around the same amount of oil.
There are also a bazillion cubic feet of natural gas trapped
in "clathrates" and "hydrates" (molecules that contain other
molecules). The problem: Extracting and processing this
oil and gas is very expensive.

Nevertheless, all three will be included in the new
energy plan because technological breakthroughs will drive
down costs. Eventually, it may become economical to go
after the stuff.

- *Geothermal.* Geothermal technology has come a long way in
  30 years but is viable largely in places like Iceland, where
  you cannot walk down the streets of Reykjavik without
  getting singed by a thermal vent. There is a small role for
  geothermal in the coming energy plan.
- *Hydropower.* The assumption is that we have maximized what
  we can do with this technology. Not true. There is a lot of
  moving water that has not been exploited. Our experience
  with massive projects like the Tennessee Valley Authority and the Boulder and Grand Coulee Dams will likely
  be examined for application to sites that have not been
  harnessed yet. There are a lot of them and this process is
  cheap, which could mean constantly replenishing energy.
  Both the Department of Energy and the Federal Energy
  Regulatory Commission, as well as states that have unreal-
  ized hydropower potential, are examining what can be done
  to realize this potential. Utilities are also studying how they
  might exploit additional hydropower resources.
- *Storage cell batteries (fuel cells).* A fuel cell would have to be as
  large as the vehicle itself to store enough energy to run the
  vehicle for any reasonable distance. However, we are very
  good at miniaturization. This is a research area that will be
  given a public sector boost.

The opportunities for attorneys across the alternative energy spectrum are vast and already growing rapidly. Each alternative energy
resource calls for additional litigators, transactional lawyers, regulatory

attorneys, and legal administrators. This practice subspecialty is huge, ranges far and wide across hundreds of industries, transcends national borders, and will impact every employment sector.

Breaking In

Launching or reinventing yourself as an energy lawyer is not difficult. Because energy law is heavily transaction and regulation oriented, any attorney at any career stage should be able not only to function but succeed as an energy lawyer.

The fact that so much of energy law is developing and evolving so rapidly also makes this a practice area that does not require much prior experience. Renewable energy resources, for example, are just now emerging as focal points of energy law practice.

At present, *the demand for energy lawyers is tremendous.* Law firms are engaged in bidding wars for experienced energy attorneys. Also, a "trickle-down" effect is in play, wherein energy practices are expanding and seeking new recruits.

While credential enhancements are not as essential to practice energy law as they might be for some other practices, they can be useful in terms of both increasing your knowledge of the field and making you a more attractive candidate worthy of higher compensation. Selected credentialing programs include the following:

- University of Denver Sturm College of Law (*www.law.du.edu*)
  - LLM in Environmental and Natural Resources Law and Policy
  - Certificate of Studies (CS) in Natural Resources Law and Policy
- Tulane University Law School—LLM in Energy & Environment (*www.law.tulane.edu*)
- University of Houston Law Center—LLM Program in Energy, Environment & Natural Resources Law (*www.law. uh.edu/eenrcenter*)
- University of Houston Bauer College of Business (*www.bauer. uh.edu/Certificates*)
  - Energy Risk Management Certificate
  - Energy Investment Analysis Certificate

- Energy Finance Certificate
- Economics of the Energy Value Chain Certificate
- University of California—Davis Extension (*http://extension.ucdavis.edu/certificates*)
    - Energy Resource Management Certificate (on-site and online)
    - Green Building and Renewable Energy Certificate (on-site and online)
    - Green Building and Sustainable Design Certificate (on-site and online)
- American Association of Professional Landmen (*www.aapl.org*)
    - Certified Professional Landman
    - Registered Professional Landman Designation
    - Registered Landman Designation
- University of Colorado—Graduate Energy Certificate Program (*http://ei.colorado.edu*)

The following membership organizations are excellent networking and information sources for anyone interested in an energy practice legal career. A number of them have local chapters around the country. Several organizations list jobs on their websites. Membership organizations are also superb resources for identifying and targeting specific employers.

- Energy Bar Association (*www.eba-net.org*)
- Federal Bar Association—Environment, Energy & Natural Resources Section (*www.fedbar.org/EENR_section.html*)
- American Bar Association—Section of Environment, Energy & Resources (*www.abanet.org/environ*)
- American Bar Association—Renewable Energy Resources Committee (*www.abanet.org/environ/committees/renewableenergy*)
- American Bar Association—Section of Public Utility, Communications and Transportation Law (*www.abanet.org/pubutil/home.html*)
- American Wind Energy Association (*www.awea.org*)
- U.S. Green Building Council (*www.usgbc.org*)
- American Solar Energy Society (*www.ases.org*)

- Association of Energy Services Professionals (*www.aesp.org*)
- Institute for Energy Law (*www.cailaw.org/iel*)
- Natural Resources Defense Council (*www.nrdc.org*)

For More Information

- Alternative Energy News (*www.alternative-energy-news.info*)
- American Coal Council (*www.clean-coal.info*)
- American Council on Renewable Energy (ACORE) (*www.acore.org*)
- American Hydrogen Association (*www.clean-air.org*)
- Association of International Petroleum Negotiators (*www.aipn.org*)
- Association of Oil Pipe Lines (*www.aopl.org*)
- Association of State Energy Research and Technology Transfer Institutions (*www.asertti.org*)
- Biomass Energy Research Association (*www.beral.org*)
- California Fuel Cell Partnership (*www.cafcp.org*)
- Clean Energy States Alliance (*www.cleanenergystates.org*)
- Coal Technology Association (*www.coaltechnologies.com*)
- Electric Drive Transportation Association (*www.electricdrive.org*)
- Electric Power Research Institute (*www.epri.com*)
- Electromagnetic Energy Association (*www.elecenergy.com*)
- Energy Efficient Lighting Association (*www.eela.com*)
- Energy Information Administration (*www.eia.doe.gov*)
- Energy Law Journal Online (*www.eba-net.org/journal.php#eljonline*)
- Energy Planet Renewable Energy Directory (*www.energyplanet.info*)
- Federal Energy Regulatory Commission (*www.ferc.gov*)
- Geothermal Energy Association (*www.geo-energy.org*)
- International Atomic Energy Agency (*www.iaea.org*)
- International Centre for Settlement of Investment Disputes (*www.worldbank.org/icsid*)
- International Energy Agency (*www.iea.org*)
- International Gas Union (*www.igu.org*)
- International Geothermal Association (*www.geothermal-energy.org*)

- National Association of Royalty Owners (*www.naro-us.org*)
- National Association of State Energy Officials (*www.naseo.org*)
- National Mining Association (*www.nma.org*)
- National Ocean Industries Association (*www.noia.org*)
- Nuclear Energy Institute (*www.nei.org*)
- Nuclear Regulatory Commission (*www.nrc.gov*)
- Organization of Petroleum Exporting Countries (OPEC) (*www.opec.org*)
- Renewable Fuels Association (*www.ethanolrfa.org*)
- Rocky Mountain Mineral Law Foundation (*www.rmmlf.org*)
- Solar Energy Industries Association (*www.seia.org*)
- U.S. Department of Energy (*www.energy.gov*)
- U.S. Department of Interior (*www.doi.gov*)
- Wave Energy Centre (*www.wavec.org*)
- Wind Energy Resource Atlas of the United States (*http://rredc.nrel.gov/wind/pubs/atlas*)
- World Trade Organization (*www.wto.org*)

FOOD AND DRUG LAW

Introduction

Food and drug regulation dates back 160 years, making this regulatory scheme the oldest in the United States. In 1848, Congress enacted the Drug Importation Act, which required the U.S. Customs Service to stop entry of adulterated drugs from overseas. In 1906, President Theodore Roosevelt signed the Food and Drug Act (21 U.S.C. 1 et seq.) and the Meat Inspection Act (21 U.S.C. 601 et seq.) on the same day.

The Food and Drug Administration (FDA) and the U.S. Department of Agriculture (USDA) have primary jurisdiction over the regulation of meat and food products in the United States and the primary responsibility for product safety. However, responsibility is shared by multiple federal agencies according to a diverse range of factors, such as the source and nature of the product, advertising, shipment method, and the like.

The FDA dates from 1938, making it one of the oldest consumer protection agencies, and monitors products—food, drugs, cosmetics, medical devices, blood supply—that account for more than 25 percent of all consumer spending. It also protects patients in clinical trials and regulates drug and device advertising.

By all accounts, the FDA today is deemed a flawed regulator—underfunded, understaffed, and unable to keep pace with scientific and technological innovation. Lately, the FDA is seen as having bowed to politics and ideology, as well as having been slow to respond to crises in the food supply (salmonella outbreaks are a prime example). The new regime in Washington, D.C., is acutely aware of these shortcomings, and a political consensus is developing that something needs to be done.

Remember Hermann's Corollary to Newton's Third Law—*for every government action, there is an equal and often greater private sector reaction.* In the food and drug law area, the renewed focus on these matters signifies a great opportunity for legal practitioners, including attorneys who lack food and drug legal education or experience.

What Is It?

Food and drug law today goes far beyond the history cited above. It also includes the following:

- Federal Trade Commission (FTC) monitoring of advertising of certain drug products
- Environmental Protection Agency (EPA) regulation of pesticides
- Consumer Product Safety Commission (CPSC) food, drug, and device regulatory activities
- U.S. Patent and Trademark Office intellectual property actions
- Department of Health and Human Services responsibilities under statutes such as the Bioterrorism Act of 2002 (Pub. L. 107-188) and research integrity regulations (42 CFR Part 93)
- Department of Agriculture regulation of animal health products and meat production

This is not a complete list. Food and drug law is "regulatory driven," and government regulation constantly expands (and struggles) in an attempt to keep up with innovation.

Food and drug law practice involves a broad spectrum of legal and regulatory activities involving the agencies listed above (and below in the next part of this section), as well as state regulators, foreign regulators, litigation, transactions, domestic and foreign intellectual property protection, and, somewhat uniquely, "crisis counseling and management" (food and drug recalls and responses to them are a growing component of the practice).

Who Does It?

Law Firms. A surprising number of major law firms *do not* have a food and drug law practice . . . at the moment. However, an interesting phenomenon is just beginning: the addition of food and drug law practices to existing health law practices in large law firms.

The Food and Drug Law Institute (*www.fdli.org*) maintains a list of member law firms on its website. The list includes not only large firms but also boutique law firms. Food and drug law practices are heavily concentrated in the Washington, D.C., area due to the intense regulatory nature of the practice and proximity to the primary regulators.

Pharmaceutical, Biotechnology, and Medical Device Companies. Geography plays a role with respect to food and drug law practice. Similar companies tend to congregate in the same locations. Pharmaceuticals, biotechs, and medical device companies are good examples, strategically situating near important research universities, such as Harvard, MIT, Princeton, Johns Hopkins, Duke, and Stanford. There are large concentrations of these companies in Boston–Cambridge, Central New Jersey (around Princeton), the I-270 Corridor in the Maryland suburbs of Washington, D.C., Research Triangle Park in North Carolina, and Silicon Valley. Large numbers of medical device companies are also located in Orange County, California, and many biotechs are in Chicago/Cook County, San Diego, New York City, suburban Philadelphia, and Seattle.

Nonprofits. Nonprofit organizations such as universities, trade and professional associations, and advocacy groups abound when it comes to food and drug matters. Hundreds of universities receive grant money for food and drug-related research (*http://mup.asu.edu/research2007.pdf*).

More than 100 trade and professional associations focus on food and drug representation (see *www.asaecenter.org*). Public interest and advocacy organizations (such as the Center for Food Safety, Community Nutrition Institute, Humane Society, U.S. Public Interest Research Group, Drug Policy Alliance, etc.), which are highly concentrated in Washington, D.C., lobby Congress and federal regulators about food and drug matters (see *www.idealist.org*). Numerous foundations provide grants for food and drug-related projects (see *www.fdncenter.org*).

U.S. Government. The federal government has created a matrix of food and drug regulation whose complexity rivals that of the agencies charged with regulating financial institutions. Federal food and drug lawyers practice in a multitude of legal and other offices, as well as in a maze of congressional committees and subcommittees:

- U.S. Department of Health and Human Services—27 offices (*www.hhs.gov*)
- U.S. Department of Agriculture—26 offices (*www.usda.gov*)
- Environmental Protection Agency—OGC—Pesticides and Toxic Substances Law Office (*www.epa.gov*)
- Federal Trade Commission—2 offices (*www.ftc.gov*)
- Library of Congress—Congressional Research Service— American Law Division (*www.loc.gov/crsinfo*)
- U.S. Court of Federal Claims (*www.uscfc.uscourts.gov*)
- U.S. Department of Justice—2 offices (*www.usdoj.gov*)
- U.S. Department of State—U.S. Mission to the United Nations, Rome, Italy—Legal Section (*www.state.gov*)
- U.S. Department of Veterans Affairs—12 offices (*www.va.gov*)
- U.S. Patent and Trademark Office—3 offices (*www.uspto.gov*)
- U.S. Department of Homeland Security—Office of General Counsel; Federal Emergency Management Agency (*www.dhs.gov*)
- U.S. Department of Commerce—National Institute of Standards and Technology (*www.doc.gov*)
- Nuclear Regulatory Commission—3 offices (*www.nrc.gov*)
- National Science Foundation—3 offices (*www.nsf.gov*)
- National Technology Transfer Center (*www.nttc.edu*)

Attorneys also work in a number of federal laboratories around the country, which conduct drug and food research and transfer technology to the private sector.

State and Local Government. State and local governments also have a role in food and drug matters. See "For More Information" at the end of this section for links to each state's and many localities' relevant agencies.

International Organizations. A number of international organizations that employ U.S. citizens have legal offices that deal with food and drug issues:

- World Health Organization—Office of the Legal Counsel, Geneva, Switzerland (*www.who.int*)
- Pan American Health Organization—Area of Legal Affairs, Washington, D.C.; Bioethics Unit, Santiago, Chile (*www.paho.org*)
- Food and Agriculture Organization—FAO Legal Office, Rome, Italy (*www.fao.org*)
- World Food Program—Legal Services Division, Rome, Italy (*www.wfp.org*)
- International Fund for Agricultural Development—OGC, Rome, Italy (*www.ifad.org*)
- Organization of American States—Department of International Legal Affairs; Inter-American Drug Abuse Control Commission, Legal Development Unit, Washington, D.C. (*www.oas.org*)
- United Nations Office on Drugs and Crime—Legal Advisory Program, New York (*www.unodc.org*)
- World Intellectual Property Organization—Office of Legal Counsel; Office of Strategic Use of Intellectual Property for Development, Geneva, Switzerland (*www.wipo.org*)
- World Trade Organization—Legal Affairs Division; Rules Division; Intellectual Property Division (*www.wto.org*)

What Does It Pay?

Private practitioners of food and drug law are handsomely rewarded for three reasons:

1. Corporate clients have among the deepest in the world.
2. Class action litigation can reap an enormous payoff.
3. The economic consequences of recalls and litigation losses can threaten a client's very existence (e.g., the recent demise of the Peanut Corporation of America following the recall of its peanut-based products tainted by *Salmonella*).

Pharmaceutical and medical device companies pay their in-house counsel office attorneys quite well, with senior attorneys earning compensation comparable to their counterparts at Fortune 500 corporations ($200,000+). Junior attorneys tend to begin at salaries just under or right around $100,000.

Medical device companies' attorney compensation is, as a rule, slightly less than what is offered by pharmaceuticals.

Public sector attorneys are paid according to the U.S. government General Schedule pay scale (see *www.opm.gov*), while state and local lawyers are paid pursuant to their jurisdiction's standard compensation scales (generally a bit lower than the federal government salary scale).

Among nonprofits, attorneys who work for the major trade associations earn fairly high compensation ($100,000+), particularly if they are involved in government relations activities, a bit less if they work in the general counsel's office. Attorneys at other nonprofits, such as public interest and advocacy organizations, earn approximately the following median salaries: chief legal officers—$95,000, government relations professionals—$86,000, staff attorneys—$48,500, legislative assistants—$41,000.

International civil servants are paid according to United Nations or other international organization pay scales. Professional positions within the UN system (most of the international organizations listed above are part of the UN system) are divided into two categories: "P" levels (P-1 through P-5) and "D" levels (D-1 and D-2). P-1 is the most junior level, roughly equivalent to a U.S. government ranking of GS-11. D-2 is the most senior level, equating to the U.S. government ranking of Senior Executive Service or Senior Foreign Service. Salaries at the entry level range from approximately $37,000 (net of taxes) for a P-1 position to $105,000 for a top director (D-2) position. Depending on circumstances, employees may also be eligible for dependency, rent, education, and other allowances. Education grants for children payable through college at the rate of 75 percent of allowable costs up to a maximum amount can be an attractive benefit for many candidates.

Post adjustments, a form of cost-of-living payment, are net of taxes and are designed to equalize purchasing power among UN duty stations worldwide. They are adjusted monthly. For some high-cost cities, such as Geneva, New York, Paris, Rome, and Vienna, these adjustments can be significant (for example, the post adjustment for a D-2 in Geneva is currently $78,000).

Future Prospects

The dynamism of food, drug, device, and related industries makes food and drug law practice a solid, secure, and exciting career endeavor upon which you can rely with a high degree of certainty. Protecting food, drugs, and related products. is universally considered one of the highest and most critical responsibilities of government. Science, technology, and globalization make that calling difficult and complex, as in these examples:

- The *Family Smoking Prevention and Tobacco Control Act (Pub. L III-31),* signed into law by President Obama in June 2009, gives the FDA the authority to regulate the smoking industry more than any other previous legislation. The new law authorizes the FDA to regulate the chemicals used in tobacco products and to restrict advertising and new product launches. The congressional mandates contained in the legislation will require the FDA to develop, issue, explain, and enforce a spate of far-reaching regulations and to hire additional attorneys for its legal and regulatory staffs.
- The FDA wants to expand *Hazard Analysis and Critical Control Point* (HACCP—pronounced "hassip") regulation to the entire food supply in an attempt to keep pace with

the increasing number of new food pathogens (certain
E. coli strains and *Salmonella* were only recognized as
dangers in the last 20–30 years), increased concern about
chemical contamination, growth in the number and diversity of food products and processes, and the enormous
increase in imported foods. HAACP is of very recent FDA
vintage (NASA and the space program have employed it
for many years), and there is a very long way to go before
FDA meets its objectives. HAACP puts tremendous burdens
on every participant in the food supply chain. Biotech, life
sciences, and genetic engineering companies are sprouting
up all over the country. The surge in technology commercialization efforts by universities and government agencies
and laboratories is contributing to this development.

- Despite a move toward consolidation in the *multinational
  pharmaceutical industry* (there are relatively few pharmaceuticals to begin with because the cost of entry is so expensive; it usually takes about ten years for a new drug to go
  from research inception to approval to market), pharmaceuticals and their outside law firms require considerable
  lawyering. The rapid and accelerating pace of change and
  technology in their industry and their multinational presence means having to deal with more than one complex
  national regulatory regime. Currently, developed countries
  account for more than 85 percent of the $625 billion of
  global pharmaceutical sales.

- The *World Trade Organization's Trade-Related Aspects of Intellectual Property Rights Agreement* (TRIPS) establishes trade
  rules for intellectual property rights, including medicines
  under patent. A major TRIPS issue is how to ensure that
  patent protection for pharmaceutical products does not
  prevent people in poor countries from having access to
  medicines. There is a very delicate balance between the
  incentive to perform R&D, which patent protection provides, and the compulsory licensing provisions of TRIPS,
  which permit poor countries access to vital medicines.
  This all requires a great deal of working out.

As with so many other practice areas, food and drug law's future is linked to the aging population of 78 million Baby Boomers who will need medications as they age in unprecedented numbers.

Righting the FDA ship will give a big boost to the practice, as will the internationalization of the FDA into China, India, and beyond.

Other stimuli certain to boost the practice include these:

- The impact of healthcare reform
- Emerging nanotechnologies
- Increasing attention to food safety and the protection of the food supply
- The proliferation of dietary supplements and food additives
- More scrutiny of clinical drug trials
- Coming court interpretations of the very vague and unde- fined Food Allergen Labeling & Consumer Protection Act (Title II of Public Law 108-282), which became effective January 1, 2006
- Increased monitoring of postmarket drug safety
- Reversal of federal stem cell research policy and restoration of science to a position of respect
- Regulatory reform with respect to food, drugs, biologics, cosmetics, and medical devices
- Regulation of "drug–device" combinations (i.e., a device coated or impregnated with a drug or biologic) by FDA's Office of Combination Products, a recent and perfect example of technology racing ahead of and prompting new regulatory initiatives
- Regulation of genetic modifications

Breaking In

You might reasonably conclude that a food and drug background and/or education are mandatory to work in this field. While they are certainly a huge advantage, they are not absolutely essential. The FDA has, for the past ten years or so, hired a substantial number of "regulatory counsel" who lacked any background in food and drug law. There are currently almost 100 such attorneys at the FDA, as well as other lawyers with other job titles who also do not have food and drug experience. The same trend is occuring even more at all of the other federal and most of the state agencies with food and drug practices.

A food and drug (especially drug) background is at a higher premium in the private sector (although there, too, lack of such a background is not always a deterrent for those doing the hiring). However, it is attainable even if you never took a relevant course in law school and never practiced in the area.

Credential Boosters
- Seton Hall University School of Law—Health Care Compliance Certification Program (FDA law is a major component) (*www.law.shu.edu*)
- Suffolk University Law School—LLM Program in Global Law and Technology, Specialization in Biomedicine and Health Law (*www.law.suffolk.edu/academic/llm/curriculum.cfm*)
- Arizona State University College of Law—LLM in Biotechnology and Genomics (*www.law.asu.edu/biotech*)
- Golden Gate University School of Law—LLM in Intellectual Property Law, Specialization in Patent and Biotechnology Law (*www.ggu.edu/school_of_law*)
- University of Maryland—Graduate Certificate of Professional Studies in Food Safety Risk Analysis (*www.umd.edu*)
- Michigan State University (*www.msu.edu*)
  - Food Regulation in the United States (online)
  - International Food Law Internet Certificate Program (online)
- Temple University—Quality Assurance and Regulatory Affairs Graduate Program (*www.temple.edu*)
  - Drug Development Certificate
  - Clinical Trial Management
  - Medical Device Certificate
- University of Florida—Pharmacy Law and Ethics Certificate Program (*www.ufl.edu*)
- Regulatory Affairs Professional Society—Regulatory Affairs Certification (specifically for the healthcare product sector) (*www.raps.org*)

- Northeastern University (*www.spcs.neu.edu*)
  - Biopharmaceutical Domestic Regulatory Affairs
    (online option)
  - Biopharmaceutical International Regulatory Affairs
    (online option)
  - Medical Devices Regulatory Affairs (online option)

Breaking In via a Law-Related Position. Most of the food and drug law-related positions have to do with regulatory affairs or regulatory compliance. Regulatory affairs positions are primarily found in government, and regulatory compliance jobs in the private sector.

Networking Organizations
- Food and Drug Law Institute (*www.fdli.org*)
- American College of Legal Medicine (*www.aclm.org*)
- American Society for Pharmacy Law (*www.aspl.org*)
- American Bar Association Section of Science & Technology
  Law (*www.abanet.org/scitech/home.html*)
- American Agricultural Law Association (*www.aglaw-assn.org*)
- American Veterinary Medical Law Association (*www.avmla.org*)

For More Information
- Government Accountability Office (*www.gao.gov*)
- Morbidity and Mortality Weekly Report, Centers for Disease
  Control (*www.cdc.gov*)
- Association of Food and Drug Officials (*www.afdo.org*)
- National Association of Boards of Pharmacy (*www.napb.net*)
- National Association of State Departments of Agriculture
  (*www.nasda.org*)
- Federation of State Medical Boards (*www.fsmb.org*)
- United States Animal Health Association (*www.usaha.org*)
- National Association of Attorneys General (*www.naag.org*)
- Conference for Food Protection (*www.foodprotect.org*)
- Association of State and Territorial Health Officials
  (*www.astho.org*)
- National Association of County and City Health Officials
  (*www.naccho.org/index.cfm*)

- National Registry of Food Safety Professionals (*http://nrfsp.com*)
- Biotechnology Industry Organization (*www.bio.org*)
- Medical Device Manufacturers Association (*www.medical devices.org*)
- Association of Medical Diagnostics Manufacturers (*www.amdm.org*)
- MedicalDeviceLink.com (*www.devicelink.com*)
- Institute for Food Laws and Regulations, Michigan State University (*www.iflr.msu.edu/index.html*)
- National Academy of Sciences (*www.nasonline.org*)
- Codex Alimentarius Commission (*www.codexalimentarius.net*)

GOVERNMENT CONTRACT AND PROCUREMENT LAW

Introduction
Government contract and procurement law is interesting because it plays out in two different modes:

1. Where you are representing clients that are government contractors
2. Where you (or your employer) *are* the government contractor

Both the military and homeland security demands on the U.S. government combine to make government contract and procurement law a vibrant, growing discipline that consumes large quantities of legal services and attorney attention. Add the massive spending ($787 billion) mandated by the American Recovery and Reinvestment Act of 2009 and you have opportunities galore at every level of government (federal, state, regional and local) and in every private sector niche, (law firms, companies, nonprofits and solo practices).

What Is It?
Government contract and procurement law is largely self-defining:

- Private practice primarily includes positioning clients to compete for government contracts; negotiating and documenting contracts, including advising and assisting with proposals and bids in response to requests for proposals (RFPs) and invitations for bids (IFBs); contract disputes (e.g., your client objects to a contract award to a competitor); and defense of contract fraud allegations.

- Corporate procurement department duties include the following:
  - Sourcing spending categories
  - Industry analyses to identify size of industry, leading players, and industry characteristics
  - Developing contracts with new suppliers or renegotiating existing contracts
  - Managing the contract negotiation process by defining the strategy, leading the sourcing process, and identifying opportunities for expanded supplier relationships
  - Identifying metrics to evaluate supplier performance and achieve best value
  - Developing close relationships with suppliers and appropriate client groups
  - Analyzing, interpreting, and overseeing procurement actions and adherence to company policies and procedures, procurement terms and conditions, government and company directives, laws and regulations
  - Conducting internal audits to identify problems and trends and recommend improvements while guiding corrective actions
- Public sector practice encompasses drafting RFPs, IFBs, and contracting documents; investigating and litigating contract dispute allegations; investigating and prosecuting contract fraud allegations; administering and terminating contracts; contract compliance; and advising policy makers on procurement matters.
- If either you or your organization is the government contractor, the practice includes drafting responses to RFPs and IFBs, advising and assisting with contract administration, executing the contract, and defending against disputes and fraud allegations.

Who Does It?

Government contract and procurement law is a huge and wide-ranging practice area, replete with numerous players. The U.S. government is the world's largest buyer of goods and services—from spacecraft and advanced scientific research to paper clips and landscaping services. Military and civilian purchases totaled more than $425 billion a year before the economy collapsed, and that figure has gone well above $1 trillion a year since. Federal agencies are required to establish contracting goals, with at least 23 percent of all government spending targeted to small business.

Tens of thousands of law firms, sole practitioners, and companies have thriving government contract and procurement practices. Non-profits such as colleges and universities, faith-based organizations, and research institutions also participate in government contracting. More than 1,000 U.S. government law offices maintain such practices and are home to several thousand government contract lawyers. In addition, the U.S. government has almost 30,000 contracting personnel (such as administrators, officers, negotiators, and managers) who work intensively with law and regulation, approximately 7,500 of whom are estimated to be attorneys. This number is certain to increase along with the increase in federal contracting activity.

Attorneys also work in a variety of capacities for the federal government's Boards of Contract Appeals, the three principal ones being the Civilian Board of Contract Appeals (*www.cbca.gsa.gov*), the Armed Services Board of Contract Appeals (*www.law.gwu.edu/asbca*) and the Postal Service Board of Contract Appeals (*www.usps.com/judicial*).

State and local governments have parallel procurement law functions and personnel.

U.S. contract and procurement attorneys also work for the legal and procurement offices of numerous international organizations, such as the World Bank, Inter-American Development Bank, European Bank for Reconstruction and Development, Pan American Health Organization, Asian Development Bank, International Finance Corporation, Multi-lateral Investment Guaranty Agency, International Centre for Settlement of Investment Disputes, and close to 200 other international and multilateral agencies in the United States and abroad.

What Does It Pay?

Compensation ranges widely, depending on type of practice, size, and geographic location of the employer and other variables. This is particularly true of private practice and corporate positions. U.S. government salaries begin at the $46,000–$56,000 range for entry-level attorneys and contract personnel and can go up to approximately $145,000 and higher. State and local salaries are typically lower.

Future Prospects

Government contract and procurement law has a bright future. Defense contracting has almost always been a thriving proposition. There is little indication that this will change much in the near future, the world being so unpredictable, unstable, and threatening.

The creation of the Department of Homeland Security gave a huge boost to U.S. government contracting ($40–$50 billion extra per year). This increase in government contracting dollars is likely to be with us for a long time.

Responses to the Great Recession, particularly the enactment of the $787 billion American Recovery and Reinvestment Act of 2009, create a bonanza for government contractors—and their legal representatives—at every level of government, injecting enormous numbers of contracting dollars into the economy. In all likelihood, the Act will be just the first step in stimulating economic recovery.

Finally, the extraordinarily ambitious Obama administration initiatives in energy, healthcare, and education also contain immediate contracting dollars of unprecedented proportions, as well as policy changes, which are likely to keep procurement dollars flowing for a long time to come.

Breaking In

Since contract law is one of the bedrocks of legal education, attorneys are natural candidates for government contract and procurement law positions in mainstream arenas—law firms, corporate in-house counsel offices, and government law offices—as well as in law-related venues, such as corporate, nonprofit, and government procurement offices. History works to the advantage of anyone interested in this field, since employers have been hiring government-contracting novices for positions for a long time.

Enhancing Your Credentials. You can enhance your employability and compensation by obtaining a government contracting degree or certificate. The following selected institutions offer these credentials:

- George Washington University Law School—LLM in Government Procurement Law (*www.law.gwu.edu*)
- Villanova University—Master Certificate in Government Contract Management (*www.villanova.edu*)
- National Contract Management Association—Certified Federal Contracts Manager (*www.ncmahq.org*)

State specialty certification in government contracting is extremely limited (Connecticut is the only state that recognizes certified specialists in government contract law).

You may be able to join one or more of the following organizations of contract professionals:

- National Contract Management Association (*www.ncmahq.org*)
- Federal Bar Association Government Contracts Section (*www.fedbar.org/govtcontracts_section.html*)
- American Bar Association Section of Public Contract Law (*www.abanet.org/contract/mission.html*)
- Boards of Contract Appeals Bar Association (*www.bcaba.org*)

You or Your Organization as the Contractor. Federal, state, and local governments increasingly outsource legal services. Traditionally, a number of primarily major law firms served as bond counsel for municipalities and special districts under lucrative contracts. That has expanded exponentially and is likely to continue to grow because outside counsel have proven their worth. Moreover, outsourcing legal services permits government to get around certain hiring restrictions that may temporarily inhibit direct hiring of attorneys.

At the federal level, the following organizations have contracted for outside legal services:

- Agricultural Research Service
- Forest Service

- Rural Development
- National Oceanic & Atmospheric Administration
- U.S. Department of Defense
- Defense Fuel Supply Center
- TRICARE Health and Medical Program of the Uniformed Services
- Department of the Air Force
- Department of the Army
- Army Corps of Engineers
- Naval Research Laboratory
- U.S. Department of Education—Office of Civil Rights
- U.S. Department of Energy
- Food and Drug Administration
- National Institutes of Health
- National Library of Medicine
- Department of Housing & Urban Development
- Bureau of Indian Affairs
- U.S. Fish and Wildlife Service
- Minerals Management Service
- National Park Service
- U.S. Department of Justice
- Federal Bureau of Prisons
- U.S. Marshals Service
- U.S. Trustee Offices
- Benefits Review Board
- U.S. Department of Labor—Office of Administrative Law Judges
- U.S. Department of Transportation
- Federal Aviation Administration
- Federal Highway Administration
- National Highway Traffic Safety Administration
- Bureau of Immigration & Customs Enforcement
- Internal Revenue Service
- U.S. Department of Veterans Affairs
- Administrative Office of the U.S. Courts
- Environmental Protection Agency
- Equal Employment Opportunity Commission

- Federal Emergency Management Agency
- Federal Communications Commission
- Federal Deposit Insurance Corporation
- General Services Administration
- Japan–U.S. Friendship Commission
- National Technology Transfer Center
- Nuclear Regulatory Commission
- Office of Personnel Management
- Pension Benefit Guaranty Corporation
- U.S. Agency for International Development

The following are the principal practice areas for which the U.S. government seeks outside legal services: real estate closings, foreclosures, patents, rule of law projects for emerging democracies and market economies, legal research and decision writing, mediation, and training in a wide variety of legal subjects. International organizations and multilateral development agencies contract for a range of legal services, particularly energy, environmental, and rule of law matters.

A significant number of subcontracts also are available for legal and law-related services. Most agencies publish a list of prime contractors, which will give you an idea of the types of subcontracting services in demand.

The states that do the most legal and law-related services contracting are California, Massachusetts, Texas, Florida, Maryland, Hawaii, and Colorado.

Very few attorneys and law firms bid on legal services contracts, so competition is rather limited.

The primary sources of information about U.S. government legal and law-related services contracts are the Federal Business Opportunities website (*www.fbo.gov*) and FedConnect (*www.fedconnect.net*). All federal contracts worth $100,000 or more are published here. Some contracts worth between $25,000 and $100,000 are also published here. Contracts worth less than $25,000 are not included.

To make sure that you or your organization receive timely information about *all* federal contract opportunities, you need to (1) identify those agencies most likely to procure the services you offer and (2) contact (ideally visit) agency-contracting offices and Small and Disadvantaged Business Utilization Offices that handle those contracts.

The U.S. government pays invoices for virtually all legal and law-related contract services within 60 days of submission. Some payments can even be made by credit card.

For More Information
- Central Contractor Registration System (CCR) (*www.ccr.gov*)
- CCR Handbook (*www.ccr.gov/Handbook.aspx*)
- Data Universal Numbering System (available from Dun & Bradstreet) (*www.dnb.com*)
- North American Industry Classification System (NAICS) Codes (*www.census.gov*)
- Standard Industrial Classification (SIC) Codes (*www.osha.gov/oshstats/sicser.html*)
- Small Business Size Standards (*www.sba.gov/services/ contractingopportunities/sizestandardstopics*)
- Federal Supply Class (FSC) Reference Guide (*www.dlis.dla.mil/hcfsch21.asp*)
- Small Business Administration (*www.sba.gov*)
- HUBZone Program (*www.sba.gov/hubzone*)
- 8(a) Business Development Program (*www.sba.gov/8abd*)
- Self-Certification Programs
  - Service-Disabled Veteran-Owned Small Business (*www.sba.gov/vets*)
  - Veteran-Owned Small Business (*www.va.gov*)
  - Women-Owned Small Business (*www.sba. gov/aboutsba/sbaprograms/onlinewbc*)
  - "Business Opportunities Course: A Guide to Winning Federal Contracts" (*www.sba.gov/training*)
  - "How to Become a Contractor—GSA Schedules Program Course" (*www.gsa.gov*)
- Office of Federal Procurement Policy (*www.whitehouse. gov/omb/procurement*)
- Acquisition Central (*http://acquisition.gov*)
- California State Contracts Register (*www.eprocure.dgs. ca.gov/default.htm*)
- Massachusetts Procurement Access and Solicitation System (*www.comm-pass.com*)

- Texas Electronic State Business Daily (*http://esbd.cpa.state.tx.us*)
- MyFloridaMarketPlace (*http://vbs.dms.state.fl.us/vbs/main_menu*)
- Maryland Office of the Attorney General RFPs
  (*http://www.oag.state.md.us*)
- Hawaii State and County Procurement Notices
  (*http://www4.hawaii.gov/bidapps*)
- Colorado Bids (*www.gssa.state.co.us/VenSols*)

LAND USE AND EMINENT DOMAIN LAW

Introduction

Land use and eminent domain law received a big boost in early 2009 with the enactment of the American Recovery and Reinvestment Act of 2009 (ARRA), which appropriated $787 billion to stimulate the economy. ARRA includes a massive infusion of funds for the development and dissemination of new construction projects and new energy sources, requiring, among other stimulants, the construction of nationwide transmission and distribution systems that either do not presently exist, require upgrading to handle energy from new sources, or attach to existing grids. These projects will take years to plan, defend, and execute, all of which is very good news for attorneys interested in land use and condemnation issues.

Eminent domain practice suddenly became front page news in 2005 when the U.S. Supreme Court decided *Kelo v. City of New London*, 545 U. S. 469 (2005). The Court in *Kelo* held, 5-4, that the use of eminent domain to transfer land from one private owner to another to further economic development was permissible under the Takings Clause of the Fifth Amendment.

Kelo prompted a barrage of criticism from some legal scholars, the president, Congress, state legislatures and the public. State reaction to *Kelo,* through ballot initiatives and legislation, was widespread. Forty-two states now have imposed restrictions on the kind of taking allowed under *Kelo.*

The law of eminent domain extends beyond real property rights to allegations of patent or copyright infringement by the U.S. government. This has begun to emerge in recent years due to the increase in public–private R&D partnerships, drug development, and related areas. The governing statute (28 U.S.C. 1498) also authorizes the government to delegate its eminent domain power over patents and copyrights to contractors and subcontractors acting on its behalf. Given the massive increase in government contracting in recent years, look for additional legal activity in this area as well.

What Is It?

Land use law includes planning, zoning, subdivision, and permitting for projects as well as any necessary related real-estate transactions. Law firms and sole practitioners provide land use services to property owners, developers, builders, government agencies, and trade associations, among others. They practice before state and federal administrative agencies and courts, as well as local zoning boards, planning commissions, and other forums.

Eminent domain (aka "condemnation") practice derives from the Fifth Amendment, which requires the government to provide just compensation to the owner of private property taken by the government for public use. Takers could include the U.S. government, a state government, a municipality, and even a private party (person or corporation) authorized to exercise functions of a public character. *Property* has been broadly defined by the courts to include not just land but also water and air rights and even certain intellectual property (see introduction to this section). The government or its surrogate takes the property through a condemnation proceeding.

Eminent domain practice is quite complex and involves many constitutional and practical nuances. It typically involves three components: negotiation, litigation, and constitutional law. This combination makes it a fascinating practice; it is both intellectually and financially rewarding.

Who Does It?

Land use and eminent domain practice has a large and growing practitioner population, including law firms of all sizes; boutique firms that focus primarily or exclusively on these matters or a subset of them; corporations, primarily those in the hospitality, recreation, retail, and other related industries; utilities; public sector agencies that have jurisdiction over land or responsibilities involving property matters (see a list of U.S. government law offices below), such as state transportation departments and local planning commissions and zoning boards; nonprofits, such as universities and especially land trusts (more than 1,300 in the United States); and special-purpose districts and authorities (e.g., Washington Metropolitan Airports Authority, Port Authority of New York and New Jersey, Chicago Transit Authority), which include 3,000+ conservation districts, over 100 port authorities and districts, water and sewer authorities, and more than 3,400 special-purpose districts in California alone.

U.S. Government Law Offices—Land Use and/or Eminent Domain Practice

- U.S. Department of Agriculture—OGC, Civil Works & Environment Section (*www.usda.gov*)
- U.S. Department of Interior—Office of the Solicitor, Division of Indian Affairs; Division of Land and Water Resources (*www.doi.gov*)
- U.S. Department of Justice—Environment and Natural Resources Division, Land Acquisition Section and General Litigation Section (*www.usdoj.gov/enrd*)
- U.S. Department of Justice—Civil Division, Commercial Litigation Branch (*www.usdoj.gov/civil*)
- U.S. Army—OGC, Civil Works and Environment Section; Corps of Engineers, OGC (*www.army.mil*)
- U.S. Air Force—Judge Advocate General's Department; Air Force Real Property Agency, Legal Division (*www.af.mil*)
- U.S. Department of Energy—Bonneville Power Administration, OGC; Western Area Power Administration, OGC; Southwestern Power Administration, OGC (*www.energy.gov*)
- U.S. Department of Transportation—Federal Highway Administration, Office of Chief Counsel, Program Services Division; Federal Lands Legal Team (*www.dot.gov*)
- Tennessee Valley Authority—Office of Executive Vice President and General Counsel (*www.tva.gov*)
- National Capital Planning Commission—OGC (*www.ncpc.gov*)
- Amtrak—OGC (*www.amtrak.com*)
- U.S. Postal Service—Law Department (*www.usps.com*)
- Library of Congress—Congressional Research Service, American Law Division (*www.loc.gov*)
- U.S. Court of Federal Claims (*www.uscfc.uscourts.gov*)

Other U.S. Government Agencies with Attorneys Practicing Land Use and/or Eminent Domain Law
- U.S. Department of Interior—Bureau of Indian Affairs, Office of the Deputy Director, Trust Services; Bureau of Land Management; Minerals Management Service; National Park Service (*www.doi.gov*)
- U.S. Army Corps of Engineers—Directorate of Real Estate, Civil Division (*www.usace.army.mil*)
- Federal Energy Regulatory Commission—Office of Energy Projects (*www.ferc.gov*)

What Does It Pay?

Law firm and corporate compensation for land use and eminent domain attorneys varies as widely as any other law firm and corporate compensation. Geographic location, size of employer, and industry type are all important variables.

Government salaries range from approximately $50,000–$60,000 at the entry level to $150,000 at senior levels (federal) and range widely at the state and local levels, starting anywhere from the low $30,000s in a municipality to $70,000+ in a major city or large state. The value of attorneys that do this kind of work is slowly being recognized by state and local government employers, and salaries are on the rise. A number of states pay such attorneys low six-figure salaries.

Attorneys who work for nonprofits, particularly land trusts, usually earn significantly lower salaries than either their private or public sector counterparts.

Future Prospects

Land use and eminent domain practice will prosper for a long time to come. In addition to the stimuli provided by actions such as *Kelo* (and the reactions to that case), ARRA, and government patent and copyright infringement cases, two additional developments ensure a bright future:

1. The political consensus around the need to fix the crumbling U.S. infrastructure will require a decades-long

commitment of resources. This effort will involve thousands
of land use issues and mean a great deal of work for attorneys who practice in this field.

2. The U.S. energy economy is transitioning from fossil fuels
to renewables. The ambitious program outlined in ARRA
and the fiscal year 2010 federal budget are just the first
shots in this campaign. This effort's timeline is also mea-
sured in decades.

Breaking In

The knowledge of the law necessary to practice in this area is not difficult
to learn. Most attorneys assigned land use or eminent domain projects
come up the learning curve quickly.

You can build upon your general legal credentials by obtaining
a relevant degree or certificate. This additional academic ticket will
enhance your employability and may have a positive impact on your
initial compensation. Selected programs include these:

- University of Denver Sturm College of Law (*www.law.du.edu*)
  - LLM in Environmental and Natural Resources Law and
    Policy, Optional Specialization in Land Use Law and
    Policy
  - Certificate of Studies in Natural Resources Law and
    Policy, Optional Specialization in Land Use Law and
    Policy
- University of Florida Levin College of Law (*www.law.ufl.
  edu/elulp*)
  - LLM in Environmental and Land Use Law
- University of California—Davis Extension (*http://extension.
  ucdavis.edu/certificates/*)
  - Certificate in Land Use and Environmental Planning
- University of Missouri—St. Louis (*http://www.umsl.edu/
  divisions/conted/certificates/index.html*)
  - Chancellor's Certificate Program in Planning and Zoning
- International Right of Way Association (*www.irwaonline.org*)
  - Right of Way Certification

A number of law-related occupations also employ land use legal principles in their daily practice. These include director of real estate (colleges and universities), land agent or landman (oil and gas companies), land acquisition manager (chain stores, hospitality and recreation companies), land law examiner (U.S. government), land preservation director (land trusts), land protection director/specialist (land trusts), and zoning administrator (municipalities).

You may wish to consider joining one or more of the following organizations to develop contacts and obtain information about land use and eminent domain practice.

- American College of Real Estate Lawyers (*www.acrel.org*)
- American Land Title Association (*www.alta.org*)
- Counselors of Real Estate (*www.cre.org*)

For More Information

- American Farmland Trust (*www.farmland.org*)
- American Planning Association (*www.planning.org*)
- American Resort Development Association (*www.arda.org*)
- California Special Districts Association (*www.csda.net*)
- Land Policy Institute (*www.landpolicy.msu.edu*)
- Land Trust Alliance (*www.landtrustalliance.org*)
- Lincoln Institute of Land Policy (*www.lincolninst.edu/index-high.asp*)
- National Association of Conservation Districts (*www.nacdnet.org*)
- National Brownfield Association (*www.brownfieldassociation.org*)
- Trust for Public Land (*www.tpl.org*)
- Urban Land Institute (*www.uli.org*)

EMPLOYMENT LAW

Introduction

The decline of organized labor—and consequently of labor law—is coterminous with employment law's rise to prominence. Three factors make employment law recession-proof:

1. Beginning with the landmark civil rights legislation of the
   1960s, Congress and the state legislatures have enacted
   numerous laws protecting the rights of workers, including the Davis-Bacon Act (Pub.L. 74-403); Equal Pay Act of
   1963 (Pub.L. 88-38); Fair Labor Standards Act (29 U.S.C.
   201–219); Architectural Barriers Act of 1968 (42 U.S.C. 4151
   et seq.); Occupational Safety and Health Act of 1970 (Pub.L.
   91-596); Title IX (20 U.S.C. 1681–1688); Rehabilitation Act of
   1973 (29 U.S.C. 701 et seq.); ERISA (29 U.S.C. 1001 et seq.);
   Vietnam Era Veterans' Readjustment Assistance Act of 1974
   (38 U.S.C. 4212); Age Discrimination Act of 1975 (42 U.S.C.
   6101 et seq.); Age Discrimination in Employment Act (29
   U.S.C. 621 et seq.); Americans with Disabilities Act (42
   U.S.C. 12101 et seq., 47 U.S.C., Chapter 5); Family and Medical Leave Act (29 U.S.C. 2601 et seq.); Contract Work Hours
   and Safety Standards Act (40 U.S.C. 3701 et seq.); Genetic
   Information Nondiscrimination Act (42 U.S.C. 2000ff et
   seq.); ADA Amendments Act of 2008 (Pub.L. 110-325); Uniformed Services Employment and Reemployment Rights Act
   (USERRA) (38 U.S.C. 4301 et seq.); and the Lily Ledbetter
   Fair Pay Act of 2009 (Pub.L. 111-2); among others.

   The large and constantly increasing number of employment protections enacted by Congress and state legislatures
   affords employees more opportunities to seek redress for
   actual and perceived wrongs, a bonanza for employment
   lawyers, regardless of the state of the economy.

   Job discrimination complaints to the Equal Employment Opportunity Commission (EEOC) rose 15 percent
   in 2008, and another record rise is expected in 2009. Age
   discrimination complaints rose 28 percent. Both represent
   the highest number of grievance filings since the agency
   opened its doors in 1965.

2. The Bureau of Labor Statistics reported that, in the first
   15 months of the Great Recession (beginning in December
   2007), more than 5 million people were laid off from their
   jobs, with many more expected to follow. In every past

recession marked by mass layoffs, there has been an upsurge in employment grievances filed with the government agencies tasked with resolving such claims, plus a large increase in employment cases filed in federal and state courts. Consequently, employment lawyers thrive during recessions.

3. The first year in which the Baby Boomer bow wave reached retirement age was 2008. The problem for Boomers, however, is that the sudden collapse of their retirement funds is causing many of them to postpone their long-desired departure from the workforce. You can bank on the fact that age discrimination complaints will increase considerably.

What Is It?

Employment law practice deals with workplace-related matters and grievances:

- Wrongful termination
- Equal employment opportunity
- Affirmative action
- Racial discrimination
- Age discrimination
- Religious discrimination
- National origin discrimination
- Disability discrimination
- Pregnancy discrimination
- Veterans' re-employment rights
- Sexual harassment
- Unemployment compensation
- Overtime issues
- Employee benefits
- Pension issues
- Family and Medical Leave
- Severance pay
- Insurance coverage after a job loss or resignation
- Denial of unemployment benefits
- Employer background checks
- Executive compensation
- Noncompete agreements
- WARN Act (Pub.L. 100-379) Notices
- Workers compensation
- Social Security
- Drug testing in the workplace
- Youth employment/ child labor laws
- Whistleblower retaliation
- *Qui tam*
- Contract compliance
- Employee handbooks and manuals

Employment law involves a great deal of client counseling and preventive law practice through the drafting and updating of employee handbooks, manuals, and policies. Employment lawyers generally have a considerable administrative litigation practice, ranging from mediations and informal hearings to formal adjudications in federal and state administrative forums under a fairly elaborate set of procedural and evidentiary rules, such as the Federal Administrative Procedure Act, 5 U.S.C. §§ 551 et seq. They may also practice before state and federal courts.

This is one practice area where the private and public sectors converge with respect to duties and responsibilities. Government employment law attorneys perform functions very similar to those of their private sector counterparts.

Who Does It?

A few law firms with offices throughout the country, notably Littler Mendelson (*www.littler.com*), Jackson Lewis (*www.jacksonlewis.com*), Ogletree, Deakins, Nash, Smoak & Stewart, P.C. (*www.ogletreedeakins.com*), Ford & Harrison (*www.fordharrison.com*), and Fisher & Phillips (*www.laborlawyers. com*), specialize in employment law. Most other large firms maintain some level of employment law practice, typically advising and defending corporate clients. However, many private practice opportunities are found in midsize, small, and boutique law firms. There is also a large sole practitioner contingent.

Every Fortune 1000 corporation and thousands of smaller companies have extensive employment law practices, as do colleges and universities, hospitals, nonprofit organizations, and government agencies at every level. The U.S. government, for example, has more than 300 separate law offices nationwide that practice employment law, plus more than 80 Alternative Dispute Resolution (ADR) offices, which focus most of their attention on employment disputes.

The U.S. government also contracts for outside employment dispute mediators. These are principal contracting agencies:

- Equal Employment Opportunity Commission (*www.eeoc.gov*)
- U.S. Postal Service REDRESS Mediation Program
  (*www.usps.com/redress*)

- U.S. Air Force Alternative Dispute Resolution Program (*www.adr.af.mil*)
- U.S. Department of Agriculture ADR Program (*www.usda.gov/cprc*)
- U.S. Department of Energy Mediation Program (*www.energy.gov*)
- Federal Deposit Insurance Corporation (*www.fdic.gov*)
- Federal Mediation and Conciliation Service (*www.fmcs.gov*)

Employment ADR is becoming more widespread, and not just within the the U.S. government. Private sector employers increasingly contract for ADR services. Many companies use employment mediators and/or arbitrators selected from the American Arbitration Association's Roster of Neutrals, a very prestigious listing. The threshold qualifications for listing are quite stringent (see *www.adr.org*).

Note: For more detailed ADR information, see the ADR section in Chapter 5: Using Your Law Degree Outside the Mainstream.

In summary, employment law is one of the most ubiquitous of practice areas: It is present in almost every large and midsize law firm, most corporations, virtually every government general counsel office, and most nonprofits with more than a handful of employees. In addition, a great many small law firms and sole practitioners practice employment law.

What Does It Pay?

Large law firms and large employment law boutique firms compensate their associates, staff attorneys, and partners on a level comparable to other large firm practitioners. Midsize and small firm attorneys' and sole practitioners' compensation varies considerably, a function of geographic location, firm size, size of the employment law practice, nature of the clients, and emphasis within the firm on this practice area.

Corporate in-house attorneys are compensated according to the norms for their employer. Compensation for corporate employment lawyers who work in the general counsel's office has increased a bit more rapidly than corporate attorney pay in general, primarily because of the central importance of their role. The variables that influence corporate employment lawyer compensation are the same as those governing corporate compensation in general: geographic location, company size, and industry. For example, an attorney with several years of experience might earn $125,000+ in a large corporation located in a major metropolitan area, whereas his or her counterpart who works for a comparable company in a rural area might earn $100,000 or less.

Corporate employment lawyers may also work in divisions other than the general counsel's office, such as human resources or compliance. Those attorneys often earn somewhat less than their general counsel office colleagues.

Public sector attorneys are paid under the Federal General Schedule and state pay schedules that apply, across the board, to almost all government professional employees (see *www.opm.gov* for current federal pay scales). This translates into starting pay around $50,000 for entry-level lawyers, ranging up to approximately $150,000, with yearly increases. State-level attorneys are generally a pay ratchet below their federal colleagues, although this varies considerably from state to state.

There is no set amount that the U.S. government compensates attorneys with whom it contracts for employment mediation services. However, this work can be quite lucrative. Several of my counseling clients make a good living doing nothing but occasional federal mediations.

Nonmainstream law-related positions (see "Breaking In" below) customarily pay somewhat less than mainstream employment law jobs.

Future Prospects

Employment law will be an interesting, diversified, and profitable practice area for years to come. First, despite the (now discredited) irrational exuberance of former Federal Reserve Chairman Alan Greenspan and his acolytes about the end of the era of economic fluctuations, economic swings won't go away. There will always be ups and downs, and that translates into positives for employment lawyers.

Second, the huge Baby Boomer population is working longer and, due to the Great Recession, going back to work, which will create more opportunities for employment lawyers.

Third, the 21st-century workplace will be increasingly unsettled. Companies will have to cope with globalization and its attendant threats of job relocation outside of the United States, technological advances, worker malaise, and corporate buyouts and acquisitions, each of which contributes to a central role for employment law and its practitioners.

Breaking In

The Learning Curve. Acquiring the substantive knowledge necessary to practice employment law is not very daunting. Any experienced or aspiring litigator can do it, regardless of where he or she has spent his or her career and regardless of what courses were taken in law school.

Any nonlitigator can also move into employment law because so much of it involves informal and formal administrative hearings, where the rules of procedure and evidence are significantly more relaxed and forgiving than trial practice before a court.

Alternative (Nonmainstream) Employment Law Options. Employment law offers many nonmainstream possibilities. The entire human resources area has become so infused with legal and regulatory compliance issues that an increasing number of employers—companies and even government agencies—have appointed attorneys to senior HR positions. In addition, employment attorneys can be found in offices other than legal departments, such as human resources, compliance, ombudsman, and others. Finally, attorneys often occupy law-related positions such as the following:

- Accessibility/compliance specialist
- ADA coordinator
- Affirmative action/ EEO officer
- Civil rights/affirmative action investigator
- Civil rights analyst
- Disability coordinator
- Diversity director
- Employee benefits manager
- Employee relations manager/specialist

- Employment and training specialist
- Equity coordinator
- Government benefits director
- Law firm recruiter
- Lawyer temporary agency manager
- Legal career counselor
- Legal search consultant
- Retirement systems administrator
- Veterans re-employment rights specialist

Law-related positions can be found in law firms, corporations, government, universities, and nonprofits, as well as other places.

Credential Enhancement. You can improve your employment law possibilities if you obtain a relevant LLM or certificate. Added to your law degree and legal experience, this type of credential can be very attractive to prospective employers.

The following selected organizations offer employment law credentialing programs:

- University of San Diego School of Law (*www.sandiego.edu/usdlaw*)
  - General LLM with Concentration in Labor and Employment Law
- Wayne State University Law School (*www.law.wayne.edu*)
  - LLM with Specialization in Labor and Employment Law
- Albany Law School (*www.als.edu*)
  - LLM in Advanced Legal Studies with Specialization in Labor & Employment Law
- New York University School of Law (*www.law.nyu.edu*)
  - LLM in Labor and Employment Law
- Golden Gate University School of Law (*www.ggu. edu/school_of_law*)
  - Graduate Law Fellowship, Women's Employment Rights Clinic
- Georgetown University Law Center (*www.law.georgetown.edu*)
  - Employee Benefits Law Certificate
- Temple University James E. Beasley School of Law (*www.law.temple.edu*)
  - Employee Benefits Certificate Program
- Villanova University School of Law (*www.law.vill.edu*)
  - Employee Benefits Certificate
- Mountain States Employers' Council (*www.msec.org*)
  - Mediating Workplace Disputes Certificate
- Expert Rating (*www.expertrating.com*)
  - Employment Law Certification (online)
- CAI (*www.capital.org*)
  - Employment Law Certification Series
- American Arbitration Association (*www.adr.org*)
  - Course in Resolution of Employment Disputes Pre-Arbitration (online)

Networking Opportunities. Joining an organization of colleagues, attending its meetings, and becoming involved in its local chapter and national activities is an excellent way of making yourself known to the community of like-minded professionals. Hundreds of my clients have landed new positions through such involvement.

The major employment law networking organizations are these:

- National Employment Lawyers Association (*www.nela.org*)
- American Bar Association—Section of Labor & Employment Law (*www.abanet.org/labor/home.html*)
- Federal Bar Association—Labor & Employment Law Section (*www.fedbar.org/labor&employ_section.html*)
- National Bar Association—Labor & Employment Law Division (*www.ogletreedeakins.com*)
- Minority Corporate Counsel Association (*www.mcca.org*)
- Society for Human Resource Management (*www.shrm.org*)

For More Information

- Elaws (U.S. Department of Labor) (*www.dol.gov/elaws*)
- National Employment Law Institute (*www.neli.org*)
- Equal Employment Opportunity Commission (*www.eeoc.gov*)
- National Labor Relations Board (*www.nlrb.gov*)
- Federal Labor Relations Authority (*www.flra.gov*)
- Occupational Safety & Health Administration (*www.osha.gov*)
- Office of Federal Contract Compliance Programs (*www.dol.gov/esa/ofccp*)
- American Arbitration Association (*www.adr.org*)

SOCIAL SECURITY DISABILITY INCOME CLAIMS REPRESENTATION

Introduction

The opportunity presented by representing Social Security Disability Income (SSDI) claimants is one of the best-kept road-to-riches-and-psychological-reward stories you may ever run across. The number of potential clients is huge and growing, a consequence of the rapid aging of the United States population. The opportunity to make an excellent living is clear. The stress associated with this kind of litigation is considerably less compared to most other areas of litigation. The satisfaction gained by helping people in need is great. Finally, the synergies with related practice areas (see the next two sections) are unique.

What Is It?

SSDI claims representation consists of advocating for disability benefits on behalf of a disabled individual who is unable to work. Advocacy can consist of assisting the claimant with the initial application for benefits, client counseling, explaining the claimant's situation to first- and second-level reviewers, representing the claimant at an SSDI hearing before a Social Security Administration administrative law judge (ALJ), and representing the claimant before the Social Security Appeals Council and, if necessary, in Federal Court.

Most claimant representation takes place at the ALJ hearing level.

While there is no legal requirement that a claimant representative (the Social Security "term of art" for this kind of representation) be a lawyer, it is very advantageous to be one for this reason: Any practitioner knows how much effort is expended in collecting fees from clients. Here, the U.S. government will collect your fee for you. You do not have to do anything. The government only does this for claimant representatives who are attorneys. The attorney is compensated out of the back benefits awarded to the claimant. The attorney gets his or her fee before the claimant gets anything. Nonattorney claimant representatives have to collect their fees the old-fashioned way, directly from the claimant.

Your next question should be: "How do I get paid if my client loses the case?"

This question merits a two-part response:

1. Around 70 percent of SSDI hearings result in victory for the claimant.
2. If you lose, you need to collect your fee directly from your client.

OK, but you're still a skeptic: "I have never tried a case in my life, and I'm intimidated by the thought of going up against someone in a courtroom."

Not to worry.

You won't be going up against anyone. SSDI hearings are not adversarial proceedings, meaning that no one is representing the other side. It's just you, your client, and the ALJ, who is there to listen to your presentation of why the claimant should be awarded benefits.

SSDI cases that go to an ALJ hearing are appeals from a denial of the claim at a lower level by civil servants who don't believe that the claim is valid or who have found flaws in the claim application. Two questions capture the essence of almost all of these cases:

1. Does the claimant have one of the designated disabilities that would entitle him or her to SSDI benefits?
2. Does the disability inhibit the claimant from performing his or her job?

This is what you, the claimant representative, have to demonstrate at the hearing.

If this is beginning to sound too good to be true . . . it gets even better.

There is presently a *backlog of more than 765,000 cases* waiting for a hearing. The system is so overwhelmed with claims that the Social Security Administration recently hired 175 new ALJs in a desperate effort to reduce this crushing backlog. That is on top of the 1,100 judges already working in the system, and more than 100 additional ALJs were to have been appointed during fiscal year 2009. Another 210 are scheduled for appointment in fiscal year 2010.

Very few of these hundreds of thousands of claimants currently have claimant representatives. Many do not know that they are entitled to representation. Others erroneously believe that they have to pay something up front if they want a claimant representative to help them. They don't. Once they get their back award of benefits, they will have plenty of money available to pay the fee.

There is no reason to wait for a claimant to be denied benefits initially for you to offer your claimant representation services. In fact, the Social Security Administration itself wishes that more claimants would engage claimant representatives for help in filing their initial claims, because statistics show that those who do are far more likely to be awarded benefits at the outset.

While the cases do require the claimant representative to make a presentation to the ALJ and often to put the claimant and perhaps others on the witness stand, many such cases follow a "script." There are nowhere near the demands on the attorney that are intrinsic to most cases.

And there are even more enticing features that make this practice attractive:

- Cases are straightforward and relatively easy to prepare.
- Hearings do not last very long.
- There are a variety of easy-to-execute and inexpensive marketing initiatives that you can implement to attract clients (see "Breaking In").
- You can practice anywhere. The Social Security Administration is one of the most omnipresent government organizations in the world, with more than 1,300 offices nationwide where claimants can file for benefits and where you can promote your services.
- Social Security has 144 hearing offices throughout the country, which means that you are never very far from one. Moreover, it is now possible for many hearings to be held by videoconference, obviating the need for travel to a hearing site.

Who Does It?

Attorneys who act as Claimant Representatives usually either are sole practitioners or work in small law firms—both general practice firms and boutique practices.

In addition, disability insurance companies often pursue SSDI benefits on behalf of their insureds, because under many disability insurance contracts, SSDI benefits offset insurance company payments, thus saving the company money. Insurance companies either do this work in-house or through subsidiaries established for this purpose.

Public sector attorneys are also involved in SSDI claims work. Several hundred attorneys work for the Social Security Administration's Office of Disability Adjudication and Review (ODAR). Their work largely consists of drafting decisions in cases heard by Social Security ALJs and advising and drafting Appeals Council decisions.

In addition, as mentioned above there are the 1,100+ Social Security ALJs, with many more to come.

What Does It Pay?

Fees are regulated by the Social Security Administration. SSDI cases pay 25 percent of the claimant's past-due benefits, or $5,300, whichever is less. For cases that have waited years to be heard (some now approaching three years), back benefits are likely to be huge, since back awards cover the entire period of time from initial application for benefits until the date when benefits are awarded.

Some claimant representatives earn well over $1 million annually handling SSDI cases.

In 2009, Social Security ALJs start at $102,000+ and could earn up to approximately $160,000, while ODAR staff attorneys and attorney-advisors begin at approximately $46,000–$73,000 and can earn up to $145,000.

Future Prospects

It is going to take years to reduce this backlog of cases to manageable proportions, meaning that there will be clients galore for a very long time. Compounding the backlog is the "age tsunami." With millions of Baby Boomers reaching senior status each year until 2026, the number of disability claims is sure to increase substantially over the current 2.8 million per year. Actuarial statistics show that once a person reaches age 50, the likelihood that he or she will incur a short-term or permanent disability skyrockets.

The utilization of claimant representatives during the SSDI claims process is increasing, stimulated by favorable changes in the governing laws and regulations and more sophistication among claimants. Moreover, the very numbers of claimants involved, as well as an increase in what are called "termination of benefits" cases, mean many more opportunities in this area than ever.

Breaking In

Because SSDI practice is largely the province of sole practitioners and small law firms, this section requires some discussion of how a practitioner would go about building the practice. The business development advice in this section is also a useful template for the practice areas described in the two following sections on Medicare appeals and veterans benefits law.

Once you have thoroughly studied the SSDI claims process, you will maximize your chances of attaining your professional and business objectives if you take a *proactive approach to letting the potential client market know you exist*. To do that effectively, you will want to develop a marketing plan—a roadmap to follow when alerting the market to your availability and interest in taking on disability cases.

The suggestions below provide you with options for inclusion in your marketing plan. While not all of them may be germane to your situation, they all represent time-tested methods that have proven successful for some of my clients.

As with marketing yourself for a job or anything else, there are three paths you can take (and you should, of course, take all three of them simultaneously):

1. Personal Path
2. Electronic Media Path
3. Print Media Path

In addition, other avenues are open to attorneys seeking to develop SSDI business. A description of those avenues follows the explanation of the three paths in the section "Supplemental Marketing Suggestions."

The Personal Path. It is a truism that networking is essential to job-hunting success. This also applies equally, if not more so, to business development.

The best way to get the word out about your capabilities is, initially, through networking; that is, communicating with as many potentially helpful contacts and intermediaries as possible.

Your best contacts are those organizations and individuals who are likely to interact with your target market: individuals with disability claims. Fortunately, there are quite a large number of potential networking contacts for this endeavor anywhere you go in the United States. It is to your advantage to contact as many of them as you can, in person, to broadcast your availability to represent Social Security disability claimants.

Personal contacts should include office visits, leaving literature (business cards at a minimum) about yourself and your services that could be passed on to prospective claimants, and periodically following-up in person. Ideally, you should seek a face-to-face meeting with your contacts, when you explain what you are doing and ask for referrals. Personal contact is better than telephone or email communication, because it leaves a stronger and more lasting impression.

Some organizations have established a formal referral roster or something similar. You should get your name placed on as many of these referral lists as possible.

The following organizations (and their employees who come into contact with prospective claimants) should be considered when formulating your marketing plan:

- *Social Security Administration local office(s).* Social Security officials who staff the 1,300 offices nationwide come into direct contact with tens of thousands of disability claimants. They answer their inquiries in person and by telephone every day, and claiments perceive them as the official experts on the subject of disability claims.

  Many Social Security office employees have come to realize the value of claimant representatives and are often favorably disposed to making referrals to them. Such representation by competent, prepared, knowledgeable, and caring claimant representatives saves the government money by making the process more efficient and greatly reducing the time it takes to resolve claims. If a claim is adequately presented in the first instance, successive reconsiderations and appeals may be avoided, at considerable cost savings to the government. Not to mention, of course, that if you can help Social Security officers resolve a claim early, you are reducing their own workload.

  As I said before, Social Security Administration local offices are everywhere. You can find the location of the ones nearest to you by looking in the U.S. government section of your local telephone directory.
- *State disability determination offices.* Each state makes the initial determination of disability for SSDI benefits purposes. Local offices that do this are ideal places for you to prospect for referrals.

- *State Vocational Rehabilitation Agency local office(s).* State "voc rehab" offices have daily contact with disabled individuals (and their families) and are often the first place a newly disabled individual goes to obtain services. They are listed in the state government section of your local telephone directory.
- *Hospital social workers.* Hospitals typically employ social workers whose function is to advise and assist patients and their families with a wide variety of problems and issues they may confront upon leaving the hospital and returning home. They almost always maintain lists of referral agencies and agents who provide services that patients might require. Alerting them to your claimant representation services is an important marketing initiative.
- *Legal services organizations.* The Legal Services Corporation funds more than 137 "Grantee Programs" with 923 offices nationwide. In addition, legal assistance is provided by local and regional legal aid societies and similar organizations.

   Legal services providers are often overwhelmed by inquiries regarding disability claims. These claims generally fall into two categories: (1) SSDI claims and (2) Supplemental Security Income (SSI) claims. Legal services organizations usually handle only SSI claims, because they are subject to a means test (i.e., a claimant must fall below a certain income level to qualify for both benefits and free legal representation). SSDI claims are not means tested. Thus, many SSDI claimants do not qualify for free legal representation.

   Consequently, legal services organizations must turn down many SSDI claims cases. However, they often maintain referral lists of claimant representatives for the benefit of the people they must turn away.

   While it is quite possible that a legal services organization will put your name on a referral list merely in response to your request, there is a way you can generate goodwill among the legal services community and enhance the likelihood of SSDI referrals. Legal services programs are often overwhelmed by requests from eligible SSI claimants, especially in tough economic times when these always underfunded programs are in even more dire straits. By offering to handle some SSI cases *pro bono,* you will be doing a legal services organization a big favor and will earn the gratitude of its staff.

Note: The procedures governing SSI and SSDI cases are virtually identical. As a result, SSI volunteer work can also serve as good training for fee-based SSDI claims cases.

- *Disability advocacy organizations.* There are more than 200 national disability organizations, ranging from large ones with millions of members, like the Disabled American Veterans, to smaller ones with narrower interests, such as the Handicapped Scuba Association. Many have local chapters. In addition, some local and regional organizations primarily focus on disability issues. All of these are prime potential networking and referral opportunities..

  These organizations often have newsletters or other means through which they communicate with their members. These publications may be receptive to articles, press releases, and/or paid advertising. This should be factored into your marketing plan under the Print Media Path, described later in this section.

- *Social service/social welfare organizations.* The extensive listings of such organizations in the Yellow Pages include a number of agencies that could potentially serve as referral agencies for you, particularly because so many of them perceive one of their major functions to be just that—acting as information clearinghouses for their constituencies.

- *Congressional offices.* Every year, members of Congress receive thousands of inquiries from constituents with respect to problems they are having with SSDI claims. Each member maintains both a Capitol Hill office and one or more state or district offices, and claims inquiries are received and acted upon by each such office. They are taken very seriously (because they mean votes). You should alert congressional staff in each office about your claimant representative services.

- *Employee assistance programs (EAPs).* A growing number of private companies and public sector agencies have instituted

EAPs, which usually consist of trained individuals whose role is to assist organizational employees in coping with a wide range of problems, such as family matters, financial difficulties, work-related issues, illness, drug and alcohol abuse, etc. EAPs maintain referral lists as one of their primary functions.

The Electronic Media Path. While nothing beats face-to-face contact, electronic advertising, in the form of the Internet, radio, and television is an integral part of attorney business marketing strategies. The Internet in particular is an inexpensive medium through which you can communicate directly with a highly targeted audience (i.e., only those people who might need your services).

Consider (1) building your own website, (2) advertising on other websites, and/or (3) writing and distributing a blog or newsletter to key potential contacts.

If you have your own website, your home page should describe your services, discuss the kind of benefits available, indicate who is eligible for them, address how the cost of representation is handled, and advise claimants how to contact you.

Electronic advertising should be designed to alert and inform not only SSDI claimants themselves but also the many intermediaries who might serve as your referral agents.

The Print Media Path. When seeking employment, the print media path includes résumés, application forms, cover letters, writing samples, letters of recommendation, reference lists, perhaps transcripts of your grades, and other such documents. Some of the same techniques also apply when you are trying to develop an SSDI business. You need to let people know you are there, available, and competent. The print media path includes the following components:

- *A formal announcement,* either placed as a display ad or notice in a trade or other journal and/or mailed to selected individuals and organizations, including other attorneys (who may often turn down SSDI cases), to proclaim your readiness to handle cases of this nature

- *A press release* to the general and trade media
- *An advertisement in the Yellow Pages (and/or comparable directories).* Advertising in the Yellow Pages is quite sophisticated these days. A modest, business card-size ad promoting your SSDI services can be eye catching and will likely stand out in many places, because SSDI claimant representation is still an emerging area of opportunity that is not yet over-subscribed. Rates for such advertisements vary from place to place but are fairly reasonable now that print media has to compete with the Internet for the advertising dollar.
- *An article that you write on some aspect of Social Security disability claims* submitted to the local media. This is a time-tested way of establishing both your credibility and your expertise. Local publications are usually eager for well-written editorial material on timely topics. While they likely will not pay you for a submission, this is a good way of getting your name and capabilities in front of a large audience.

Supplemental Marketing Suggestions

- *Offer yourself as a speaker.* Many civic and other organizations have a regular need for speakers on topics of interest to their membership and community. Such speaking occasions are invaluable promotional opportunities. It may be that a good number of audience members will be interested in your SSDI claims information for themselves or for family members or friends.
- *Become active in the community as a disability volunteer.* Disability organizations constantly need volunteers. Whether you volunteer as a reader for a local radio reading service for the visually and physically challenged, or take part in fundraising activities on behalf of such organizations, there are many opportunities for volunteer service in every U.S. community.
- *Join the National Organization of Social Security Claimants' Representatives (NOSSCR) (www.nosscr.org).* NOSSCR is a national organization of 2,000+ claimant representatives. It publishes a monthly newsletter, *The Forum,* strongly recommended

for anyone contemplating this practice area, and operates a referral service of members who are available to serve claimants in particular communities.

For More Information
- Social Security Administration (*www.ssa.gov*)
- Social Security Administration Office of Disability Adjudication and Review Hearings, Appeals and Litigation Law Manual (*www.ssa.gov/OP_Home/hallex/hallex.html*)
- Online Social Security Handbook (*www.ssa.gov/OP_Home/handbook/handbook.html*)
- Social Security Program Operations Manual System (*https://s044a90.ssa.gov/apps10/poms.nsf/partlist?OpenView*)
- Administrative Procedure Act (*www.law.cornell.edu/uscode/5/usc_sup_01_5_10_I_30_5_40_I.html*)
- Code of Federal Regulations, Title 20, Employees' Benefits (*www.gpoaccess.gov/CFR/INDEX.HTML*)
- National Organization of Social Security Claimants' Representatives (NOSSCR) (*www.nosscr.org*)
- National Association of Disability Representatives (*www.nadr.org*)
- Social Security News (*http://socsecnews.blogspot.com*)
- American Association of People with Disabilities (*www.aapd-dc.org/index.php*)
- DisabilityInfo.gov (*www.disabilityinfo.gov*)
- House of Representatives Social Security Subcommittee (*http://waysandmeans.house.gov/committees.asp?formmode=detail&comm=4*)
- National Association of Disability Examiners (*www.nade.org*)
- Government Accountability Office (*www.gao.gov*)

MEDICARE APPEALS

Introduction
This practice area demonstrates the magic of *synergy;* that is, how you can take the knowledge and expertise you gain from handling Social Security Disability Income (SSDI) cases to another practice area where your new skills can be easily transferred, thereby supplementing your SSDI practice.

There is no reason why you have to limit yourself to SSDI claims. If you decide to represent SSDI claimants, it is a no-brainer to expand your entrepreneurial strategy to Medicare appeals.

In addition to the natural affinity between the two, there is an intriguing extra potential opportunity: As an "appointed representative" for Medicare appeals, you can represent not only individuals but also any healthcare providers that have disputes with Medicare.

Of course, you can elect to handle Medicare appeals without also serving as an SSDI claimant representative.

What Is It?

Medicare is the government health insurance program for people age 65 or older, people under age 65 with certain disabilities, and people of all ages with end-stage renal disease (kidney failure in people who need dialysis or a kidney transplant). Medicare has four major components:

- *Part A. Hospital Insurance,* for which people usually pay through payroll tax contributions while they are working. Part A covers inpatient care in hospitals and nursing facilities (but not custodial or long-term care), as well as hospice and some home healthcare.
- *Part B. Medical Insurance,* for which most recipients pay a monthly premium. Part B covers medically necessary visits to the doctor and outpatient care plus certain medical services not covered by Part A (e.g., physical and occupational therapy and some home healthcare expenses).
- *Part C. Medicare Advantage Plans.* You must have both Part A and Part B to join Medicare Advantage plans. The plans provide all Part A and Part B services and generally additional ones as well. One usually pays a monthly premium and copayments that will likely be less than the coinsurance and deductibles under original Medicare. In most cases, these plans also offer Part D prescription drug coverage. These plans are offered by private insurance companies approved by Medicare. Costs and benefits vary by plan.
- *Part D. Prescription Drug Coverage,* also requiring beneficiaries to pay a monthly premium. This program began in 2006.

Like SSDI, Medicare cases are heard by federal administrative law judges (ALJs). However, instead of hearings before the Social Security Administration, cases are heard by judges at the relatively new Office of Medicare Hearings and Appeals (OMHA) in the Department of Health and Human Services.

Another incentive for enering this field is that *the Medicare appeals procedures are governed by the same statute as SSDI hearings,* the Administrative Procedure Act (5 U.S.C. 551 et seq.).

OMHA provides a forum where individuals and organizations dissatisfied with Medicare determinations affecting their participation in the Medicare program may administratively appeal in accordance with the Administrative Procedure Act and the Social Security Act (42 U.S.C. 301 et seq.).

OMHA maintains four offices: Arlington, Virginia; Cleveland, Ohio; Miami, Florida; and Irvine, California. You must be wondering if you will have to pay a fortune to travel to one of these four hearing sites to act as an appointed representative. The answer is no.

Virtually all Level 3 hearings are done by videoconference at one of hundreds of video-teleconference (VTC) sites. Moreover, in the extremely rare case when a VTC site is not viable, judges have the discretion to authorize a telephone hearing. If the judge wishes to hold a VTC hearing and you have to travel more than 75 miles to a VTC site, travel expenses may be paid by the government.

Like SSDI claims, Medicare cases can go through multiple levels of determination (five in this case). An individual files an initial claim (Level 1) that, if rejected, goes to an automatic reconsideration (Level 2). If the claim is once again rejected, either the claimant or the appointed representative can request a Level 3 hearing before an OMHA judge. Again, SSDI, a Level 3 hearing is non-adversarial (i.e., there is no opposing counsel). You are not going up against anyone representing "the other side." There is no "other side."

A Medicare claimant may have an appointed representative at any stage of the claims process. The appointed representative's fee must be approved by the ALJ presiding in the case.

Who Does It?

Like SSDI practice, Medicare appeals are largely the province of sole practitioners and small law firms. However, some larger law firms may provide these services to certain institutional healthcare clients who are pursuing reimbursement claims.

Public sector attorneys work for OMHA in one of its four locations. Each office consists of ALJs and staff attorneys whose work primarily consists of drafting ALJ decisions.

What Does It Pay?

Medicare appeals compensation for private practitioners depends on both the volume of cases handled and the appointed representative's abilities. Like their ODAR counterparts, OMHA attorneys are paid according to the U.S. government General Schedule pay scale (see *www.opm.gov/flsa/ oca/09tables/html/gs.asp* for 2009 compensation tables, excluding locality pay adjustments). OMHA ALJs start at a minimum of $102,000 per year and earn up to $165,000.

Future Prospects

Medicare appeals are certain to increase significantly, if only because the Medicare population is going to increase tremendously with the aging of the Baby Boom generation.

In addition, consider these interesting statistics:

- Each year more than 1 billion Medicare claims are processed. This is not a misprint. *One billion medicare claims.* And the number is climbing . . . fast.
- Of these claims, payment is approved for approximately 90 percent, and payment is denied for approximately 10 percent.
- The most common reasons for denying a claim are
  - the services were determined not to have been medically necessary;
  - Medicare did not cover the services; or
  - the beneficiary was not eligible for services.

Now, here is where the numbers get *really* interesting. Translate the percentages of annually approved and denied claims, and you come up with the following hard numbers:

- 900 million claims approved
- 100 million claims denied
- Only a little more than 100,000 denied claims are ever appealed

If you do the math, you will come to the startling conclusion that only a little more than one-tenth of 1 percent of denied claims are appealed.

That leaves us with *99.9 percent of denied claims that never are appealed.* That represents a huge, heretofore untapped, potential market for your services.

Here are some additional intriguing "opportunity" numbers:

- 65 percent of Medicare Parts A, B, and C claims are fully or partially approved on appeal.
- 40 percent of Part D claims win on appeal.

Not quite as good as the SSDI reversal rate, but not bad.

Another benefit of the Medicare appeals program is that these appeals must be heard within 90 days. That is a better timeframe than the SSDI appeals process.

At this point, you probably have two questions:

1. How come the OMHA reversal rate of initially denied claims is so high?
2. How come so few denied claims are appealed?

The answer to Question 1 is simple: Guess who the Level 1 reviewer is? The Medicare carrier—the insurance company that would be out the money if the claim were approved! The Level 2 review is conducted by another private company, which also has a financial incentive to deny claims: If these secondary companies want their lucrative contracts with the Medicare carrier to be renewed, they have to be careful how much largesse they hand out in approved claims.

Small wonder, then, that there is some bias against claimants at Levels 1 and 2. So why does the situation suddenly favor the claimant at Level 3? Again, the answer is consistent with what happens at Levels 1 and 2—the nature of the decider—but the outcome is very different. It is different because the Level 3 decider—the ALJ—is part of an independent corps of judges with virtually guaranteed job security regardless of how they decide cases. In other words, they have considerable freedom to decide claims on their merits, regardless of the "politics" involved. Consequently, they tend to be sympathetic to elderly and disabled claimants.

Question 2's answer is also not complicated. Just like SSDI claimants, the vast majority of individual Medicare claimants (a) tend to trust the decisions of institutional authorities, such as insurance companies and supposedly independent government contractors, (b) do not possess the sophistication to jump through the necessary bureaucratic hoops to protest a denial of a claim, (c) are often aged and intimidated by the system, and (d) do not understand their rights.

Breaking In

The techniques I recommended for generating SSDI business work quite well with Medicare appeals. In fact, it is easier to sell your Medicare appeals services, for two reasons:

1. There are so many senior-focused media outlets and senior-directed organizations.
2. Healthcare provider organizations have a stake in favorable appeals outcomes (i.e., ensuring that they get paid for their services); at the same time, they can act as additional, free conduits of information about your services to their patients.

For More Information

- Office of Medicare Hearings and Appeals (*www.hhs.gov/omha*)
- American Association of Retired Persons (*www.aarp.org*)
- Center for Medicare Advocacy (*www.medicareadvocacy.org*)
- Centers for Medicare and Medicaid Services (*www.cms.hhs.gov*)
- Medicare Official Website (*www.medicare.gov*)
- Medicare Appeals Forms (*www.medicare.gov/basics/forms/default.asp*)

- Medicare and You 2008 (*www.medicare.gov/publications/pubs/pdf/10050.pdf*)
- Government Accountability Office (*www.gao.gov*)

VETERANS BENEFITS LAW

Introduction

This practice area is relatively new, having emerged as a result of legislation in mid-2007 (see below).

The process by which veterans can appeal an initial denial of benefits presents another synergistic opportunity for attorneys who handle Social Security Disability Income (SSDI) cases and/or Medicare appeals. These practice areas focus on the nexus between law and medicine and, as such, are a natural fit with one another.

We live in a dangerous and uncertain world, as evidenced by the September 11, 2001, terrorist attacks. The resulting conflicts in Iraq and Afghanistan have returning veterans applying for benefits in great numbers.

The United States could be involved in long-duration occupations, wars, and peacekeeping missions around the world. The United States will be forced to maintain large military forces for the foreseeable future. This, in turn, will mean a huge law practice potential with respect to veterans' issues, primarily veterans benefits.

Veterans benefits law is unaffected by economic fluctuations. Veterans have never been a more politically powerful interest group than now, as evidenced by the virtually unanimous support for veterans benefit legislation in Congress and the state legislatures, regardless of funding constraints. This was most striking when, in March 2009, President Obama proposed making combat veterans pay for their own healthcare through private insurance rather than the Veterans Administration. The uproar by veterans and Congress was so powerful that the president reversed himself the next day and withdrew the proposal.

Nobel economist Joseph Stiglitz conservatively estimates that the Iraq War will ultimately cost America $3 trillion, much of it to care for disabled veterans. Stiglitz also calculates that the residual costs of the war will be around $500,000 per soldier.

What Is It?

The vast majority of such appeals are of claims for disability benefits. Veterans can also appeal the denial of other benefits, such as education and home loan guarantees, (see list at the end of this section). In some cases, veterans' dependents also have standing to appeal.

The initial process is administrative, and the follow-up is a judicial appeal. The process begins with a veteran who files a claim with his or her local Veterans Affairs (VA) office (there is at least one in each state) or, alternatively, online. Help with filing a claim is sometimes available from one of the veterans service organizations, such as the Disabled Veterans of America or the Paralyzed Veterans of America, or from a VA-recognized agent.

If the claim is denied, the veteran can file a Notice of Disagreement (NOD) with the local VA office within one year of the date that the original decision is mailed. The NOD is a request that the claimant's file be reviewed by a Decision Review Officer (DRO) from the local office. This is the stage in the claims process where the possibility of private attorney representation kicks in.

The DRO reviews the entire file and may also hold a Personal Hearing with the claimant and his or her representative. If the denial of the claim is upheld, the local office prepares a Statement of the Case (SOC), which is a detailed explanation of evidence, laws, and regulations it used to decide the claim. The SOC is mailed to the claimant along with a VA Form 9, "Substantive Appeal Form" (also available at the Board of Veterans Appeals (BVA) website (*www.vba.va.gov*).

If the claimant wishes to appeal the decision, he or she must file the completed VA Form 9 with the local office within 60 days of the mailing of the SOC or within one year of the mailing of the original decision, whichever is later. The form should state (1) the requested benefit, (2) any mistakes noted in the SOC, and (3) if the claimant wants another Personal Hearing (i.e., a meeting between the claimant, his or her representative, and either a local office official or a member of the BVA). If a board member is requested, the hearing can take place either at board headquarters in Washington, D.C., via videoconference at the local office, or at the local office with a board member in person. Videoconference is the quickest way to get a hearing.

The hearing is informal and customarily lasts about an hour. It is non-adversarial, and the claimant is permitted to add evidence at the hearing. The hearing transcript then goes to the Board along with the appeal.

At this stage, the Board will either allow or deny the claim or remand it to the local office for reconsideration. If the claim is denied, the claimant can either (1) go back to the local office and try to reopen the claim, (2) file a motion for reconsideration by the Board or a new review, (3) file an appeal to the U.S. Court of Appeals for Veterans Claims, or (4) do nothing.

The Board's jurisdiction is broad, encompassing virtually all kinds of veterans benefits in addition to disability claims. It also includes claims for the following:

- Pension benefits
- Insurance benefits
- Education benefits
- Home loan guaranties
- Vocational rehabilitation
- Dependency and indemnity compensation
- Healthcare delivery

Who Does It?

To date, veterans claim representation is largely the preserve of sole practitioners and very small law firms. The practice is so new that it is difficult to tell how this might play out in the future.

The practice opportunity is not limited just to private practitioners. The BVA is comprised of more than 350 attorneys (including 60 Veterans Law Judges) and has traditionally had rather high turnover (75 new attorney hires in fiscal year 2008). Given the inevitable surge in veterans claims resulting from our ongoing wars and other military obligations (we currently have military missions in more than 130 countries!), plus the additional issues faced by returning veterans (principally the return of Reservists and National Guard soldiers to their civilian jobs), this practice area should expand for years to come.

What Does It Pay?

For 144 years, veterans who disputed a decision on their benefits claim were severely restricted from hiring an attorney. The restriction dated from the Civil War era when concern about attorneys preying on sick and disabled veterans resulted in legislation limiting attorney fees to $10.

The $10 limit was repealed in 2006. Beginning June 20, 2007, a veteran could hire an attorney after an NOD is filed in a case. The new law still does not permit a veteran to hire an attorney at the beginning of the application process.

The new "Attorneys for Veterans" Act (Pub.L. 109-461) authorizes the VA to regulate attorney qualifications and standards of conduct and to review fee agreements between attorneys and claimants. Generally, a fee not exceeding 20 percent of the past due amount of benefits awarded is presumed reasonable.

Future Prospects

The fiscal year 2008 Report of the chairman of the BVA to the secretary of Veterans Affairs states that the Board issued a record number of decisions on appeals of veterans claims decisions (more than 43,750), and held a record number of appeals hearings (10,600+). In addition, the report noted that appeals are increasing at a rate of approximately 10 percent per year.

The number of potential clients is enormous. According to the U.S. Census Bureau,

- there are currently more than 25 million U.S. veterans.
- close to 10 million veterans are over age 65.
- almost 2 million troops have already served in Iraq and Afghanistan since 2001.
- there are more than 8 million Vietnam-era veterans.
- more than 10 percent of veterans receive service-connected disability benefits.
- the U.S. government spends over $65 billion a year on veterans benefit programs.

Every state also has its own veterans benefit programs. Many of these state programs supplement federal government benefits.

Hundreds of thousands of veterans are being diagnosed with Post-Traumatic Stress Disorder (PTSD) resulting from military service and becoming eligible for veterans benefits. PTSD is so widespread among combat veterans that the Department of Veterans Affairs has established a National Center for PTSD. This is likely to encourage even more benefit claims, resulting in more work for attorneys.

Benefits for veterans came into full being after World War II with the enactment of the "GI Bill of Rights." Benefits were slowly whittled down over the next 60 years but were revived in 2008 with the enactment of the Post-9/11 Veterans Educational Assistance Act of 2008, 38 U.S.C. Ch. 33, which returned veterans' educational benefits to World War II levels beginning in August 2009. This development is also likely to mean more legal work and employment opportunities.

Breaking In

Roughly the same marketing techniques recommended above for SSDI business development can operate effectively for a veterans benefits claims practice. Promoting yourself to the many veterans organizations (some of which are listed below) is important, mindful that veterans service organizations sometimes provide free assistance to disabled vets who are pursuing claims. Nevertheless, veterans sometimes inquire of these organizations about referrals to private attorneys.

Volunteering to assist veterans in some capacity is also a good marketing mechanism. In addition, you can also advertise your services in veterans' publications and websites.

For More Information

- U.S. Department of Veterans Affairs (*www.va.gov*)
- Board of Veterans Appeals (*www.vba.va.gov*)
- Veterans Employment & Training Service, U.S. Department of Labor (*www.dol.gov/vets*)
- U.S. Court of Appeals for Veterans Claims (*www.vetapp.uscourts.gov*)
- 38 U.S. Code (*http://uscode.house.gov/usc.htm*)
- 38 Code of Federal Regulations (*www.access.gpo.gov/nara/cfr*)
- Veterans' Choice of Representation & Benefits Enhancement Act of 2006, 38 USCS §5904
- 38 C.F.R. §20.603—Representation by attorneys-at-law
- Uniformed Services Employment & Reemployment Rights Act, 38 U.S. Code, Ch. 43.
- National Organization of Veteran's Advocates (*www.vet advocates.com*)
- Afghan War Veterans Organization (*www.afghanistanwar veterans.org*)

- Iraq War Veterans Organization (*www.iraqwarveterans.org*)
- PTSD Information Center (*www.ncptsd.va.gov/ncmain/information*)
- Blinded Veterans Association (*www.bva.org*)
- Disabled American Veterans (*www.dav.org*)
- National Association of State Directors of Veterans Affairs (*www.nasdva.net*)
- National Veterans Legal Services Program (*www.nvlsp.org*)
- Veterans Assistance Foundation (*www.veteransassistance.org*)
- Vietnam Veterans of America (*www.vva.org*)
- Wounded Warrior Project (*www.woundedwarriorproject.org*)
- Veterans Legal Support Center (*www.jmls.edu/veterans*)

ELDER LAW

Introduction

You cannot overlook a potential market of 80 million people, plus their family members.

There has never been anything like this in recorded human history: The United States is about to be engulfed by an unprecedented age wave . . . and, more importantly for our purposes, great accompanying wealth, notwithstanding the multi-trillion-dollar losses caused by the Great Recession?. The most populous and prosperous generation ever of Americans is "aging up."

Baby Boomers still have money, and many of them believe that "60 is the new 40" and that "80 is the new 60." However, the realities of aging will hit them eventually, just as they have every prior generation.

As of January 1, 2007, the U.S. population age 65 and older numbered more than 38 million, and those age 85 and older numbered 5 million. The 65+ age group has doubled in size in one generation, and the number of really old codgers—those 85 and older—is growing even more rapidly. By 2010, there will be an additional 3 million seniors and an additional 1 million "ancients." By 2020, when the Baby Boom hits the Golden Years with a vengeance, there will be 55 million seniors and more than 7 million Methusalehs.

Life expectancy statistics are also interesting: An American age 65 in 2009 can expect to live almost 20 more years, and an 85-year-old will likely live an additional 7.5 years.

To support these tens of millions of individual seniors and their families, an enormous institutional market caters to their needs:

- 4,000+ adult day care facilities
- 33,000 assisted living facilities
- 4,500 dialysis centers
- Almost 9,000 home healthcare services

- Almost 3,000 hospices
- 7,500+ hospitals
- 2,600+ ambulatory surgery centers
- 16,000+ nursing homes
- 7,700+ retirement homes

Many other elder-oriented institutions do not fit under any of these categories, such as rehabilitation facilities and senior centers.

This is not like winning the lottery. You will, of course, have to invest some "sweat equity"—in terms of getting to know the issues of importance to this population, as well as acquiring legal know-how on this topic—to position yourself for the extraordinary opportunity that this age sector represents. However, unlike Powerball or MegaMillions, your odds of hitting the jackpot are far better.

What Is It?

Elder law is still a "young" practice and is still evolving. At present, the practice includes the following:

- Estate and gift planning
- Disability planning
- Knowledge of senior programs and services
- Retirement living
- Living wills
- Advanced medical directives
- Healthcare proxies
- Powers of attorney
- Reverse mortgages
- Medicare eligibility and appeals

- Medicaid eligibility and planning strategies
- Long-term care insurance
- Social Security Old Age and Survivor's Insurance & Disability Insurance
- Federal and state tax planning for seniors
- State conservator and guardianship laws
- Financial abuse and fraud on seniors

- Other elder abuse and neglect
- Nursing home rights
- Age discrimination
- Grandparent visitation rights
- Veterans benefits

The activism and political clout of the Baby Boom generation is certain to add to this list.

Demand for elder law advice and legal services is not exclusively from the elderly. Many elder law issues originate with their Generation X and Y family members concerned about financial, succession, caregiving, and quality-of-life issues for their aging relatives.

Who Does It?

Private practice elder law is almost exclusively for small law firms and sole practitioners. There is not enough money in individual elder law matters to interest most large firms. The only exception is very large estates, where a large firm prepares the estate plan and then handles any collateral elder law matters as a courtesy to the client.

There are a handful of public sector elder law practices. Most of these focus on one or a few subspecialties, such as Social Security, elder abuse, or age discrimination. At the federal level, the following legal and other offices practice elder law:

- Corporation for National & Community Service—Office of General Counsel (OGC) (*www.cns.gov*)
- Social Security Administration (*www.ssa.gov*)
  - Office of Disability Adjudication and Review (ODAR)
  - Office of the Chief Counsel to the Inspector General
  - OGC & Regional Chief Counsel Offices
- U.S. Department of Health and Human Services (*www.hhs.gov*)
  - Food and Drug Administration—Center for Devices and Radiological Health
  - Office of Medicare Hearings and Appeals Headquarters and Field Offices
  - OGC—Children, Families, and Aging Division

State governments have established specific agencies to deal with elder issues, usually focusing on elder abuse (financial and/or physical), end-of-life healthcare, nursing home rights, and age discrimination. Representative agencies include the following:

- California Office of Attorney General—Bureau of Medi-Cal Fraud & Elder Abuse (*www.ag.ca.gov*)
- Pennsylvania Office of Attorney General—Elder Abuse Unit; Health Care Section (*www.attorneygeneral.gov*)
- Texas Department on Aging and Disability Services— Office of General Counsel (*www.dads.state.tx.us*)
- New York State Office of Children & Family Services— Division of Legal Affairs (*www.ocfs.state.ny.us/main*)
- Illinois Department on Aging—Legal Services Developer (*www.state.il.us/aging*)
- Florida State Long Term Care Ombudsman's Office (*http://ombudsman.myflorida.com/index.php*)
- Virginia Office of the Attorney General—Medicaid Fraud Control Unit (*www.oag.state.va.us*)
- North Carolina Board of Examiners for Nursing Home Administrators—Board Attorneys (*www.ncbenha.org*)
- Arizona Department of Health Services—Office of Administrative Counsel & Rules (*www.azdhs.gov*)

Local governments, especially large municipalities, also have comparable offices.

What Does It Pay?

Private practice elder law compensation ranges widely and often depends on how well the attorney or firm markets the practice, as well as the size of the local senior market.

While there are no compensation studies to which one can refer, anecdotal evidence suggests that practitioners who are certified elder law specialists do somewhat better than those who do not seek or are ineligible for certification (see later in the section).

Government elder lawyers are paid according to the same scales that apply to federal, state, or local employees in their jurisdictions. U.S. government attorneys begin at approximately the $46,000–$56,000 level and move up to a maximum of approximately $150,000. As a general rule, state and local lawyers are paid at somewhat lower levels.

Elder lawyers who work for nonprofits generally earn less than their public sector and private practice counterparts.

Future Prospects

The demographics alone make elder law very promising. The first Baby Boomers reached age 62 in 2008. The last official Baby Boomer will not reach this age until 2026.

Presumably, the national and world economies will recover and emerge from the Great Recession, and, consequently, Baby Boomers will reinforce their status as the wealthiest generation in history. They and their families will need the advice and services that elder lawyers provide and probably additional counsel and services that have not yet materialized. Modern life complexities, lengthening life spans, healthcare reform, and other factors will see to that.

Breaking In

Elder law is open to attorneys of all ages and levels of experience. Certification as an elder law specialist is advantageous, but you cannot become certified until you have practiced law for five years. Nevertheless, it is still possible to develop a successful elder law practice without being certified. There are more noncertified elder law attorneys than there are those who are certified. For example, Sun City Center, Florida, a retirement community of more than 20,000 senior residents, has only one certified elder law specialist.

There are a number of other credential enhancements that you can obtain to assist in establishing your *bona fides* as an elder law attorney:

- University of Kansas School of Law (*www.law.ku.edu/ academics/elderlaw/llm/index.shtml*)
  - LLM Program in Elder Law

- Western New England College School of Law (*http://www1. law.wnec.edu/llm*)
  - LLM Program in Estate Planning and Elder Law (on-site or online)
- Albany Law School (*www.albanylaw.edu*)
  - LLM in Advanced Legal Studies with Specialization in Family and Elder Law
- Stetson University College of Law (*www.law.stetson.edu*)
  - Elder Law LLM Program
- University of Toledo (*www.utoledo.edu*)
  - Graduate Certificate in Elder Law (online)
- Washington Online Learning Institute (*www.woli.com*)
  - Certificate of Specialization in Probate and Elder Law
- Center for Insurance Education and Professional Development (*www.insuranceeducation.org*)
  - Long-Term Care Professional (LTCP) Designation
- Cleveland State University (*www.csuohio.edu/ce*)
  - Patient Advocacy Certificate Program (online)

Membership organizations for elder law attorneys are good vehicles for making contacts, developing business, identifying job opportunities, and keeping up with law and practice developments. The following organizations should be considered:

- National Academy of Elder Law Attorneys (*www.naela.org*)
- American Association of Trusts, Estates and Elder Law Attorneys (*www.aateela.org*)
- American Academy of Estate Planning Attorneys (*www.aaepa.com*)
- American College of Trust & Estate Counsel (*www.actec.org*)
- National Guardianship Association (*www.guardianship.org*)

The following states recognize elder law certification for members of their state bars. Certification may carry over if you relocate from one of the following states to another, provided that you also meet the new state's bar admission requirements:

- Alabama
- California
- Delaware
- Florida
- Idaho
- Indiana
- Maine
- Minnesota
- Mississippi

- New Hampshire
- New Jersey
- New York
- Ohio
- Pennsylvania
- South Dakota
- Tennessee
- Vermont
- Wisconsin

Since so many elder law attorneys fly solo or work for small firms, the following law marketing websites are recommended:

- Law Marketing Portal (*www.lawmarketing.com*)
- Hieros Gamos (*www.hg.org/marketing.html*)
- Smart Marketing (*www.smartmarketingnow.com*)

For More Information

- American Bar Association Commission on Law and Aging (*www.abanet.org/aging*)
- National Elder Law Foundation (*www.nelf.org*)
- National Senior Citizens Law Center (*www.nsclc.org*)
- Healthcare and Elder Law Programs Corporation (HELP) (*www.help4srs.org/home.htm*)
- Elder Law Blog (*www.abajournal.com/blawgs/elder_law_blog*)
- Nursing Home Law Blog (*www.abajournal.com/blawgs/ nursing_ home_law_blog*)
- Nursing Home Abuse Blog (*www.abajournal.com/blawgs/ nursing_home_abuse_blog*)
- Aging in Place Blog (*www.abajournal.com/blawgs/aging_in_place*)
- Centers for Medicare and Medicaid Services (*www.cms.hhs.gov*)
- U.S. Department of Health and Human Services (*www.hhs.gov*)
- RetirementHomes.com (*www.retirementhomes.com/ North_America/index.htm*)
- National Citizens Coalition for Nursing Home Reform (*www.nccnhr.org*)

NONTRADITIONAL FAMILY LAW

Introduction

The traditional family model—a mother, father, and children—now accounts for only about 25 percent of the nation's households. Incrementally, legal recognition is being extended to the other 75 percent: cohabiting families, single-parent families, blended families and step-families (generally created by divorce and remarriage, where biologically unrelated children may live in the same household), grandparent-led families, families where the adults are gay or lesbian, commuter families, foster families, and group home families.

Sixty percent of all children spend some of their lives in single-parent families, 88 percent of which are headed by women. Eight percent of U.S. children live in households headed by their grandparents.

Children may be raised by a gay or lesbian single parent or two gay or lesbian parents. The children may come to them from a heterosexual parent relationship or may have been adopted or conceived by assisted reproductive technologies. One parent may be the genetic parent, and the other parent the adoptive parent.

The U.S. government and 41 states have adopted Defense of Marriage Acts. Yet these laws have not slowed the growing societal and legal acceptance and recognition of nontraditional families, such as through civil unions. Numerous private companies, governments, municipalities, service industry businesses, and nonprofits have adopted domestic partner policies that give benefits and rights to unmarried heterosexual and same-sex couples.

Courts throughout the United States are recognizing nontraditional family relationships and rights.

Thirty years ago, single-parent adoptions were rare. Today, about one-third of all U.S. adoptions are by single parents, including a growing number of men.

Nontraditional family policy changes are unusual in that they have been fostered from the bottom up—by corporations and municipalities—rather than by legislation.

There are many different family structures, and family law is only now dealing with them. The legal needs of nontraditional families are often different from those of the traditional family, and they present a growing opportunity for legal representation

What Is It?

Nontraditional family law is still evolving. Representation includes counseling clients on formalizing domestic partnerships, pursuing benefits, domestic and international adoption, alternative reproduction, financial matters, as well as all of the issues customarily part of the end of relationships (including divorce when only one partner is gay, lesbian, transgender, or bisexual). More specifically, the practice includes the following:

- Drafting partnership, coparenting, donor, surrogacy, and dissolution agreements
- Legal validation of same-sex marriages
- Alternative and assisted reproduction
- Adoption proceedings
- *De facto* parent status
- Nontraditional family dissolution
- Guardianship
- Custody, including issues such as custody of sperm donations
- Visitation rights
- Child support following a nontraditional family dissolution
- Property division following a nontraditional family dissolution
- Mediation
- Estate planning for nontraditional families

Who Does It?

Like traditional family law, nontraditional family practice is primarily done by small law firms and sole practitioners. Government plays a small but growing role in this practice area, and nonprofits—primarily advocacy organizations—are proliferating.

What Does It Pay?

Much depends on geographic location. Jurisdictions that recognize gay marriage or civil unions are likely to be more lucrative places in which to practice than more restrictive states. Similarly, locations where large companies have adopted liberal benefit provisions for nontraditional couples make for higher potential compensation, as do states that offer benefits for same-sex partners of state employees (17 as of 2008: Alaska, Arizona, California, Connecticut, District of Columbia, Hawaii, Illinois, Iowa, Maine, Montana, New Jersey, New Mexico, New York, Oregon, Rhode Island, Vermont, and Washington).

As this book goes to press, six states recognize same-sex marriage (Connecticut, Iowa, Maine, Massachusetts, New Hampshire, and Vermont). However, the trend is moving toward recognition (four of the six states granted such recognition in 2009). The New York State legislature is currently considering a gay marriage bill. California briefly recognized gay marriage, but that policy was overturned by the voters in November 2008 (Proposition 8). Rhode Island and New York recognize same-sex marriages from other states. New Jersey authorizes civil unions between same-sex couples. California, Hawaii, Oregon, and Washington extend most or all state-level spousal rights to unmarried, same-sex couples.

Future Prospects

A few demographic and other statistics from the U.S. Bureau of the Census and other sources make the point about the prospects for nontraditional family law:

- There were 37 million nontraditional households in the United States in 2007, a number that is growing with each passing year.
- 30+ percent of American children are born out of wedlock.
- 51 percent of gay Baby Boomers don't have a will.
- One in five gay men are unsure who will take care of them when the need arises.
- In the last five years, membership in the American Academy of Matrimonial Lawyers has increased by 25 percent.

The idea of a Uniform Domestic Partnership Act is gaining some traction, the idea being that marriage as legally defined in most jurisdictions today fails to fulfill the expectations of most families—traditional and nontraditional. Such an act would allow parties to select from several forms of domestic partnerships and leave marriage under the control of religious institutions.

State recognition of same sex unions from other states (and Canada, which recognizes gay marriage and civil unions) is likely to expand. When New York Governor David Paterson, in May 2008, ordered that state agencies recognize such relationships, it was estimated that up to 1,300 New York laws and regulations were involved. With the political tides having swung towards Democrats in the last two national elections (Democrats now control 28 state houses, up from 18 in 2000), look for more states to follow New York's lead. There is a long way to go here, since even Massachusetts, which permits gay marriage, does not permit gay residents from other states to be married there if their home states prohibit same-sex unions.

Defining *marriage* is a hot button issue; defining a *family* less so. Rather, the definition of family is ever evolving and expanding to include relationships not previously mentioned in this section, such as siblings living together and senior citizen couples who do not marry because of Medicaid or other rules. Every expansion of the definition means new legal matters to be addressed.

Nontraditional couples need retirement planning, too, and the difficulties they face as part of the aging population of Baby Boomers are far more vexing than those faced by married heterosexual couples. Health insurance, Medicaid, and Social Security limitations are just some examples of these restrictions. While the laws that protect married couples do not apply, there are ways to work around them, and nontraditional couples need legal advice to realize these benefits.

An Oklahoma statute barring recognition of adoptions by same-sex couples was recently held unconstitutional by the 10th U.S. Circuit Court of Appeals as violating the Full Faith and Credit Clause (*Finstuen v. Crutcher,* 496 F.3d 1139 [2007]). The ruling is binding in the 10th Circuit (Colorado, Wyoming, Utah, Kansas, and New Mexico) and has persuasive authority in the rest of the United States.

Nontraditional family law practice is dynamic. The issues are wide-ranging and cutting-edge. There is much yet to be resolved concerning matters such as shared parenting agreements, second parent adoptions, international adoptions, third-party assisted reproduction, same-sex divorce, employee benefits, and other issues.

The tide in favor of recognition of nontraditional family rights (and obligations) is likely unstoppable. This is a practice area that will only expand with this tide.

Breaking In

Increasingly, Continuing Legal Education (CLE) providers offer courses in nontraditional family law. State bar associations may provide and orient these to their own members, which limits their utility. However, national CLE providers have also begun to offer similar courses with a more universal approach. The West LegalEd Center (*http://westlegaledcenter.com*), for example, offers an audio webcast on this topic that you can listen to online from any location and that is currently accredited for CLE in 20 states. The National Business Institute (*www.nbi-sems.com*) offers a "bricks-and-mortar" seminar on *Effectively Representing the Nontraditional Family* at various locations around the country. See also ALI-ABA (*www.ali-aba.org*).

Attending conferences and seminars is both a good way to advance your knowledge of the field and to make useful contacts with practitioners. The American Bar Association Section of Family Law (*www.abanet.org/family/*) offers 1.5-hour teleconferences and materials on family law issues each month as well as CLE programs at locations around the country.

Credentialing. The following LLM programs include courses relevant to nontraditional family law:

- Chicago-Kent College of Law
  (*www.kentlaw.edu/academics/llm/family*)
  - LLM Program in Family Law
- Loyola University Chicago School of Law
  (*www.luc.edu/law/academics/graduate/child_family.html*)
  - LLM in Child and Family Law
- Hofstra University School of Law
  (*http://law.hofstra.edu/LLMAdmissions/llmadm_fl.html*)
  - LLM in Family Law

The following states sponsor certification programs in family law or expressly permit practitioners to advertise that they are family law specialists:

- Alabama
- Alaska
- Arizona
- California
- Connecticut
- Delaware
- Florida
- Idaho
- Indiana
- Louisiana
- Maine
- Minnesota
- Mississippi
- Nevada
- New Hampshire
- New Jersey
- New Mexico
- New York
- North Carolina
- Ohio
- Pennsylvania
- South Carolina
- Tennessee
- Texas
- Vermont
- Wisconsin

Information and Networking Organizations.
- American Academy of Estate Planning Attorneys (*www.aaepa.com*)
- American Academy of Matrimonial Lawyers (*www.aaml.org*)
- American Bar Association Section on Family Law (*www.abanet.org/family*)
- National Association of Counsel for Children (*www.naccchildlaw.com*)
- National Association of Guardians ad Litem (*www.nagalro.com*)
- National Lesbian, Gay, Bisexual, and Transgender Law Association (*www.lgbtbar.org*)

For More Information
- Nontraditional Family Law (*www.nontraditionalfamilylaw.com*)
- U.S. Bureau of the Census (*www.census.gov/population/www. socdemo/hh-fam.html*)
- Drobac, Jennifer Ann and Antony Page, "A Uniform Domestic Partnership Act: Marrying Business Partnership and Family Law." *Georgia Law Review*, 2007 (*http://ssrn. com/abstract=929269*)
- Amato, Paul R., Alan Booth, David R. Johnson, and Stacy J. Rogers. *Alone Together: How Marriage in America Is Changing.* Cambridge: Harvard University Press, 2007.

- What is a Family? (*www.courtinfo.ca.gov/programs/cfcc/pdffiles/ 7_Friendly.pdf*)
- Association of Family and Conciliation Courts (*www.afccnet.org*)
- American Bar Association Center on Children and the Law (*www.abanet.org/child*)
- The International Commission on Couple and Family Relations (*www.iccfr.org*)

TAX CONTROVERSY PRACTICE

Introduction

What they say about "death and taxes" is unassailable, at least until humans are cloned or a flat tax replaces the Internal Revenue Code. Until that time, tax practice will flourish, and tax controversy practice will thrive even more because, unlike tax planning and tax transactional practice, it is impervious to economic fluctuations.

Tax controversy practices are also intellectually stimulating and less stressful than most litigation, involving much less discovery (and, thus, discovery disputes) and the gamesmanship so often a part of litigation. A certain collegiality exists among tax practitioners that is mostly absent elsewhere. Both private and government tax practitioners are held to a higher standard than what is generally expected of attorneys.

Even more enticing, tax controversy lawyers tell me that there are not enough qualified tax controversy lawyers.

Internal Revenue Service (IRS) enforcement efforts have been increasing for a number of years, and the rate of increase is accelerating. In fiscal year 2007, the IRS audited 84 percent more returns (31,382) of individuals with incomes of $1 million or more than during 2006. Overall, enforcement revenue reached $59.2 billion, up from $48.7 billion in 2006 and nearly $34.1 billion in 2002.

Here is a breakdown of these interesting figures:

- *Individuals.* One out of every 11 individuals with incomes of $1 million or more faced an audit in 2007. Overall, total individual returns audited increased by 7 percent to 1,384,563 in 2007. Audits of individuals with incomes more than $200,000 reached 113,105 returns, up

29.2 percent from the prior year. The IRS also increased audits of individual returns with incomes of $100,000 or more, auditing 293,188 of these returns in 2007, up 13.7 percent from the prior year. The IRS filed 3.8 million levies and almost 700,000 liens during 2007, an increase from the previous year and a substantial increase from five years earlier.

- *Businesses.* Business audits in general rose to 59,516, an increase of almost 14 percent in just one year. The IRS continued efforts to review more returns of "flow-through entities"—partnerships and S corporations. The IRS increased its focus on midmarket corporations—those with assets between $10 million and $50 million dollars. Audits of S corporations increased to 17,681 during 2007, up 26 percent from the prior year. Audits of partnerships increased to 12,195 during 2007, up almost 25 percent. Audits of midmarket corporations increased to 4,473, up 6 percent.

The IRS and U.S. Department of Justice have also increased their enforcement efforts against abusive tax shelter promoters and participants. Moreover, the IRS shares its information with the states, making for even more tax controversy practice opportunities.

What Is It?

Tax controversy attorneys represent clients in disputes with the IRS and state and local tax authorities. Clients generally turn to tax controversy lawyers during complicated audits, often leaving more mundane audits to their accountants.

Representation usually begins during the audit stage and may continue with an appeal of the audit result through the IRS or state administrative appeals process. Most cases are fully resolved at the audit and appeals stages. A few are litigated.

The specifics of tax controversy practice include the following:

- Representing taxpayers in disputes or potential disputes with federal, state, and local tax agencies

- Advising clients on tax returns, reporting positions, the civil aspects of white-collar criminal investigations involving tax charges, and tax strategies and their acceptability to taxing agencies
- Tax litigation in the U.S. Tax Court, District Courts, Bankruptcy Courts, Court of Federal Claims, Courts of Appeal, and Supreme Court and state courts
- Related tax practice and procedure

The tax examination "life cycle" is also a good way of viewing the practice:

- Examination risk analysis
- Pre-examination audit readiness analysis
- Examination planning and representation
- Representation before the IRS Examination and IRS Appeals Office, in ADR forums, at the IRS National Office, and before the U.S. Competent Authority, as well as in state and local venues
- Litigation
- IRS Service Center matters
- Computations of IRS and state and local tax penalties and interest
- Compliance assistance
- Representation before the U.S. Department of Labor on ERISA and ESOP matters

Potential clients run the gamut from individuals to estates to C, S, and LLC corporations, partnerships, foreign corporations, tax shelter promoters, charitable trusts, foundations, other tax-exempt organizations, trade and professional associations, fiduciaries, and retirement plan sponsors. No industry or economic sector is excluded.

Almost 95 percent of all federal tax controversies are settled at the administrative appeal level. That makes it a given that a taxpayer should always appeal if frustrated by the IRS agent conducting the audit. It is virtually guaranteed that a taxpayer will secure a more favorable settlement on administrative appeal.

The IRS recognizes the value of closing cases before they get into court. Consequently, it has instituted an array of settlement initiatives as alternatives to the traditional Appeals Office conference:

- Early Referral from the Examination or Collection Division to Appeals. Revenue Procedure 99-28 (*www.irs.gov/businesses/ article/0,,id=180750,00.html*)
- Mediation (nonbinding). Revenue Procedure 2002-44; Internal Revenue Manual (IRM) 35.5.5.4–35.5.5.8(2), Mediation (*www.irs.gov/irm/index.html*)
- Arbitration. Revenue Procedure 2006-44 (*www.irs.gov/ irb/2006-44_IRB/ar10.html*)
- Fast Track Mediation. IRS Publication 3605 (*http://www.irs. gov/pub/irs-pdf/p3605.pdf*)
- Post-Appeals Mediation and Arbitration for Offer in Compromise (OIC) and Trust Fund Recovery Penalty (TFRP). Two-year pilot program launched in 2008. (*www.irs.gov/ newsroom/article/0,,id=200750,00.html*)
- Pre-Filing Agreements (large and midsize businesses) IRM 4.30.1 (*www.irs.gov/irm/part4/ch28s01.html*); PFA Orientation Guide (*www.irs.gov/businesses/article/0,,id=201340,00.html*)
- Industry Issue Resolution Program (*www.irs.gov/businesses/ article/0,,id=109645,00.html*)
- The IRS Restructuring and Reform Act of 1998 (Pub.L. 105-206) added IRC Sec. 7123, which codifies alternative appeals dispute resolution procedures. (*www.law.cornell. edu/uscode/html/uscode26/usc_sup_01_26.html*)

Who Does It?

Law Firms. Tax controversy is a very lucrative practice for law firms of all sizes and locations, and it is particularly rewarding for firms and sole practitioners located in the Washington, D.C., area and in state capitals. The practice also gives rise to a substantial number of boutique firms that practice tax law exclusively or primarily. Some of these boutiques are quite large.

The list below represents the most recent Chambers rankings of top tax controversy practices among major law firms and includes the cities where they maintain such practices:

- Baker & McKenzie (Chicago, Palo Alto, Washington, D.C.) (*www.bakernet.com*)
- Mayer Brown (Chicago, Washington, D.C.) (*www.mayerbrown.com*)
- McKee Nelson (Washington, D.C.) (*www.mckeenelson.com*)
- Miller & Chevalier (Washington, D.C.) (*www.millerchevalier.com*)
- Skadden Arps Slate Meagher & Flom (New York, Washington, D.C.) (*www.skadden.com*)
- Fulbright & Jaworski (Houston, New York) (*www.fulbright.com*)
- McDermott Will & Emery (Chicago, Washington, D.C.) (*www.mwe.com*)
- Chamberlain Hrdlicka White Williams & Martin (Atlanta, Philadelphia) (*www.chamberlainlaw.com*)
- Latham & Watkins (Los Angeles, Washington, D.C.) (*www.lw.com*)
- Sutherland Asbill & Brennan (Atlanta, Washington, D.C.) (*www.sablaw.com*)
- Alston & Bird (Washington, D.C.) (*www.alston.com*)
- Caplin & Drysdale (Washington, D.C.) (*www.capdale.com*)
- Cooley Godward & Kronish (Palo Alto, California) (*www.cooley.com*)
- Ivins Phillips & Barker (Washington, D.C.) (*www.ipbtax.com*)
- Morgan Lewis & Bockius (Philadelphia, Washington, D.C.) (*www.morganlewis.com*)
- Pillsbury Winthrop Shaw Pittman (New York, Washington, D.C.) (*www.pillsburylaw.com*)
- Roberts & Holland (New York, Washington, D.C.) (*www.robertsandholland.com*)
- White & Case (New York, Washington, D.C.)(*www.whitecase.com*)

In addition to the firms listed above, several boutique firms specialize in tax controversy practice:

- Real Property Tax
  - Feld, Hyde, Wertheimer, Bryant & Stone (Birmingham, Alabama) (*www.feldhyde.com*)
  - Hyden, Miron & Foster (Little Rock, Arakansas) (*www.taxlawyer.com*)
  - Hochman, Salkin, Rettig, Toscher & Perez (Beverly Hills, California) (*www.taxlitigator.com*)
  - Sarnoff & Baccash (Chicago, Illinois) (*www.sarnoffbaccash.com*)
- International Tax
  - Lourie & Cutler (Boston, Massachusetts) (*www.louriecutler.com*)
  - Vacovec, Mayotte & Singer (Newton, Massachusetts) (*www.vacovec.com*)
- Property Tax
  - Barnes, Broom, Dallas and McLeod (Flowood, Mississippi) (*www.wealthmanagement.net*)
  - Korf & Rosenblatt (Morristown, New Jersey) (*www.kork rosenblatt.com*)
  - Popp, Gray & Hutcheson (Austin, Texas) (*www.property-tax.com*)
- Ad Valorem Property Tax Disputes & Planning
  - Brusniak | Blackwell, Dallas, Texas (*www.txtax.com*)

Accounting Firms. What I said previously about clients turning to tax controversy attorneys for the more complex cases means that they turn to their accounting firms for the less complex ones. A growing number of accounting firms have tax controversy attorneys on staff to help with these, as well as more complicated cases. An attorney who wishes to work for an accounting firm should be cognizant of unauthorized practice of law rules in his or her jurisdiction.

Corporations. Many corporations invest their tax function to their General Counsel office. However, a large number break out the function and place it in a separate Tax Office. This is more often the case in corporations that "self-represent" in tax controversy cases (although most large corporations outsource tax controversy matters to their outside law firms).

Tax department positions sometimes have specialized requirements, such as a JD plus a CPA, an LLM in Tax, or a master's degree in Taxation.

Tax-Exempt Organizations. Most large tax-exempt organizations (i.e., nonprofits) farm out their tax controversy matters to outside law firms. However, a number of them handle the function in-house.

Federal, State, and Local Governments. Working for the IRS or a state or local tax authority, such as the California Franchise Tax Board, the New York State Department of Taxation and Finance, or the Philadelphia Revenue Department, offers lawyers another perspective on the practice. Nationwide, thousands of attorneys are engaged in tax controversy work for various government tax authorities.

U.S. government tax controversy practice is centered in the IRS, primarily in the Office of Chief Counsel, both in the National Office in Washington, D.C., and in Chief Counsel Field Offices nationwide. Almost 600 attorneys work in the National Office, and more than 700 work in 36 Field Offices.

While concentrated in the IRS, tax controversy work also goes on to a much more limited extent in other federal government law offices, principally these:

- U.S. Department of Treasury—Office of Tax Policy; Office of Tax Legislative Counsel; Office of the Benefits Tax Counsel; Office of Technical Assistance; Office of the Chief Counsel, Alcohol & Tobacco Tax and Trade Bureau; and Office of Chief Counsel, Treasury Inspector General for Tax Administration (*www.treas.gov*)
- Small Business Administration—Office of Interagency Affairs, Office of Advocacy (*www.sba.gov*)
- U.S. Court of Federal Claims—Staff Attorneys Office (*www.uscfc.uscourts.gov*)
- U.S. Department of Justice—Office of the Chief Counsel, Bureau of Alcohol, Tobacco and Firearms; and Tax Division (*www.usdoj.gov*)
- U.S. Tax Court (*www.ustaxcourt.gov*)
- State and local tax authorities (*www.irs.gov/taxpros/article/ 0,,id=100236,00.html*)

Legal and Tax Specialty Publishers. A large print and online publishing industry devoted to tax matters, including tax controversy practice. Attorneys are hired as legal researchers and editors. A selected list of legal and tax publishers follows:

- American Bar Association (*www.abanet.org*)
- American Institute of Certified Public Accountants (*www.aicpa.org*)
- Bureau of National Affairs (*www.bna.com*)
- CCH (*www.cch.com*)
- Corporate Tax Publishers (*www.ctpistatetax.com*)
- Matthew Bender (*http://bender.lexisnexis.com*)
- National Association of Tax Professionals (*www.natptax.com*)
- PLC (*www.practicallaw.com*)
- RIA (*http://ria.thomsonreuters.com*)
- Tax Analysts (*www.taxanalysts.com*)
- Tax Management (*www.bnatax.com*)
- Thomson Reuters (*www.thomsonreuters.com*)

What Does It Pay?

Tax controversy in private practice pays very well. There is often a lot at stake, and clients are willing to ante up to avoid adverse tax consequences. Law and accounting firms pay the most (experienced attorneys can earn $200,000+), followed by government (salaries range from approximately $50,000 at the entry level to $150,000), with legal and tax publishers paying the least (approximately $45,000 to $100,000).

One of my Washington, D.C., area counseling clients worked on tax controversy matters for a small CPA firm and earned close to $200,000. When he opened his own solo practice, soon he reached the same compensation level, which he subsequently exceeded.

Future Prospects

The IRS and state tax authorities have every incentive to continue increasing their enforcement efforts. Historically, tax authorities have been impervious to economic cycles. They've gone about their business regardless of economic ups and downs. However, the Great Recession is different. Its negative impact on tax revenues has changed the thinking of the IRS and its state and local counterparts, since empirical evidence says that stepped-up enforcement brings in a large amount of revenue. Do not expect the tax authorities to pull back as the economy turns around. It is an obvious choice for them to continue to go full throttle after this money.

Tax controversy practice is constantly evolving in response to changes in the way government tax authorities conduct audits. IRS keeps involving its own tax controversy attorneys earlier in the process and for multiple purposes; hence, taxpayers find it important to do the same.

Tax examinations appear to be growing in complexity, meaning more potential work for attorneys and correspondingly less for accountants.

The IRS is on a continuous mission to streamline its procedures for early identification and confrontation of corporate and individual taxpayer noncompliance. Congress has also steadily given taxpayers additional procedural protections, while at the same time rendering more punitive the consequences of losing a tax dispute.

An increasing number of individual and corporate taxpayers (10+ million is the best estimate) owe the IRS more than $100 billion. More than 5 million taxpayers have failed to file one or more federal income tax returns past any available extension date. IRS reporting requirements are increasing, as are demands for information via letters, summons, and subpoenas. Financial transactions, including tax shelters, offshore credit card schemes, and USA Patriot Act money tracing, are being increasingly challenged. State tax authorities are following suit.

All of this makes for a bright future for tax controversy attorneys.

Breaking In

The Importance of Tax Education. Tax controversy practice is demanding. It requires extensive knowledge of the Internal Revenue Code, Revenue Rulings, Treasury issuances, etc. and knowledge of and facility with the many procedures and options inherent in the practice. If you also contemplate a state and/or local practice, you will have to become conversant with those codes and procedures, too.

Specifically, some of the most important items you should know include the following:

- The latest issues and trends in administrative and judicial enforcement of tax disputes

- The latest audit techniques, enforcement initiatives, dispute resolution procedures, general defense strategies, and defense strategies in special situations
- How to advise a client during examination of a tax return or appeal of a proposed deficiency
- Judicial forums available to dispute a proposed tax assessment and how to file an action in each
- Guidelines for offers in compromise and installment agreements
- Settlement options at various procedural stages
- Options for paying additional tax assessments
- Ethical issues affecting practitioners
- Your professional responsibilities and exposures when representing taxpayers
- The Office of Professional Responsibility and the recent legislative enhancements to that division's disciplinary authority

The best way to prepare for a tax controversy practice is to enroll in one of the many Tax LLM programs offered by U.S. law schools. From the standpoint of career entry and advancement, the two most compelling programs are those offered by New York University School of Law and Georgetown University Law Center. However, accomplished tax controversy practitioners have emerged from every one of the LLM programs that has been around for more than a few years.

The large number of Tax LLM programs means that you can find one that suits your budget. You can find out about Tax LLM programs by accessing the *Graduate Law Degree Program Directory* at *www.attorneyjobs. com,* a Thomson Reuters subscription service.

Tax certificate programs are also available through law schools. Law schools offering such programs include San Diego, Denver, Georgetown, St. Thomas (Florida), DePaul, Chicago Kent, John Marshall (Illinois), New York University, Capital University, Cleveland Marshall, Temple, and Villanova.

Other selected providers offering tax certificate programs include Southern New Hampshire University (*www.snhu.edu*), Bentley College (*www.bentley.edu*), and the National Business Institute (*www.nbi-sems.com*).

Tax Networking Organizations
- American College of Tax Counsel (*www.actonline.org*)
- American Property Tax Counsel (*www.aptcnet.com*)
- American Taxation Association (*http://aaahq.org/ata/index.htm*)
- Institute for Professionals in Taxation (*www.ipt.org*)
- National Association of Tax Practitioners (*www.natptax.com*)
- National Tax Association (*http://ntanet.org*)

Law-Related Positions. There are a variety of tax controversy positions that draw on your legal background but are not attorney positions. Most of these can be found in the larger CPA and consulting firms, such as the Big Four (Deloitte Touche, Ernst & Young, PricewaterhouseCoopers, and KPMG) and some of the national CPA firms down a level, such as Towers Perrin, Grant Thornton, and BDO Seidman. Some of the job titles to watch for are these:

- Tax Controversy Senior Manager
- Tax Controversy Manager
- Tax Controversy Specialist
- Tax Manager (SALT)—Controversy

Related Work Often Generated by Tax Controversies. One of the best things about tax controversy work is its almost unique ability to bring in additional business from the same client. Types of related work include:

- Real estate
- Commercial transactions
- Corporate matters
- Intellectual property
- Banking
- Divorce and separation
- White-collar crime
- Asset forfeiture
- Bankruptcy/insolvency
- Lending/investment/finance

- Estate planning
- Internal investigations

For More Information

- Internal Revenue Service (*www.irs.gov*)
- Nath, Robert G. *The Unofficial Guide to Dealing with the IRS.* Arco, 1999 (*www.allbookstores.com/author/Arco_Publishing.html*)
- CCH Tax Practice Guides (*www.cch.com*)
- Miller & Chevalier Tax Controversy Alert (*www.millerchevalier.com*)
- IRS Training Materials (*www.irs.gov*)

Chapter 3

Countercyclical
Opportunities

THIS CHAPTER LOOKS AT three practice areas—bankruptcy law, corporate reorganization, and real estate distress law—that are classically countercyclical. That is, they do very well in bad economies and not so well in good ones. Their success in dismal times is due to the fact that they focus on adversity and negative results (such as insolvencies, business failures, and real estate foreclosures) and provide the specific legal services to deal with them.

But what happens when the economy turns around again? When a recession ends and growth resumes, fewer individuals and organizations have to cope with job loss, client abandonment, and the disappearance of their businesses. Consequently, these three practice areas wane. In many cases, practitioners must reinvent themselves to keep working, eating, and paying the mortgage.

None of the three sections in this chapter contains a "Future Prospects" discussion. The fact that these are countercyclical opportunities means that their future prospects once the economy begins to grow again are not particularly enticing. However, the organizations that practice real estate distress law are the ones most likely to perform reasonably well in a positive economy, because they will be able to make the transition to practicing the "upside" of real estate law—development, projects, transactions—with relative ease.

BANKRUPTCY LAW

Introduction

Total U.S. bankruptcy filings increased 31 percent in 2008 over 2007, according to the Administrative Office of the U.S. Courts, totaling an incredible 1,117,771. Fourth-quarter 2008 filings exceeded 300,000.

2008 was the first year since the implementation of the Bankruptcy Abuse Prevention and Consumer Protection Act of 2005 (Pub.L. 109-8) that bankruptcies surpassed 1 million. The American Bankruptcy Institute (ABI) predicts that bankruptcy filings will continue to rise in 2009. ABIs and other organizations' estimates range from 1.4 million to 3 million.

The 43,546 business bankruptcy filings in 2008 represented a 54 percent increase over 2007. ABI says that business bankruptcy filings in the first quarter of 2009 were up over 30 percent at an annualized rate. Even more compelling is how big the filers are becoming. There were 60 debtors in 2008 with assets of more than $1 billion, compared with just 7 in 2007.

Following are the states with the highest per capita filing rate (total filings) for the 12-month period ending December 31, 2008 (listed in order by per capita filing rate):

- Tennessee
- Nevada
- Georgia
- Alabama
- Indiana
- Michigan
- Ohio
- Kentucky
- Arkansas
- Illinois

The Federal Judicial Districts with the highest percentage increase in total filings for 2008 (compared to 2007) are as follows:

- Central District of California: 93.5%
- District of Arizona: 78.9%
- Eastern District of California: 78.1%
- Southern District of California: 76.6%
- District of Delaware: 73.9%

The Federal Reserve says that household debt is at a record high relative to disposable income. This has led to increased household delinquencies and bankruptcies and threatened the health of lenders. Household debt is now more than ten times the level it was in 1980.

Bankruptcy law may emerge from the Great Recession in better shape than is typical of countercyclical law practices, for these reasons. Unemployment, which prompts victims to declare bankruptcy, will likely continue to rise even after economic indicators turn upward. People who were able to find new jobs during the downturn will often find themselves underemployed and at greater risk of insolvency as a result. Many previously two-income families have become one-income families, meaning less revenue coming in. Individuals and families who lost their health insurance or had to cut back on it will incur medical expenses that may force them into bankruptcy (unless healthcare reform, under debate in Congress as this book goes to press, comes to pass and eases that burden). And consumer debt is at historic highs and will not likely decline to noncrisis levels for many years.

What Is It?

The American Bankruptcy Institute has the following bankruptcy code explanations:

- *Chapter 7* of the Bankruptcy Code is available to both individual and business debtors. Its purpose is to achieve a fair distribution to creditors of the debtor's available nonexempt property. Unsecured debts not reaffirmed are discharged, providing a fresh financial start. Chapter 7 is essentially a liquidation.
- *Chapter 11* of the Bankruptcy Code is available for both business and consumer debtors. Its purpose is to rehabilitate a business as a going concern or reorganize an individual's finances through a court-approved reorganization plan.

- *Chapter 12* of the Bankruptcy Code is designed to give special debt relief to a family farmer with regular income from farming.
- *Chapter 13* of the Bankruptcy Code is available for an individual with regular income whose debts do not exceed specific amounts. It is typically used to budget some of the debtor's future earnings under a plan through which unsecured creditors are paid in whole or in part.

Who Does It?

Bankruptcy law is practiced by law firms (large, midsize, and small), sole practitioners, corporate in-house counsel offices, financial institutions, and consulting firms that advise on bankruptcies and creditors' rights. Thirty-two U.S. government practices do bankruptcy law; following are the principal ones:

- U.S. Bankruptcy Courts (*www.uscourts.gov/bankruptcycourts.html*)
- U.S. Courts of Appeals (*www.uscourts.gov/courtsofappeals.html*)
- U.S. Department of Justice (*www.usdoj.gov*)
  - Executive Office for U.S. Trustees
  - U.S. Trustees' Offices Nationwide
  - Civil Division—Commercial Litigation Branch
  - Criminal Division—Fraud Section
  - Tax Division
  - U.S. Attorneys' Offices Nationwide
- U.S. Department of Treasury (*www.treas.gov*)
  - Internal Revenue Service—Office of Chief Counsel Nationwide
  - Office of General Counsel (OGC)
  - Office of Domestic Finance—Legal Counsel
  - Office of Thrift Supervision—Office of Chief Counsel
  - Financial Stability Oversight Board—OGC
- Federal Reserve Board—Division of Banking Supervision & Regulation (*www.federalreserve.gov*)
- Federal Deposit Insurance Corporation—Legal Division (*www.fdic.gov*)
- Securities and Exchange Commission—OGC (*www.sec.gov*)
- Commodity Futures Trading Commission—OGC (*www.cftc.gov*)

- Pension Benefit Guaranty Corporation—Office of the Chief Counsel and OGC (*www.pbgc.gov*)
- U.S. Department of Commerce—Office of the Assistant General Counsel for Finance and Litigation (*www.commerce.gov*)
- U.S. Department of Defense—Defense Finance and Accounting Service—OGC (*www.defenselink.mil*)
- U.S. Department of Transportation—Maritime Administration—Office of Chief Counsel, Division of Ship Financing Contracts (*www.dot.gov*)

Law-Related Job Titles.
- Bankruptcy analyst
- Chapter 13 trustee
- Credit examiner
- Loan workout officer
- Assistant U.S. trustee

What Does It Pay?

In times of great economic stress, bankruptcy becomes a very high-volume practice and can be very lucrative. Attorney fees for Chapter 7 liquidations typically range from $1,000 to $2,000, Chapter 13 bankruptcies from $1,500 to $5,000, the higher figures applying primarily to sole proprietorships; and Chapter 11 bankruptcies from $5,000 for very small, incorporated businesses to over $100,000 for larger companies.

Fees also affected by the complexity of a case, the number of creditors, and geographic location (fees are customarily higher in large metropolitan areas).

Savvy bankruptcy attorneys will ask for an up-front retainer because, once a case is filed, certain restrictions may apply to professional services fee payments.

Breaking In

The demand for bankruptcy lawyers during severe economic downturns is huge, which translates into easier entry into the practice than in good times. Both debtors and creditors need legal advice and assistance. Moreover, a bankruptcy case often generates multiple parties with varying interests, each requiring independent representation.

Because so much of bankruptcy practice is codebased, the learning curve is quite rapidly achieved. Attorneys with no bankruptcy experience can usually handle a simple Chapter 7 liquidation without much background or preparation.

Bankruptcy Job Websites
- U.S. Bankruptcy Courts (*www.uscourts.gov/employment.html*)
- U.S. Trustee Offices (*www.usdoj.gov*)
- Association of Corporate Counsel (*www.acca.com*)
- Real Estate Investment Trust and Related Jobs (*www.nareit.org*)
- Pension Real Estate Association (*www.prea.org*)

Education and Training
- American Board of Certification (*www.abcworld.org*)
  - Business Bankruptcy Certificate
  - Consumer Bankruptcy Certificate
  - Creditors' Rights Law Certificate
- UCLA School of Law—LLM Specialization in Business Law, Bankruptcy and Commercial Law Track (*www.law.ucla.edu*)
- St. John's University School of Law—LLM in Bankruptcy (*www.stjohns.edu/academics/graduate/law/academics/llm*)

Networking Organizations
- American Bankruptcy Institute (*www.abiworld.org*)
- American College of Bankruptcy (*www.amercol.org*)
- American College of Real Estate Lawyers (*www.acrel.org*)

For More Information
- Corporate Yellow Book (*www.leadershipdirectories.com*)
- Federation of Defense and Corporate Counsel (*www.thefederation.org*)
- Financial Yellow Book (*www.leadershipdirectories.com*)
- Directory of Corporate Counsel (*www.aspenpublishers.com*)
- Commercial Real Estate Development Association (*www.naiop.org*)

CORPORATE REORGANIZATION LAW

Introduction

It was a toss-up whether to place this section here or in Chapter 4 "Hot Practice Areas during the Great Recession." All three locations might arguably be appropriate.

The objective of a reorganization is to put the company on a firmer footing, assure its survival, and return it to profitability.

When companies experience periods of economic and financial crisis, a whole new range of legal, financial, and management considerations emerge. Corporate reorganization is in the air. In the Great Recession, few companies are immune from having to rethink how they are structured, what they produce, with whom they do business, etc. Overlaying all of these immediate considerations are the longer-term inducements to corporate reorganization and renewal—globalization; outsourcing; the threat of product, service, and delivery substitution that results from competitor innovation; and other impacts that portend either opportunity or disaster. These survival issues make it essential that organizations have the expertise on board or on call to cope with such upheavals.

Corporate reorganization practitioners are increasingly essential to the reorganization, restructuring, renewal, and/or turnaround process. They serve as interim managers, general counsels, or consultants, even temporarily replacing company CEOs, or may serve as advisors to a troubled company's board of directors.

What Is It?

Corporate reorganization means much more than Chapter 11 bankruptcy. It can be the conversion of all outstanding shares to common stock or achieving a reverse stock split (i.e., combining outstanding shares into a smaller number of shares). It can mean getting bad assets and distressed debt off the books. It can include renegotiating labor and employment agreements (as in the examples of General Motors and Chrysler). It often includes downsizing the workforce through layoffs, attrition, hiring freezes, etc. It can encompass spinoffs and divestitures, strategic alliances and partnerships, and mergers and acquisitions. It may include recasting the board of directors and officers, amending the bylaws and other documents, changing the legal nature of the company, rebranding, changing product lines and service offerings, and much more. As a rule, corporate reorganization is a combination of one or more such strategies. It can also be international when it involves a multinational corporation.

In addition to troubled companies, clients may be debtors, debtors-in-possession, creditors, creditors' committees, shareholders, shareholders' committees, U.S. Trustees' Offices, U.S. Bankruptcy Courts, financial institutions, or even tort claimants.

Who Does It?

Generic and specialized management consulting firms are the primary employers in this discipline, but law firms are playing catch-up. The Great Recession has prompted numerous law firms to establish corporate reorganization practice groups under such labels as Global Financial Restructuring, Financial Stabilization, Distressed Assets, and Corporate Turnaround.

The following selected law and consulting firms have corporate turnaround practices:

- AEG Partners LLC (*www.aegpartners.com*)
- Alix Partners (*www.alixpartners.com*)
- Bain & Company (*www.bain.com*)
- Deloitte & Touche Corporate Finance (*www.deloitte.com*)
- Ernst & Young (*www.ey.com*)
- FTI Consulting Inc. (*www.fticonsulting.com*)
- Haskell Slaughter (*www.hsy.com*)
- Houlihan Lokey (*www.hlhz.com*)
- Hunter Higgins Miles Elam & Benjamin PLLC (*www.greensborolaw.com*)
- Katsy Korins LLP (*www.katskykorins.com*)
- MCA Financial Group Ltd. (*www.mca-financial.com*)
- McGlinchey Stafford PLLC (*www.mcglinchey.com*)
- Morris Nichols Arsht & Tunnell (*www.mnat.com*)
- Ohio Key Bank (*www.keybank.com*)
- Pepper Hamilton LLP (*www.pepperlaw.com*)
- PricewaterhouseCoopers (*www.pwc.com*)
- Rivenrock Advisors (*www.rivenrockadvisors.com*)
- Rosenthal & Rosenthal Inc. (*www.rosenfact.com*)

- Vedder Price Kaufman & Kammholz (*www.vedderprice.com*)
- Weir & Partners LLP (*www.weirpartners.com*)

Government gets involved, too. Whenever, for example, the Federal Deposit Insurance Corporation takes over a failed bank, it attempts to perform whatever corporate reorganization might be viable and necessary to make the bank attractive to a purchaser. In that case, a government attorney often becomes the *de facto* bank general counsel or even CEO during the resolution period.

Most corporate reorganization specialists are not locked into a particular industry. Rather, they transcend industries. As they become more visible and the fruits of their labors are more widely reported, companies engage them earlier and earlier, often now at the first signs of trouble.

What Does It Pay?

Corporate reorganization practitioners and turnaround specialists in private practice command high fees, thanks to the nature of what they do and the expertise they bring to the table. Their public sector counterparts are compensated according to their respective government pay scales, with the exception of attorneys who work for federal financial regulatory agencies, who are compensated at a significantly higher rate than other government attorneys ($200,000+ annual compensation is not out of the ordinary for federal financials regulators).

Breaking In

Recent law school graduates can, of course, compete for positions with large law firms. Consulting firms generally want attorneys with relevant experience. Government agencies, particularly during stressful economic times, hire both recent law graduates and experienced lawyers.

Credentialing Programs

- Turnaround Management Association—Certified Turnaround Professional Certificate Program (*www.turnaround.org*)
- Association of Insolvency and Restructuring Advisors (*www.airacira.org*)
- Certified Insolvency and Restructuring Advisor
- Certification in Distressed Business Valuation

For More Information
- Association of Certified Turnaround Professionals (*www.actp.org*)
- Association of Insolvency and Restructuring Advisors (*www.airacira.org*)
- Spinoff and Reorg Profiles (*www.spinoffprofiles.com*)

REAL ESTATE DISTRESS LAW

Introduction

Other than bankruptcy, no practice is more countercyclical than real estate distress law. Traditional, "upside" real estate law may virtually disappear when the economy turns sour, but real estate distress practices boom. The Great Recession, triggered by the collapse of the real estate market, has only intensified this phenomenon this time around.

As of this writing, approximately 11,000 foreclosures are taking place daily in the United States. This gives some indication of the breadth and depth of the real estate distress crisis. In addition, thousands of real estate securities based on subprime mortgages have tanked. Moreover, mortgage modifications so desperately sought by millions of Americans are made much more complicated by the exotic nature of the mortgage securities that evolved out of the subprime mortgage boom. Consequently, the number of attorneys who traditionally practiced real estate distress law is suddenly inadequate to the task.

What Is It?

Real estate distress law is the combination of all that needs to be done when the profitable aspects of real estate—deals, projects, developments, mortgages, real estate securities—go bad. The work consists of workouts and restructuring of loans, settling defaulted loans and deeds in lieu of foreclosure, handling foreclosures and certain refinancings, marshalling and disposing of real estate assets and nonperforming loans, etc.

Foreclosure is a good example of the diversity of real estate distress practice. Plaintiff foreclosure attorneys represent lenders, creditors, and loan servicers with collections; conduct judicial and nonjudicial foreclosure sales and forfeiture proceedings; collect on collateral and deficiency balances; draft deeds in lieu of foreclosure and loan forbearance; modify sale agreements; manage troubled assets in lender loan portfolios; help recoup capital investments; pursue repossessions; litigate judicial foreclosures, quiet title actions, and postforeclosure evictions; and represent clients in bankruptcy court.

Defense foreclosure lawyers protect property owners' rights and attempt to avoid foreclosure. They advise homeowners on available nonbankruptcy options and on debt relief available under the Bankruptcy Code; negotiate forbearance and refinancing agreements, short sales, mortgage modifications, and alternative payment plans to avoid foreclosure; pursue predatory lending claims; mitigate fees and improper prepayment penalties; and advise clients of their rights under federal and state unfair debt collection practice laws.

Commercial foreclosure is more complicated because it often involves additional issues such as tenant rights; assignments of rents; separate sales of pledged collateral; and UCC liens on equipment, furniture, goods, and other items of personal property not connected to real estate.

The Great Recession has prompted a continuous evolution of foreclosure law in many states, with an eye to streamlining the process and helping homeowners remain in their homes and businesses remain in business.

The U.S. government has also gotten heavily into the act, establishing a variety of programs and enacting sweeping legislation (the Helping Families Save Their Homes Act (Pub.L. 111-22) and the Fraud Enforcement and Recovery Act (Pub.L. 111-21), signed into law by President Obama in late May 2009). The nonlegislative program initiatives have done little to help homeowners weather the crisis (the Bush administration's Hope for Homeowners program, for example, had modified one loan up to mid-2009, making it one of the most colossal government failures of all time).

The two laws cited above are likely to make a significant dent in the foreclosure barrage. The Helping Families Save Their Homes Act provides financial incentives to homeowners, mortgage lenders, and servicers and makes certain previously voluntary (on the part of lenders and servicers) measures mandatory. The Fraud Enforcement and Recovery Act (FERA) extends federal bank fraud statutes to cover mortgage brokers and certain other previously nonregulated or federally insured financial institutions. FERA also authorizes over $340 million to beef up federal departments and agencies that have enforcement authority under this and related laws, including the Department of Justice, Department of Housing and Urban Development, FBI, Secret Service, Securities and Exchange Commission, and the U.S. Postal Inspection Service. A good deal of this new funding authority will be used to hire attorneys.

Who Does It?

Real estate distress positions are found in many places: law firms of all sizes and sole practitioners; real estate developers; colleges and universities; energy companies; banks and financial services institutions, including insurance companies; retailers with substantial real property holdings; the hospitality and recreation industry; transportation companies; public utilities; pension funds with real estate investments; Real Estate Investment Trusts (REITs); consulting firms that provide real estate distress advice and services/loan workouts and/or disposition of properties and bad related assets; and federal, state, and local governments (including Federal Home Loan Banks, Farm Credit Banks, and government-sponsored enterprises like Fannie Mae and Freddie Mac). Much of these government agencies' work in recessionary times involves real estate distress.

Real estate distress practice, while concentrated in organizations that deal exclusively with the real estate market downside, is also found in institutions that deal with both good and bad real estate markets. These institutions have at least some work regardless of the state of the economy.

What Does It Pay?

Real estate distress law generally pays quite well, because of two factors:

1. The large dollar amounts involved, especially in commercial contexts
2. The urgent desire of clients to be rid of the albatrosses— properties, projects, loans, bad assets—around their necks

Of course, commercial and financial practices compensate at much higher rates than residential real estate practices.

Within the public sector, real estate distress positions can pay quite a bit more than is customary in government legal and law-related employment, especially in certain U.S. government agencies. For example, attorneys who work for one of the federal financial regulatory agencies earn considerably more (20–50 percent) than their attorney counterparts at other federal departments and agencies, pushing into the $200,000 range for nonsupervisory and nonexecutive legal positions.

Breaking In

The easiest route to a real estate distress law position is to work for a public sector agency (see below). They are the most likely employers of recent law graduates. They also always staff up to handle the distress issues presented by economic crises. For example, the FDIC almost doubled its budget from fiscal year 2008 to fiscal year 2009 (the budget for its receivership operations increased by almost 700 percent) to resolve failed financial institutions that collapsed during the Great Recession. They also, of course, look for attorneys with experience. Outside of major law firms, virtually all other employers seek experienced attorneys.

Note: Do not assume that government employment is necessarily more secure than that in the private sector once the economic crisis passes. After the savings-and-loan debacle of the early 1990s, the FDIC laid off numerous attorneys.

Principal U.S. Government Real Estate Distress Law Practices

- Federal Housing Finance Agency—Office of General Counsel (OGC) (*www.fhfa.gov*)
- Federal Deposit Insurance Corporation—Legal Division (*www.fdic.gov*)
- U.S. Department of Housing and Urban Development— OGC (*www.hud.gov*)
- U.S. Department of the Treasury (*www.treas.gov*)
  - Financial Stability Oversight Board—OGC
  - Internal Revenue Service—Office of Chief Counsel
- U.S. Department of Veterans Affairs—OGC and Regional Counsel Offices (*www.va.gov*)
- Federal National Mortgage Association (*www.fanniemae.com*)
- Federal Home Loan Mortgage Corporation (*www.freddiemac.com*)

Credentialing
- University of Miami School of Law—LLM in Real Property Development (relevant courses in Distressed Property Workouts, Bankruptcy) (*www.law.miami.edu*)
- John Marshall Law School (Illinois)—LLM in Real Estate Law (relevant courses in Bankruptcy and Insolvency Laws Affecting Real Estate, Securitization of Real Estate) (*www.jmls.edu*)

Networking Organizations
- American College of Real Estate Lawyers (*www.acrel.org*)
- Counselors of Real Estate (*www.cre.org*)
- Real Estate Investors Association (*www.nationalreia.com*)

For More Information
- Mortgage Bankers Association (*http://mbaa.org/default.htm*)
- Commercial Real Estate Development Association (*www.naiop.org*)
- U.S. foreclosure laws (*www.foreclosurelaw.org*)
- American Real Estate Society (*www.aresnet.org*)
- International Association of Corporate Real Estate Executives (*www.nacore.org*)
- National Association of Real Estate Investment Trusts (*www.nareit.org*)
- *Pensions & Investments* newspaper (*www.pionline.com*)

Chapter 4

Hot Practice Areas During the Great Recession

"ANGRY INVESTOR" CHALLENGES

The volume of litigation and other actions resulting from the Great Recession and its attendant financial meltdown, credit crunch, housing market collapse, rampant foreclosures, and toxic assets—along with the actions and inaction of George W. Bush and assorted skullduggery—is prodigious. The list of defendants and the besieged reads like a "Who's Who" of American and global movers and shakers and malefactors of great wealth. It's not only accused investment manager Bernie Madoff and his merry band of scammers.

Between home values and investments, Americans have lost somewhere between $15 trillion and $30 trillion so far. With 401(k) balances down by 50 percent or more and home values down by similar margins in many markets, including millions of houses where the value is now less than the mortgage, no wonder individuals are just as upset as the managers of pension funds and other institutions that suffered major losses.

Plaintiffs believe that in the absence of a government bailout, somebody has to pay, both in the remunerative and retributive sense. They are filing suit against anything that moves and has a deep or not-so-deep pocket. No potential target is safe. Judges and attorneys will be busy sorting out this mess for at least a few years to come.

Even investors who have received bailouts are suing ... each other. A number of financial firms are trying to make up the difference between what they received via taxpayer largesse and what they lost.

Moreover, "angry investor" activities have expanded beyond litigation to include (1) an array of challenges designed to oust bank, insurance, and other company board members (Citigroup, Bank of America, and AIG, among many others, are prime targets); (2) formal complaints to the Securities and Exchange Commission (SEC), urging the no-longer-reluctant regulator to take action; and (3) complaints by investors to the Financial Industry Regulatory Authority (FINRA), already resulting in an increase in disciplinary actions against securities brokers and dealers (they are almost triple what they were three years ago). Angry investors are hardly restricted to U.S. citizens, companies, and regulators. Litigation and other challenges have crossed national borders. Deutsche Bank AG of Germany, for example, has sued Reserve Fund (U.S.) for the $72 million of its $500 million money market investment that has not been paid back.

Anytime people lose money, litigation picks up. But never before like this.

What Is It?

Angry investor challenges come in diverse and sometimes creative manifestations. Its origins were with subprime mortgages and the securitized paper that derived from that fiasco. At first, the focus was on suits against financial institutions: mortgage lenders, investment and commercial banks, hedge funds, insurance companies, securities brokers and dealers, money market funds, etc. A Stanford University study found that almost one-third of all financial firms were named as a defendant in a securities class action in 2008.

Now, all limits and all bets are off. The litigation and shareholder onslaught has expanded to include defendants far distant from the financial services sector. A class action filed in late 2008 in California, for example, targeted NextWave Wireless for allegedly issuing materially false and misleading statements regarding the company's business and financial results. The next day, NextWave's share price declined by 67 percent.

Federal securities class-action filings (267) in 2008 increased 37 percent over 2007. Here is a partial list of angry investor class-action defendants in lawsuits filed in March 2009:

- Insight Enterprises
- Steel Dynamics
- Citigroup
- CV Therapeutics
- Gevity HR
- Prudential Financial
- Perrigo Company
- Corus Bankshares
- Sprint Nextel
- Century Aluminum
- SunTrust Banks
- Heartland Payment Systems
- Barclays Bank
- General Electric

While approximately 40 percent of class action suits are dismissed, the other 60 percent survive a Motion to Dismiss and usually settle, making filing a gamble worth taking.

Moreover, regulators have awakened to the fact that there are problems and are going after companies on their own initiative. The most active regulators to date have been the SEC and the New York State Attorney General's Office. In addition, states and municipalities (usually because of losses to their employee pension funds) have joined in the action.

Shareholder attacks on corporate boards of directors are gaining momentum. Not only have shareholder annual meetings gone from the stodgy to the very lively, but companies have felt compelled to make changes to their boards to head off such unpleasantness.

All of this requires a lot of lawyering: filing lawsuits and administrative actions, representing shareholders (individuals and institutions) intent on ousting company directors, and penning formal complaints to regulatory agencies. Not to mention all the lawyers on the other side.

Employment is largely with plaintiffs' law firms and secondarily in government regulatory agencies such as the SEC (*www.sec.gov*), Commodity Futures Trading Commission (*www.cftc.gov*), Federal Trade Commission (*www.ftc.gov*), state attorney general offices (*www.naag.org*), and state securities commissions (*www.seclaw.com*).

For More Information

- Class Action World (*www.classactionworld.com*)
- Securities Docket (*www.securitiesdocket.com*)
- Stanford Law School Securities Class Action Clearinghouse (*http://securities.stanford.edu*)
- Yahoo Finance (*http://finance.yahoo.com*)
- PACER (*http://pacer.psc.uscourts.gov*)
- Financial Industry Regulatory Authority (*www.finra.org*)

FINANCIAL REGULATORY REFORM

Question 1: How many U.S. government agencies share responsibility for financial regulation?

Answer: At least nine agencies with multiple offices.

Question 2: How many new federal regulators have been proposed to be added to this matrix?

Answer: Three.

Question 3: How many new federal and state entities with financial regulatory authority have been established as a result of the American Reinvestment & Recovery Act?

Answer: As of June 2009, there have been 33, with additional ones pending.

Question 4: How many agencies have been—or would be—eliminated by financial regulatory reform?

Answer: Four would be gone, but there would be a net gain of two agencies. The Office of Federal Housing Enterprise Oversight, the regulator of Fannie Mae and Freddie Mac, was abolished earlier in 2009, along with the Federal Housing Finance Board. Both agencies' functions were transferred to a new Federal Housing Finance Agency (FHFA). (Net loss: one agency). In addition, the administration proposes eliminating the Office of Thrift Supervision and the Office of the Comptroller of the Currency, the Treasury Department agencies that charter and regulate savings and loan associations and national banks, respectively, and replacing them with a National Bank Supervisor. The thrift charter would be eliminated. This makes a lot of sense because there is so little difference now between thrifts and commercial banks. (Aggregate net loss: two agencies).

Question 5: Who currently regulates nonbank lenders, hedge funds, venture capital funds, private equity firms, foreign exchange trading, over-the-counter derivatives trading, ratings agencies, and the U.S. Treasury securities market?

Answer: No one.

> *The current U.S. financial regulatory system has relied on a fragmented and complex arrangement of federal and state regulators—put into place over the past 150 years—that has not kept pace with major developments in financial markets and products in recent decades. As the nation finds itself in the midst of one of the worst financial crises ever, the regulatory system increasingly appears to be ill-suited to meet the nation's needs in the 21st century. Today, responsibilities for overseeing the financial services industry are shared among almost a dozen federal banking, securities, futures, and other regulatory agencies, numerous self-regulatory organizations, and hundreds of state financial regulatory agencies.*

From *Financial Regulation: A Framework for Crafting and Assessing Proposals to Modernize the Outdated U.S. Financial Regulatory System.* Government Accountability Office. GAO-09-349T (2009) (*www.gao.gov*)

The Obama administration's financial regulatory reform proposals represent the largest overhaul of financial regulation since the Great Depression. Existing financial regulators would receive broad additional authority. That means many more attorney jobs in places like these:

- The *Federal Deposit Insurance Corporation (FDIC),* the agency that insures bank and savings and loan deposits, examines state-chartered banks that do not join the federal system and seizes failing banks before they collapse and "resolves" them. Under the administration proposal, the FDIC's seizure and resolution authority would, at the behest of the Treasury Department, be expanded beyond banks and thrifts to the largest financial companies. The bevy of new regulations and compliance and reporting requirements that the FDIC would promulgate means an enormous new legal workload for the agency as well as the regulated financial institutions and their law firms.

- The *Federal Reserve Board (Fed)* is the agency that controls monetary policy and supervises state-chartered banks that opt into the federal system. The Great Recession vastly expanded the Fed's role in the economy, and the regulatory reform proposal would expand it even more. Under the reform plan, the Fed would become the principal "systemic risk regulator" and supervise the largest financial services companies. If the plan is enacted, look for the Fed, these companies, and their law firms to hire hundreds of attorneys.
- The *Securities and Exchange Commission (SEC)* regulates public corporations, stock exchanges, brokers, mutual funds, municipal bonds, and corporate auditors. The SEC's new chair, Mary Schapiro, is aggressively expanding the agency's investigative and enforcement roles in a so-far successful effort to retain its existing powers in the face of financial regulatory reform. So far, she is winning this battle. The SEC's investor protection watchdog role would likely survive reform initiatives, even if a new financial consumer protection agency is created (see discussion later in this section). The SEC would be given expanded authority to promote transparency in disclosures to investors, as well as new tools to promote fair treatment of investors, including establishing a fiduciary duty for broker-dealers offering investment advice and harmonizing the regulation of investment advisors and broker-dealers. Moreover, because the SEC's regulatory and enforcement jurisdiction would expand to cover an array of previously unregulated entities and financial instruments, the agency and the newly regulated entities would require large additions to their legal staffs.
- The *U.S. Department of the Treasury* would receive broad new authority in a variety of areas, including the power to direct the resolution of bank holding companies and nonbank financial companies that might pose a systemic risk.
- The *Federal Trade Commission* would lose some of its authority to the new Consumer Financial Protection Agency (see the discussion later in this section), but would also receive additional resources to go after financial fraud and related abuses.

The Obama administration has also proposed the addition of three entirely new financial regulatory agencies and one new nonregulatory agency. If Congress goes along, look for the following new organizations to be added to the already Balkanized federal financial regulatory matrix:

- A *Consumer Financial Protection Agency (CFPA)* to write and enforce rules on fair lending and other matters and, inter-mediate between financial institutions and consumers. The CFPA would protect consumers in the financial products and services markets, except for investment products and services already regulated by the SEC or CFTC. The new agency would have to staff up quickly with attorneys and other professionals. Similarly, the financial institutions that would come under its jurisdiction would have to cope with a vast array of new regulatory reporting requirements, which means more lawyer jobs.
- A *Financial Services Oversight Council* chaired by the Treasury Department and comprised of the heads of the new National Bank Supervisor, Fed, FDIC, Consumer Financial Protection Agency, SEC, and FHFA. The Council would monitor the financial system for systemic risks in concert with the Fed. It is unclear whether the Council will have its own staff or will borrow or detail staff from its member agencies.
- A *Financial Consumer Coordinating Council* to address poten-tial gaps in consumer and investor protection and to pro-mote best practices across different markets. The Coordi-nating Council would consist of the heads of the SEC, FTC, Department of Justice, and CFPA or their designees, and heads of other state and federal agencies. It would identify gaps in consumer protection across financial products and facilitate coordination of consumer protection efforts.
- An *Office of National Insurance (ONI)* within the Treasury Department to gather information, develop expertise, negotiate international agreements, and coordinate policy in the insurance sector. The ONI would be designed to over-come the lack of federal government expertise regarding the insurance industry, which was highlighted by the financial

crisis, specifically the AIG collapse and bailout. The ONI would be responsible for monitoring all aspects of the insurance industry, gathering information and being responsible for identifying the emergence of any problems or gaps in regulation that could contribute to a future crisis.

- *Reform of the government-sponsored enterprises (GSEs) Fannie Mae and Freddie Mac.* Options on the table include: (1) returning them to their previous status as GSEs with the paired interests of maximizing returns for private shareholders and pursuing public policy home ownership goals; (2) gradually winding down their operations and liquidate their assets; (3) incorporating the GSEs' functions into a federal agency; (4) following a public utility model where the government regulates the GSEs' profit margin, sets guarantee fees, and provides explicit backing for GSE commitments; (5) converting to providing insurance for covered bonds; or (6) dissolving Fannie Mae and Freddie Mac into many smaller companies.

Financial regulatory reform probably will not touch or greatly alter the following existing regulators:

- The *Commodity Futures Trading Commission (CFTC)*, the independent agency that oversees commodity and financial futures and exchanges. The administration favors merging the CFTC into the SEC, but that combination is unlikely due to spirited resistance from both agencies and the congressional committees that separately oversee the SEC and CFTC and do not want to give up their jurisdictions. Instead, the administration would direct the SEC and CFTC to harmonize their regulations.
- The *National Credit Union Administration,* the independent agency that regulates credit unions
- The *Farm Credit Administration,* the independent agency that regulates and examines the banks, associations, and related entities of the Farm Credit System (FCS), including the Federal Agricultural Mortgage Corporation (Farmer Mac).

- The *Federal Housing Finance Agency.* (See the discussion of
  this recently created agency, above.)

At the state level, financial regulation is the province of at least three
agencies in each state: the Office of the Attorney General, the state banking regulator and the state securities regulator.

The most vexing problems for financial regulatory reform are
international ones. Capital flows across national boundaries simply by
a keyboard touch, unfettered by any domestic regulatory restraints and
free of any oversight. As the Great Recession strikingly demonstrated,
a financial institution collapse in one country can adversely affect the
entire planet.

The London G-20 summit in April 2009 partially addressed these
issues but without providing much detail. The presidents and prime min-
isters delegated broad new authority to the International Monetary Fund
to provide early warning of serious financial problems. They also pledged
to regulate hedge funds, including multinational ones. Recognizing that
financial stress can spread easily and quickly across national boundaries, the Obama administration intends to promote international initiatives consistent with its domestic reform proposals with respect to four
core issues: regulation of capital standards, oversight of global financial
markets, supervision of internationally active financial firms, and crisis
prevention and management. These initiatives would also generate new
jobs for attorneys, primarily with the following international agencies:
the International Monetary Fund, the Financial Stability Board, and the
Basel Committee on Banking Supervision.

Nowhere does Hermann's Corollary to Newton's Third Law (*"For every
government action, there is an equal or greater private sector reaction."*) apply
with more impact than here.

Law firms, consulting firms, financial institutions, and other companies are beginning to position themselves for this regulatory revival
and the advent of a new and much more expansive and intrusive regulatory regime.

There are now and will be many opportunities for lawyers in all
realms of financial regulatory reform: law firms, financial institutions,
corporations, government regulatory agencies and their law offices, and
self-regulatory organizations. In addition, the private sector—law firms,

corporations, and consulting firms—will have to hire additional attorneys to (1) make sense of the new regulatory regime for themselves and their clients and (2) handle the volumes of litigation, transactions, and regulatory responses and international regimes certain to emerge from financial regulatory reform.

For More Information
Principal Federal Financial Regulatory Law Practices

- U.S. Department of Treasury (*www.treas.gov*)
  - Office of the General Counsel (OGC)
  - Financial Crimes Enforcement Network—Office of Chief Counsel
  - Office of Foreign Assets Control—Office of Chief Counsel
  - Office of Thrift Supervision—Office of Chief Counsel
  - Office of the Comptroller of the Currency—Office of Chief Counsel & District Counsel Offices Nationwide
  - Office of Domestic Finance—Office of Financial Stability—Office of Chief Counsel
  - Office of Inspector General—Office of Counsel
- Federal Reserve Board (*www.federalreserve.gov*)
  - Legal Division
  - Division of Banking Supervision and Regulation
  - Division of Consumer and Community Affairs
  - Office of Counsel to the Inspector General
- Federal Deposit Insurance Corporation (*www.fdic.gov*)
  - Legal Division
  - Division of Bank Supervision
  - Inspector General Office of Counsel
  - Office of Legislative Affairs
  - Office of the Executive Secretary
  - Regional Offices Nationwide
- National Credit Union Administration—OGC (*www.ncua.gov*)
- Federal Housing Finance Agency—OGC (*www.fhfa.gov*)
- Securities and Exchange Commission (*www.sec.gov*)
  - Office of Administrative Law Judges

- Office of Compliance Inspections and
- Examinations—Office of Chief Counsel
- Division of Corporation Finance
- Division of Trading and Markets
- Division of Enforcement
- Division of Investment Management
- OGC
- Office of the Inspector General
- Office of International Affairs
- Office of Risk Assessment
- Regional Offices Nationwide
- Commodity Futures Trading Commission (*www.cftc.gov*)
  - Regional Offices Nationwide
  - Division of Market Oversight
  - Division of Enforcement
  - Clearing Intermediary
  - OGC
  - Executive Staff
  - Office of Proceedings
- Federal Trade Commission (*www.ftc.gov*)
  - Bureau of Consumer Protection
  - Bureau of Competition
  - OGC
  - Office of International Affairs
  - Office of Administrative Law Judges
  - Office of Policy Planning
  - Regional Offices Nationwide
- Federal Financial Institutions Examination Council (*www.ffiec.gov*)
- Farm Credit Administration—OGC (*www.fca.gov*)

Self-Regulatory Organization Law Offices (and Other SRO Offices Employing Attorneys)

Note: Self-regulatory organizations (SROs) are nongovernmental organizations empowered by federal financial regulatory agencies to create and enforce industry regulations and standards.

- Financial Industry Regulatory Authority (FINRA) (*www.finra.org*)
  - Office of General Counsel
  - Enforcement
  - Regulatory Policy
  - Market Regulation
  - Member Regulation
  - Dispute Resolution Offices Nationwide
  - District Offices Nationwide
- Public Company Accounting Oversight Board (PCAOB) (*www.pcaob.org*)
  - Office of the Secretary and General Counsel
  - Division of Enforcement and Investigations
  - Division of Registration and Inspections
  - Office of International Affairs
- Municipal Securities Rulemaking Board (MSRB) (*www.msrb.org*)
- New York Stock Exchange (NYSE) (*www.nyse.com*)
- American Stock Exchange (AMEX) (*www.amex.com*)
- Chicago Board Options Exchange (*www.cboe.com*)
- Options Clearing Corporation (*www.theocc.com*)
- Chicago Mercantile Exchange (*www.cme.com*)
- Depository Trust and Clearing Corporation (*www.dtcc.com*)
- NASDAQ Stock Market—Office of General Counsel (*www.nasdaq.com*)
- National Futures Association (*www.nfa.futures.org*)
- National Stock Exchange (*www.nsx.com*)

International Regulators
- International Monetary Fund (*www.imf.org*)
- Bank for International Settlements—Legal Service (*www.bis.org*)
- Financial Services Forum (*www.fsforum.org*)

Additional Information Resources
- Government Accountability Office (*www.gao.gov*)
- *Who Regulates Whom? An Overview of U.S. Financial Supervision.* Congressional Research Service (2009) (*http://opencrs.com/document/R40249*)

Chapter 5

Using Your Law Degree Outside the Mainstream: Law Related Careers

U NTIL RECENTLY, LAW SCHOOLS that invited me to speak to their students and/or alumni would often instruct me not to mention what an attorney could do other than practice law in private practice, a corporation in-house counsel office, or a government general counsel office. Today, they expressly ask me to address alternative legal career options, because the traditional legal market has become extremely tight and nonmainstream careers thus appear more enticing.

Law is the most fungible of professions, meaning that lawyers can do so many things in the professional world. Moreover, society and the workplace have come to the realization that, since law increasingly infuses virtually every human endeavor, attorneys are ideally educated and experienced to fill many roles that go beyond pure legal practice.

However, the legal profession itself is probably the slowest to come around to this enlightened way of thinking and has even resisted it to some extent. Consequently, it is worth thinking about both the short-term

163

and long-term implications of making a career switch out of mainstream law before making the leap. The following discussion of the pros and cons of moving out of mainstream law is designed to get you to think through these implications.

Pros

Greater civility, less contention. Most law-related careers are non-adversarial. There is usually no other side or opposing counsel. The professionals you interact with will respect your legal education and background—an advantage to you in your business relationships.

Few geographic limitations. Most law-related careers do not have rigorous state licensing requirements or expensive fees associated with getting licensed. You can largely work anywhere. This is true for virtually all law-related careers, even those purportedly regulated by state licensing authorities. Unlike for law—the most heavily regulated and closely scrutinized of all occupations—most professional regulation has been *pro forma* at best, making relocation easier.

Fungibility and marketability. Because law translates so well into a large number of law-related careers, employment sectors, and industries, opportunities are everywhere. An attorney can, for example, move from claims management to risk management to compliance and back into mainstream law without requiring an employer to make a major leap of faith. Lawyering develops numerous transferable skills.

Once technical legal skills are honed, attorneys find that they can move with relative ease among a wide range of practice areas. Savvy employers know, for example, that a regulatory attorney accustomed to dealing with common carrier matters before the Federal Communications Commission has all the tools to handle matters in other regulatory areas, such as utility rate cases before the Federal Energy Regulatory Commission or state public service commissions. Any diligent lawyer can learn the essential substantive law in a new area in a fairly short time.

Possible increased value of your nonlegal education and work experience. Few attorneys find that they can use their nonlegal education and work experience in their law practices. This can change dramatically when they move out of mainstream law: Suddenly, college majors and minors, as well as graduate school degrees, can play an important role in a career change.

Undergraduate degrees in a scientific field, computer science, business, economics, accounting, marketing, criminal justice, journalism, or international affairs can lead directly to alternative careers that require knowledge of both law and your additional academic disciplines. Moreover, a pre-law work background often meshes well with your legal training.

Law degree a plus during the job application process. When competing for a law-related position, possession of a law degree and/or legal experience immediately distinguishes you from most other candidates and gives you an automatic advantage (if you know how to exploit it)—an advantage that will remain with you throughout your law-related career.

Possibly increased job security. If you have worked in a law firm, you understand the "up-or-out" nature of the partnership track. Law-related fields generally offer something different: As long as you perform your own job well and get along with your colleagues, you can reasonably anticipate remaining with the organization as long as it remains viable. You will not be asked to leave or feel like a failure because someone else was selected for promotion. In addition, the fact that you have legal training or are an attorney is good protection against layoffs, because you may be perceived as being able to contribute to the organization in more than one area.

Better life-work balance. Non-mainstreamers work a 40-hour week for the most part, an unattainable goal for the vast majority of mainstream attorneys.

No more lawyer jokes.

Cons

Reduced earning potential. Attorneys are among the most highly compensated professional groups. Six-figure incomes are the norm, and even seven-figure compensation is not all that unusual. Even attorneys who work in government and follow a normal career path normally earn a six-figure income. Sole practitioners and lawyers in small law firms and smaller corporations (both publicly traded and closely held) can also earn exceptional compensation.

This is less true of nontraditional careers, where the trade-off for the upsides discussed above (which can be summarized as a reduction of risk and stress and an increase in job security and collegiality) is often lower compensation and less earning potential. Only a handful of legal career alternatives lend themselves to something equivalent to a solo or small firm practice and share that entrepreneurial spirit and earning potential.

Beyond those select law-related careers, the highest earning potential can probably be found among those that we call *intrapreneurial*, where within an organizational context, you are given (often considerable) autonomy to develop or expand an activity that earns money for your employer and where your compensation depends, to some extent, on what you bring in.

What these careers have in common is the potential for either increasing organizational revenues or cutting expenses. Both objectives are highly prized for obvious reasons, and the reward for success is often a financial bonus or a share of the revenues or savings.

Supervisors with less education than you. If your education intimidates your prospective boss, you may not get the position at all. On the other hand, because you have more education, an enlightened boss will regard you with greater respect and will often defer to your judgment. You will be perceived as a value-added resource and, correspondingly, will have more influence than other colleagues.

Loss of prestige. Your self-esteem may suffer if you move into a law-related career where you believe your new job title is less distinguished than "Attorney." If it pains you to have to respond that you are an Alternative Dispute Resolution Specialist or a Compliance Officer or a Risk Manager, then think twice about such a move. However, you will find that, among a random group of attorneys at a social event, you are not alone in having gone down a nontraditional career path. Many lawyers may even envy you.

Stigma attached by attorneys to those who leave the law. This is closely linked to the perceived loss of prestige suffered by people who leave the law, as well as to the possible difficulties you might encounter returning to traditional practice (see below).

In the 1990s, when abandoning a mainstream legal career path was a much rarer event than it is today, attorneys who left the law were viewed with a certain amount of contempt by those who remained in the profession. That is changing rapidly as more people move out of the mainstream and report success and satisfaction with their move. Today, the stigma is much reduced but is not gone.

Possible difficulty returning to mainstream practice. This is perhaps the most important potential downside risk of a transition to an alternative legal career, although it is becoming less of a risk every year. Some 15 years ago it was difficult to leave the law for something else and then decide to return. The legal community viewed such departures from the normal, ordinary course of a legal career as signs of weakness. But the macho-muscle days of practicing law are for the most part diminishing, replaced by a more humane and realistic philosophy of life and work. When combined with the other major paradigm shift affecting employment in general—more frequent job changes becoming an accepted part of many careers—this kind of shifting in and out no longer automatically brands you as an unemployable pariah.

Law-Related Careers

If you have weighed all the considerations and decided that a transition into law-related work will be agreeable to you, you'll want to zero in on those careers that thrive in any economy. The following law-related careers are like their mainstream law practice counterparts in that their future is not linked to the economy. This does not mean they are completely unaffected by economic ups or downs. On the contrary, law-related careers that do well in good times often do even better in bad times, but that does not make them countercyclical. For example, the first two careers discussed in this section—regulatory compliance and risk management—were very dynamic and experienced tremendous growth in recent years while the economy was growing. Now they are faring even better precisely because the economy has turned south, bolstered by the collapse of the financial industry and frozen credit markets.

Litigation management is impervious to economic fluctuations because litigation itself never goes away, regardless of the economy. People and organizations sue each other constantly, regardless of the economy.

Globalization has rendered economic development vitally important to state, regional, and community well-being. The state of the economy only plays a role because, in bad times, fewer companies are likely to implement expansion or relocation plans, thus requiring economic development agencies to exert themselves even more to meet their goals. Extra effort means the need for more economic development personnel, lawyers included.

Intellectual asset management is going to grow regardless of the economy because (1) it is a relatively new phenomenon and a very exciting one for companies seeking new revenue centers and (2) it requires very little additional spending or exertion relative to the opportunity to realize more revenue from existing resources. The rewards are enormous, very attractive in good times and even more so in bad times.

Government affairs is of paramount importance to companies in all economic times. Government, regardless of the state of the economy, is increasingly in the business of picking winners and losers, so keeping tabs on—and influencing—what is happening in Washington, D.C., and in state capitals is more important than ever.

Government has steadily increased its scrutiny of elementary, secondary, and higher education, and its tentacles continue to insinuate themselves ever more deeply into what is going on in academe. Compliance requirements imposed on academic institutions by law and regulation have increased by the hundreds in recent years, with no end in sight. More compliance mandates mean more compliance professionals.

The immense volume of litigation flooding the courts and administrative fora has focused new light on the advantages of alternative dispute resolution mechanisms designed to keep costs to both litigants and government down while streamlining and expediting the resolution of contentious issues. Dispute resolution alternatives to courtroom dramas are proliferating everywhere and, once in place, never disappear.

REGULATORY COMPLIANCE

Introduction

Regulatory compliance is the fastest growing career in corporate America, according to the Society of Corporate Compliance and Ethics (*www.corporatecompliance.org*)

The regulatory compliance discipline is as old as regulation. Lately, however, it has become considerably more important and is central to the activities of most organizations. Publicly traded companies find that,since the enactment of the Sarbanes-Oxley legislation in 2002, it is virtually impossible to function without a compliance staff. The sheer omnipresence of this discipline—in any economy—makes it a viable choice for job-seeking attorneys. There has even been a "trickle-over" effect on closely held corporations and nonprofits.

What Is It?

Regulatory compliance in its broadest definition means systems, departments, procedures, and processes that ensure that an organization— corporation, government agency, university, etc.—is in compliance with relevant laws and regulations. Compliance can be general or quite specific (e.g., healthcare compliance, financial compliance, securities compliance, or tax compliance).

The compliance function goes far beyond regulatory reporting. It often also includes the following:

- Giving compliance advice
- Developing and updating Codes of Conduct
- Developing compliance policies and procedures
- Training employees
- Monitoring regulations and regulatory changes
- Analyzing new laws and rules for their impact on the organization
- Performing regulatory risk assessments
- Interacting with regulators
- Advising senior management on compliance matters
- Responding to alleged violations of rules, regulations, policies, procedures, and the code of conduct by evaluating or recommending the initiation of investigative procedures or undertaking the actual investigation
- Reporting violations or potential violations to the appropriate enforcement agencies

Who Does It?

Corporate Compliance Department. The corporate compliance function has expanded exponentially in recent years, prompted by four federal laws that placed substantial compliance burdens on many U.S. companies.

1. *Health Insurance Portability and Accountability Act of 1996 (HIPAA)* (Pub.L. 104-191) established national standards to protect the privacy of personal health information.

2. *Graham-Leach-Bliley Financial Modernization Act of 1999* (Pub.L. 106-102) protects the privacy of consumer information held by *financial institutions,* a term encompassing a wide variety of organizations.

3. *Public Company Accounting Reform and Investor Protection Act of 2002* (Sarbanes-Oxley) (Pub.L. 107-204) established sweeping new or enhanced standards for all U.S. public company boards, management, and public accounting firms.

4. *USA Patriot Act* (Pub.L. 107-56) increased the ability of law enforcement agencies to search phone and email communications and medical, financial, and other records; eased restrictions on foreign intelligence gathering within the United States; and expanded the Secretary of the Treasury's authority to regulate financial transactions, particularly those involving foreign individuals and entities.

In very large companies, compliance departments may be further divided into multiple units by function or product area.

Compliance duties can vary from one industry to another. Bank compliance officers, for example, may spend much of their time concerned with financial institution regulatory agencies, such as the Federal Reserve Board, the Federal Deposit Insurance Corporation, state bank regulatory agencies, as well as the Securities and Exchange Commission. Hospital compliance officers may focus their attention on the U.S. Department of Health and Human Services, the state health department, the state insurance commission, the Center for Medicare and Medicaid Services, and state professional licensing boards. Tax compliance personnel concentrate on the Internal Revenue Service and state and local tax authorities.

Certain corporations combine compliance with the ethics and/or risk management function(s).

U.S. Government Compliance Monitoring Offices. A large number of U.S. government law offices have a compliance-monitoring function. The following are representative of federal compliance-monitoring offices:

- U.S. Department of Labor—Office of Federal Contract Compliance Programs (*www.dol.gov*)
- Environmental Protection Agency—Office of Enforcement & Compliance Assurance (*www.epa.gov*)
- U.S. Department of Commerce—Office of the Chief Counsel for Industry and Security, Office of Antiboycott Compliance (*www.doc.gov*)
- Food and Drug Administration—Office of Regulatory Affairs (*www.fda.gov*)
- U.S. Department of Housing and Urban Development— Office of General Counsel, Office of Finance and Regulatory Compliance (*www.hud.gov*)

U.S. Government Inspector General Offices. The mission of all U.S. government Inspector General (IG) offices is to identify and rectify fraud, waste, mismanagement, and abuse in U.S. government programs, contracts and grants. Consequently, IG offices are very business oriented.

There are currently 64 statutory IG Offices in the federal government (i.e., IG offices authorized by the Inspector General Act of 1978, as amended, 5 USC App.§§ 1-12 [2007]). These offices

- conduct independent and objective audits, investigations and inspections;
- prevent and detect waste, fraud, and abuse;
- promote economy, effectiveness, and efficiency;
- review pending legislation and regulation; and
- keep the agency head and Congress fully and currently informed.

While by law, IGs are under the general supervision of the agency head or deputy, neither official can prevent or prohibit an IG from conducting an audit or investigation.

IGs are authorized to do the following:

- Have direct access to all records and information of the agency.
- Have ready access to the agency head.

- Conduct such investigations and issue such reports as the IG thinks appropriate (with limited national security and law enforcement exceptions).
- Issue subpoenas for information and documents outside the agency.
- Administer oaths for taking testimony.
- Hire and control their own staff and contract resources.

Slightly more than 50 percent of the federal IG offices have a legal counsel's office.

While the auditing function predominates, auditing has a slightly different meaning in an IG context. In addition to auditing agency financial statements, IG auditors also audit thousands of government programs to gauge their effectiveness.

Each of the following federal IG offices has a legal office:

- Agency for International Development
- Department of Agriculture
- Amtrak
- Department of Commerce
- Corporation for National & Community Service
- Department of Defense
- Department of Education
- Department of Energy
- Environmental Protection Agency
- Equal Employment Opportunity Commission
- Farm Credit Administration
- Federal Communications Commission
- Federal Deposit Insurance Corporation

- Federal Housing Finance Board
- Federal Reserve Board
- General Services Administration
- Department of Health and Human Services
- Department of Homeland Security
- Department of Housing and Urban Development
- Department of the Interior
- Department of Justice
- Department of Labor
- National Aeronautics and Space Administration
- National Labor Relations Board
- National Science Foundation

- Nuclear Regulatory
  Commission
- Office of Personnel
  Management
- Pension Benefit Guaranty
  Corporation
- Securities and Exchange
  Commission
- Small Business
  Administration
- Smithsonian Institution
- Social Security
  Administration
- Tennessee Valley
  Authority
- Department of
  Transportation
- Department of the
  Treasury
- U.S. Postal Service
- Department of Veterans
  Affairs

There is also a Special IG for Iraq Reconstruction (*www.sigir.mil*).

Self-Regulatory Organizations. Self-regulatory organizations (SROs) are non-governmental organizations empowered by regulatory agencies such as the Securities and Exchange Commission and the Commodity Futures Trading Commission to create and enforce industry regulations and standards. The following selected SROs have broad regulatory compliance responsibilities:

- *Financial Industry Regulatory Authority (FINRA)* (*www.finra.org*). FINRA regulates U.S. securities brokers and dealers. The following FINRA divisions monitor regulatory compliance:
  – Office of General Counsel
  – Market Regulation Department
  – Member Regulation Department
  FINRA has offices in Washington, D.C., Rockville, Maryland, and 15 District Offices nationwide.
- *Public Company Accounting Oversight Board (PCAOB)* (*www. pcaob.org*). PCAOB was created by the Sarbanes-Oxley Act to oversee the auditors of public companies. Compliance monitoring duties are vested in the Division of Registration and Inspections.
- *Municipal Securities Rulemaking Board (MSRB)* (Alexandria, Virginia) (*www.msrb.org*). The MSRB develops rules regulating securities firms and banks involved in underwriting,

trading, and selling municipal securities (i.e., bonds and notes issued by states, cities, and counties or their agencies to help finance public projects).

- *New York Stock Exchange (NYSE)* (New York) (*www.nyse.com*). The NYSE is a subsidiary of NYSE Euronext, which operates the world's largest and most liquid exchange group and offers the most diverse array of financial products and services. NYSE Regulation is the subsidiary unit responsible for most regulatory compliance-monitoring activities.
- *American Stock Exchange (AMEX)* (New York) (*www.amex.com*). AMEX's Office of the Chief Regulatory Officer has primary responsibility for AMEX compliance monitoring.

Other SROs with extensive regulatory compliance programs include these:

- Chicago Board Options Exchange (*www.cboe.com*)
- Options Clearing Corporation (*www.theocc.com*)
- Chicago Mercantile Exchange (*www.cme.com*)
- Depository Trust and Clearing Corporation (*www.dtcc.com*)
- National Futures Association (*www.nfa.futures.org*)
- National Stock Exchange (*www.nsx.com*)

State and Local Inspector General Offices. The IG concept is becoming increasingly widespread at the state and local levels. There are hundreds of state and local IG offices, the powers and duties of which may vary considerably from one jurisdiction to another.

There are three primary IG models at the state and local levels:

1. One IG Office responsible for the entire state or local government
2. Individual IG offices in one or more state or local government agencies that focus exclusively on that agency
3. States and localities with one overall IG as well as agency-specific IGs

Here are some examples of state IG offices:

- Office of the Chief Inspector General, Florida Governor's Office (*www.flgov.com/ig_home*)
- Office of Inspector General, Florida Department of Transportation (*www.dot.state.fl.us/InspectorGeneral*)
- Office of Inspector General, Kentucky Transportation Cabinet (*http://transportation.ky.gov/oig*)
- Inspector General, Texas Department of Criminal Justice (*www.tdcj.state.tx.us/inspector.general/inspector.gnl-home.htm*)

Here are some examples of local government IG offices:

- Inspector General, City of Philadelphia (*www.phila.gov/oig*)
- Office of Inspector General, Chicago Board of Education (*www.cps.edu/About_CPS/Departments/Pages/InspectorGeneral.aspx*)
- Office of Inspector General, Chicago Transit Authority (*www.transitchicago.com/business/office_of_inspector_general.aspx*)
- Office of Inspector General, Port Authority of New York and New Jersey (*www.panynj.gov/DoingBusinessWith/inspector/html/index.html*)
- New York City (54 separate Inspector General offices)

What Does It Pay?

Private sector compensation for regulatory compliance professionals is quite high, often several hundred thousand dollars, and can go as high as seven figures. This reflects the critical nature of these positions for U.S. companies, as well as the vastly expanded responsibilities that come with compliance positions. The high salaries also reflect the fact that compliance officers can be the first to go if their companies are sanctioned by the government for noncompliance. Compensation has skyrocketed in recent years, in some cases doubling in three years.

Public sector pay is, of course, considerably less and is in line with general government pay schedules at every level—federal (see *www.opm.gov*), state, and local.

Future Prospects

Regulatory compliance opportunities are growing rapidly. In just the last three years, the AttorneyJobs.com database listed almost 1,400 corporate compliance positions.

The United States entered into an intense regulatory phase in the 1930s, one that lasted roughly 35–40 years. The subsequent 35–40 year period was largely one of deregulation and regulatory suspension. Now we have entered another era of regulatory activism. If the cycle continues, regulatory compliance should prosper for a very long time. The prospects for compliance work are made even brighter by the legacy of the Great Recession.

Growing trends in this field are international compliance and compliance with laws and regulations of foreign countries. As business becomes increasingly global, compliance becomes both more complex and central to business success. Globalization has complicated this function and increased demand for corporate compliance professionals, who now must be concerned with compliance requirements in multiple jurisdictions.

Breaking In

Attorneys are naturally suited to regulatory compliance positions through education and/or experience. This is evidenced by two facts:

1. The large number of attorneys who serve in compliance positions in corporations and government, many coming into their jobs without a compliance credential
2. Recent graduates who have gone directly into corporate compliance positions. (By contrast, corporate in-house counsel offices almost always require some experience.)

However, you can expand your compliance employability and fungibility if you earn an additional credential.

Credentialing Opportunities
- The Association of Health Care Compliance Professionals—Certificate in Healthcare Compliance (*www.hcca-info.org*)
- Seton Hall University School of Law—Health Care Compliance Certification Program (*www.law.shu.edu*)

- St. Thomas University (Florida) School of Law—International Tax Law Program: Anti-Money Laundering and Compliance Certificate (*www.stu.edu/lawschool*)
- Financial Industry Regulatory Authority—Compliance Boot Camp (*www.finra.com*)
- National Safety Council—Certificate in OSHA Compliance (*www.nsc.org*)
- National Regulatory Services—Investment Adviser Compliance Certificate (*www.nrs-inc.com*)
- Institute of Certified Bankers—Certified Regulatory Compliance Manager (CRCM) (*www.aba.com/ICBCertifications*)
- Credit Union National Association—Regulatory Training and Certification Program (*http://training.cuna.org*)
- Society of Corporate Compliance & Ethics—Certified Compliance and Ethics Professional (*www.corporatecompliance.org*)
- ABS Consulting—Environmental and Quality Certification Programs (*www.absconsulting.com*)
  - Clean Air Compliance (CAC) Specialist
  - Clean Water Compliance (CWC) Specialist
  - Regulatory Compliance Specialist (RCS)
- Northeastern University (*www.spcs.neu.edu*)
  - Biopharmaceutical Domestic Regulatory Affairs (online option)
  - Biopharmaceutical International Regulatory Affairs (online option)
  - Medical Devices Regulatory Affairs (online option)
- International Import-Export Institute—Certified U.S. Export Compliance Officer (*http://expandglobal.com*)
- San Diego State University (*www.ces.sdsu.edu/regulatoryaffairs.html*)
  - Advanced Certificate in Regulatory Affairs (pharmaceuticals, biologics, medical devices)

Networking Organizations
- Society of Corporate Compliance and Ethics (*www.corporatecompliance.org*)
- Association of Insurance Compliance Professionals (*www.aicp.net/*)

- Health Care Compliance Association (*www.hcca-info.org*)
- Ethics and Compliance Officers Association (*www.theecoa.org*)
- International Compliance Association (*www.int-comp.org*)
- Regulatory Compliance Association (*www.ccouniversity. org/aboutrca.phtml*)
- American Bar Association Center for Regulatory Compliance (*www.aba.com/Compliance/default.htm*)

Compliance Job Titles. Regulatory compliance job titles come in many variations. The following list illustrates the wide variety of compliance job titles.

- Compliance trust officer
- Compliance manager
- Claims legal and regulatory compliance director
- Director, sales and marketing compliance
- Assistant vice president—compliance
- Compliance consultant manager
- Procurement analyst—compliance
- Director, compliance/audit
- Director of operational compliance
- Corporate compliance director
- Campus security compliance officer
- Grants and contract compliance specialist
- Academic compliance affairs officer

- Bank investment compliance officer
- Compliance officer (bank regulation)
- Compliance officer (commodities/securities)
- Securities compliance examiner
- Accessibility/compliance specialist
- ADA compliance manager
- Equal Opportunity compliance specialist
- Legal compliance officer
- Environmental compliance manager
- Professional regulation compliance analyst
- Healthcare compliance officer
- Re-employment rights compliance specialist
- Import compliance specialist

- Manager of export/ import compliance
- Wage and hour law compliance specialist
- Professional licensing board compliance officer
- Regulatory compliance officer
- Regulatory impact analyst
- Regulatory implementation manager
- Telecommunications regulatory analyst

For More Information

- Society of Corporate Compliance and Ethics (*www.corporate compliance.org*)
- Society of Corporate Secretaries & Governance Professionals (*www.governanceprofessionals.org*)
- Open Compliance and Ethics Group (*www.oceg.org*)
- International Association of Risk & Compliance Professionals (*www.risk-compliance-association.com*)
- Professional Association for Compliance and Ethics (*www. pacecompliance.com*)
- Federation of Regulatory Counsel (*www.forc.org*)
- Sarbanes Oxley Compliance Professionals Association (*www.sarbanes-oxley-association.com*)
- National Association for Athletics Compliance (*www.nacda.com*)

RISK MANAGEMENT

Introduction

Risk management has been a rising law-related profession for almost two decades, and it's one in which attorneys can make a significant mark and have a very solid career. In fact, by one estimate, approximately 20 percent of risk managers have a law degree.

The principal reason risk management favors a legal education or background is that attorneys are trained and experienced in evaluating and mitigating risk. We do this every day in virtually every legal capacity, so much so that it becomes second nature. The risk management community is very aware that attorneys possess these capabilities and prizes them.

A second reason is that, like attorneys, risk managers have to be quick studies and become knowledgeable about a large number of issues. They must be able to absorb and synthesize information rapidly and apply it in the real world.

The perceived value of a law degree and legal background is underscored by the large number of organizations that send their nonlawyer risk managers to law school to obtain a JD.

What Is It?

Risk management is the process of identifying and managing threats to an organization, including threats to its very survival. Risk managers evaluate risks and try to eliminate or mitigate them through insurance buys, self-insurance, the institution of safety measures and instructions, employee training, etc.

A fundamental first step in identifying risks is learning all there is to know about the organization's operations, which makes risk managers even more valuable and secure in their jobs.

Originally, risk management was all about insurance. However, the increase in government scrutiny of organizational activities and operations through rules, regulations, compliance requirements, and investigations has brought increased prominence to the profession and an expansion of risk management into areas beyond insurance.

Financial risk management, while falling within the general definition above, has some additional nuances. It involves the use of financial instruments to manage exposure to and hedge against risk, with an emphasis on credit risk, market risk, currency fluctuations, liquidity risk, inflation, and other financial risk. Financial risk management is qualitative, like general risk management, but it also has an emphatic quantitative component.

Risk managers save their organizations a great deal of money, which makes their function even more valuable in tough economic times.

Who Does It?

Currently, the most common employers of risk managers are healthcare providers, financial services firms, municipalities, and higher education. Three of these four sectors are experiencing significant growth in risk management positions. Financial services, being in the throes of a meltdown, is not one of those three. However, the regulatory reforms arising out of the financial markets debacle portend plentiful opportunities for financial risk managers down the road.

The financial market crisis has given new prominence to the central role of the financial risk manager. Look for mandatory requirements for objectivity and independence to emerge from the turmoil. Risk managers in many financial services firms are likely to rise to senior management-level positions.

A rough rule of thumb is that a hospital needs to have at least 200+ beds to support a risk management office. There are more than 1,650 such hospitals in the United States at present.

A variety of other healthcare provider and supplier and advisory organizations also hire risk managers. They include health maintenance organizations, pharmaceutical companies, management consulting firms, insurance companies, biotechnology firms, physicians groups, and medical device manufacturers. In addition, there is a thriving placement practice for healthcare risk managers operated by both generic and specialty executive search firms.

The Public Risk Management Association's membership consists of more than 2,000 public sector risk management entities, including cities, counties, townships, school districts, parks authorities, and risk pools, in 1,800 public organizations.

What Does It Pay?

Risk manager compensation is increasing faster than compensation in most other professional fields.

Healthcare risk managers (starting salaries: $65,000–$135,000) earn more than their counterparts in public sector agencies (starting salaries: $50,000–$120,000) who, in turn, earn more than academic risk managers (starting salaries: $40,000–$85,000). As a rule, larger organizations pay more than their smaller counterparts.

Financial services risk managers have historically been at the top of the risk management pay scale, with many senior people earning $200,000+ per year in addition to handsome bonuses. An educated guess as to compensation is that base pay will remain high and, given the central role of financial risk managers in the new regulatory environment to come, will go higher. Bonuses, however, will not be nearly as generous as in the past, thanks to the recent spate of bonus abuses by the top executives of so many companies.

Future Prospects

Risk management is approaching maturity as a profession, but it is not there yet. Its value is reinforced every day, as additional savings are realized and liability exposures reduced.

The 21st century has, to date, been the Age of Uncertainty. Starting with the intelligence failures that led to the September 11, 2001, terrorist attacks and the Iraq War, and the regulatory neglect that contributed mightily to the sudden financial meltdown and ensuing Great Recession, we are living in an era that is both confusing and replete with risks. In other words, it's the Perfect Storm if you seek a risk management career. Healthcare and financial services, as indicated above, are likely to be the most promising industries for attorneys seeking a risk management career.

Breaking In

Credential Enhancement. While a number of attorneys have secured risk management positions based solely on their law degrees and legal experience, the risk management field offers a variety of credential enhancement opportunities that expand one's employment possibilities. Supplemented by an Associate in Risk Management (ARM) certification or comparable credential, an attorney is well armed to compete for a position in this burgeoning field. An ARM, a very prestigious credential, can be earned in a short period, via three levels of online courses plus an online examination at the end of each of the three stages, for a modest amount of money (typically around $900).

A résumé that begins with

JANE JONES, JD, ARM

is compelling to the growing number of organizations who value the risk management function.

The ARM designation program was developed and is sponsored by the Insurance Institute of America. The program teaches would-be risk managers what they need to know to supplement their legal training and experience and compete effectively for risk management positions. The program consists of three online courses—Risk Assessment, Risk Control, and Risk Financing. At the end of each course, the candidate takes a two-hour examination, which he or she must pass to receive the ARM designation.

If you are interested in working for a public sector organization, such as a municipality, you can take an additional course—Risk Management for Public Entities—and earn the ARM–P (for Public Entities) designation.

The ARM and ARM–P study and examination programs are offered by a number of organizations that have been licensed by the Insurance Institute, including the following:

- American Institute for CPCU (*www.aicpcu.org*)
- AB Training Center (*www.abtrainingcenter.com*)
- KEIR Educational Resources (*www.keirsuccess.com*)
- Insurance Educational Association (*www.ieatraining.com*)

The ARM is by no means the only helpful credential available to an aspiring risk manager. While it is the baseline, generic credential, a number of more specialized risk management credentials also merit examination. The following list includes a representative sampling from the fields of banking and finance, healthcare, food safety, education, employment, energy, and sports:

- Global Association of Risk Professionals (*www.garp.com*)
  - Financial Risk Manager Certification
  - The International Certificate in Banking Risk and Regulation
- Professional Risk Managers' International Association (*www.prmia.org*)
  - Professional Risk Manager Certification
- American Hospital Association Certification Center (*www.aha.org*)
  - Certified Professional in Healthcare Risk Management (online)
- American Society for Healthcare Risk Management (*www.ashrm.org*)
  - Barton Certificate Program in Healthcare Risk Management

- University of Maryland (*www.umd.edu*)
  - Graduate Certificate of Professional Studies in Food Safety Risk Analysis
- National Alliance for Insurance Education & Research (*www.scic.com*)
  - Certified School Risk Managers (CSRM) Designation
- Mountain States Employers' Council (*www.msec.org*)
  - Workplace Risk Management Certificate Program
- University of Houston Bauer College of Business (*www.bauer. uh.edu*)
  - Energy Risk Management Certificate
- United States Sports Academy (*www.ussa.edu*)
  - Sports Law and Risk Management Certificate (online)

Networking Organizations. The risk management profession has produced an impressive number of membership organizations that offer opportunities for networking for jobs and careers. They include the following:

- American Risk and Insurance Association (ARIA) (*www. aria.org*)
- American Society for Healthcare Risk Management (*www. ashrm.org*)
- Association of Insurance & Risk Managers (*www.airmic.com*)
- Association of Threat Assessment Professionals (ATAP) (*www.atapworldwide.org*)
- Professional Risk Managers International Association (*www. prmia.org*)
- Public Agency Risk Managers Association (PARMA) (*www. parma.com*)
- Public Risk Management Association (*www.primacentral.org*)
- Risk and Insurance Management Society (*www.rims.org*)
- State Risk and Insurance Management Association (*www. strima.org*)
- University Risk Management and Insurance Association (*www.urmia.org*)

For More Information

- *Risk Management* magazine (*www.rmmagazine.com*)
- International Risk Management Institute (*www.irmi.com*)
- National School Safety Center (*www.nsscl.org*)
- Nonprofit Risk Management Center (*www.nonprofitrisk.org*)
- Public Entity Risk Institute (*www.riskinstitute.org*)
- Public Risk Database Project (*www.prdp.org*)
- Risk Management Resource Center (*www.eriskcenter.org*)

LITIGATION MANAGEMENT

Introduction

Eighty percent of my disability insurance referrals (I advise disability insurers on the issues presented by attorneys receiving disability benefits) are attorneys burned out by litigation. Litigation management is one of the best careers to move into if you have had it with litigation.

Litigation management departments first appeared many years ago in insurance companies. In recent years, litigation management has become a more broadly popular function primarily because litigation is, by far, the largest expense item for virtually every corporate legal office. Anything that promises to reduce the costs of litigation is welcomed with open arms.

What Is It?

Typical litigation management duties could include these:

- Overall management of lawsuits against the organization
- Interviewing and selecting outside counsel
- Actively directing retained outside counsel, including strategizing the litigation
- Assisting outside counsel in trial preparation, including case staffing, witness preparation, and other activities
- Managing the course of litigation to minimize legal costs and organizational exposure
- Monitoring, critiquing, and correcting outside counsel performance

- Auditing/assessing outside counsel billing, fees, litigation performance, and guideline compliance
- Reviewing, evaluating, negotiating, and settling nonlitigated matters and claims
- Working with insurance carriers on successful resolution of covered claims and lawsuits
- Preparing legal documents related to claims (releases, stipulations, etc.)
- Advising management as to best practices and avoidance of professional liability exposures and drafting organizational policies to accomplish this
- Reviewing marketing materials and internal documents to avoid legal exposures
- Collecting and analyzing data on the organization's case handling and management
- Developing and maintaining litigation management tools, including software

Litigation management consultants advise and assist their clients with some or all of these duties, depending on the engagement.

Who Does It?

Corporations. Litigation management, historically the province of the corporate general counsel's office, has been separated out in some companies—particularly those that are burdened with a large number of lawsuits (such as pharmaceuticals, construction engineering firms, and manufacturers)—and such separation is the industry standard in the insurance industry. In some large companies, the function is divided by geographic scope or type of litigation.

Litigation managers also work for a number of major nonprofit corporations.

Major CPA Firms with a Consulting Practice. Litigation management has spawned numerous consulting opportunities for attorneys. Corporations hire litigation management consultants to advise them on cost control, selection of outside counsel, case strategizing, and other components of effective litigation management.

The "Big Four" CPA firms (Deloitte Touche, PriceWaterhouseCoopers, Ernst & Young, and KPMG) were early entrants into this business and have found it to be a lucrative and steady profit center. They have offices in every major city. Their aggressive approach to client development has prompted their smaller national, regional, and local competitors also to offer litigation management services. Here are the major CPA firms with a consulting practice:

- Deloitte Touche
  www.deloitte.com
- PriceWaterhouseCoopers
  www.pwc.com
- Ernst & Young
  www.ey.com
- KPMG
  www.kpmg.com
- Grant Thornton
  www.grantthornton.com
- BDO Seidman
  www.bdo.com

Management Consulting Firms. Both major and small management consulting firms have also ventured into the litigation management consulting arena. While many of them are latecomers, they had no choice but to go into this business once CPA firms began offering litigation management consulting services and began hiring attorneys (among others) as consultants. Following is a list of the major management consulting firms that offer litigation management:

- Accenture
  www.accenture.com
- Arthur D. Little
  www.adlittle.com
- A.T. Kearney
  www.atkearney.com
- Bain & Company
  www.bain.com
- Bearing Point
  www.bearingpoint.com
- Booz Allen Hamilton
  www.boozallen.com
- Boston Consulting Group
  www.bcg.com
- Capgemini
  www.capgemini.com
- Corporate Executive Board
  www.executiveboard.com
- Fujitsu
  www.fujitsu.com
- McKinsey & Co.
  www.mckinsey.com
- Oliver Wyman
  www.oliverwyman.com
- Towers Perrin
  www.towersperrin.com

Legal and Professional Services Consulting Firms. Professional services and law practice management consulting firms are specialty firms that perform management consulting exclusively for professional services firms, law firms, corporation in-house counsel offices, and/or government legal offices. They also hire attorneys as litigation management consultants. Following is a list of some of the significant firms in this category:

- Altman Weil Pensa (*www.altmanweil.com*)
- Hildebrandt International (*www.hildebrandt.com*)
- BTI Consulting Group (*www.bticonsulting.com*)
- Jaffe Associates (*www.jaffeassociates.com*)
- LawBiz Management Company (*www.lawbiz.com*)
- Robert Denney Associates (*www.robertdenney.com*)

Law Firm Subsidiaries. A number of large law firms have subsidiaries that provide litigation management services:

- Armstrong Teasdale—Lawgical Choice (*www.lawgicalchoice.com*)
- Duane Morris—Wescott Analytics LLC (*www.wescottanalytics.com*)
- Foley & Lardner—Litigation Support Services (*www.foley.com*)
- Holland & Hart—Persuasion Strategies (*www.persuasion strategies.com*)
- Howrey & Simon—CapAnalysis (*www.capanalysis.com*)
- Hunton & Williams—Litigation Support Group (*www.hunton.com*)

Government
- Architect of the Capitol—OGC (*www.aoc.gov*)
- Federal Defender Organizations Nationwide (*www.fd.org*)
- Legal Services Corporation—Office of Legal Affairs (*www.lsc.gov*)
- Social Security Administration—OGC, Office of General Law; Office of Program Law (*www.ssa.gov*)
- U.S. Department of Agriculture—OGC, Civil Rights Division (*www.usda.gov*)
- U.S. Department of Defense—Office of Counsel, U.S. Army Sustainment Command (*www.afsc.army.mil/gc/index.htm*)
- U.S. Department of Energy (*www.energy.gov*)
  - OGC, Idaho National Laboratory

- OGC, Sandia National Laboratories
- Office of Laboratory Counsel, Los Alamos National
  Laboratory—Litigation Management Practice Group;
  Employment Law and Litigation Practice Group
- U.S. Department of Justice—Antitrust Division
  (*www.usdoj.gov*)

What Does It Pay?

Typical salary ranges for insurance company litigation managers range from approximately $90,000 to $145,000, depending upon the geographic and supervisory scope of the responsibilities of the position, the size of the company, its industry, as well as other factors. Other corporate litigation managers can earn considerably more, primarily because corporations outside the insurance industry generally provide higher compensation to their professionals. Consulting firm compensation is closer to corporate compensation levels. Government litigation managers are paid at the same scales that apply to their professional colleagues (see *www.opm.gov* for U.S. government compensation), which is almost always less than what the private sector pays, with the exception of senior litigation managers, who can earn up to $150,000.

Future Prospects

There is a constant demand for former litigators to serve in this capacity. It is highly unlikely that this demand will ever wane, given the litigious propensities of Americans and the fast-changing legal and business environments of our times, which lead to countless opportunities for disputation. Moreover, the barrage of new laws and regulations sure to be enacted and promulgated means more litigation and more opportunities for litigation managers.

Breaking In

You will have a career advantage if, in addition to a litigation background, you also know how to evaluate the costs and benefits of litigating versus settling a case, as well as how to bring management principles to bear on legal fee and performance auditing (in other words, some business background or sense and a facility with numbers). JD/CPAs and JD/MBAs are very attractive to employers of litigation managers. The addition of the joint degree may also have a bearing on compensation. It is also an advantage to have represented corporate clients.

Credentialing. While credentialing is usually not necessary for litigation management positions, a few certificate programs are available:

- LitWorks—Certified Litigation Support Manager (*www.litworks.com*)
- Americans for Effective Law Enforcement Legal Center— Litigation Professional (LP) Designation (*www.aele.org*)

Networking Organizations
- Council on Litigation Management (*www.litmgmt.org*)
- International Litigation Management Association (*www.litigationmanagement.org*)

For More Information
- International Litigation Management Association (*www.litigationmanagement.org*)
- Federation of Defense and Corporate Counsel (*www.thefederation.org*)
- Defense Research Institute (*www.dri.org*)
- Council on Litigation Management (*www.litmgmt.org*)

ECONOMIC DEVELOPMENT

Introduction

Economic development has never been more important. Governments, as well as businesses that have a stake in expanding local, regional, and state economies, are devoting more resources to economic development than ever.

The complexities of attracting new businesses, and of persuading and enticing existing businesses to remain and expand, increasingly call for the involvement of attorneys. The result is that economic development offices (EDOs) now often employ lawyers to help them and their prospects uncover, translate, and manage the maze of legal and related policy and business issues that arise in a typical economic development transaction.

What Is It?

The International Economic Development Council defines *economic development* as "a program, group of policies, or activity that seeks to improve the economic well-being and quality of life for a community, by creating and/or retaining jobs that facilitate growth and provide a stable tax base."

For the purposes of this section, the term *economic development* is more narrowly defined as "business attraction or retention," wherein states and municipalities attempt to entice businesses to relocate, open new facilities, or remain in their jurisdictions and then assist them in establishing their local offices and/or plants.

Who Does It?

EDOs function as individual entities and, in some cases, as departments of state or local governments. Their role is to seek out new economic opportunities and retain existing business wealth.

Economic development positions for attorneys are very high-profile. Their activities are usually aligned closely with the governor's or mayor's office. This is so that, when a business has been attracted to, retained by, or convinced to expand in the state, city, or county, the governor and/or mayor can bask in the credit.

Other organizations, whose primary function is not economic development, work in partnership with economic developers because they benefit from economic development. They include foundations, utilities, healthcare providers, colleges, universities, technology parks, and research institutions. Some economic development professionals work for public agencies, others for chambers of commerce, private nonprofit organizations, public/private partnerships, or universities. Some work with private-sector consulting firms, and a few are sole practitioners.

The U.S. government also plays a role in economic development, principally through the following agencies and their law offices:

- U.S. Department of Commerce (*www.commerce.gov*)
    - Economic Development Administration—Office of Chief Counsel and Regional Counsel Offices
    - Minority Business Development Agency—Office of the Chief Counsel

- Appalachian Regional Commission—OGC (*www.arc.gov*)
- National Capital Planning Commission—OGC (*www.ncpc.gov*)
- Tennessee Valley Authority—Office of Executive Vice President & General Counsel (*www.tva.gov*)
- Trade and Development Agency—OGC (*www.ustda.gov*)
- U.S. Department of Agriculture—OGC, Rural Development Division (*www.usda.gov*)
- U.S. Department of Transportation (*www.dot.gov*)
  - Office of Chief Counsel, Federal Transit Administration
  - Office of Chief Counsel, St. Lawrence Seaway Development Corporation
- U.S. Department of Treasury—Community Development Financial Institutions Fund, Legal Counsel Office (*www.cdfifund.gov*)
- Federal Housing Finance Agency—OGC (*www.fhfa.gov*)
- National Indian Gaming Commission—OGC (*www.nigc.gov*)

What Does It Pay?

Pay varies widely from place to place, with larger states (like Texas) and major metropolitan areas (like Houston and Dallas) paying the most. Compensation can be quite lucrative—into six figures—for these high-stakes positions that contribute to bringing jobs and revenue to the locale.

Government EDOs in some states operate under a higher pay system than their civil service peers.

Future Prospects

The competition among nations, states, and communities to attract and retain business, create jobs, and improve tax bases is fierce and is becoming more intense each year. Many variations of economic incentives are offered to the potential business, such as tax incentives, help with investment capital, donated land, regulatory concessions, and many others. The use of tax, finance, and regulatory incentives to attract jobs and investment has grown exponentially over the past two decades and shows no sign of letting up. If anything, there will be more pressure on jurisdictions to attract and retain business than ever before.

In addition, EDOs are becoming more sophisticated when it comes to doing deals. The use of "clawbacks"—performance measures, defined in an incentive contract, that must be met by the business party within a set time for it to keep the incentive—is increasing. This makes for tough bargaining and complex agreements, which means a need for legal input.

Economic development positions are superb vehicles for individuals who want to meet and work with senior corporate and governmental officials, and they can serve as terrific boosts to future jobs and careers. In one sense, economic development jobs are a networker's dream.

Breaking In

One of my legal career transition counseling clients wanted to break into this field. She read that her state legislature was debating whether the state should open overseas offices for the purpose of attracting foreign businesses to the state. Although she had no direct experience in economic development, she contacted the chief aide to the chair of the relevant legislative committee and volunteered to assist in information gathering and drafting policy papers and analyses on the topic. The thinly staffed committee was eager for assistance. She threw herself into the project, and after six weeks, she was asked to prepare the key points to be covered in a draft bill to open overseas offices. The bill eventually became law, and she was offered a position with the new International Division of the state EDO.

Lawyers who work in this field usually have excellent interpersonal and communication skills, as well as a broad-based knowledge of law and regulation. The former skills are important because economic development professionals meet with high-level business executives and attempt to persuade them to locate, remain, or expand within a jurisdiction. Knowledge of law and regulation is important because businesses need help negotiating their way through the maze of tax and regulatory incentives, securing financing, obtaining land, etc. and other legal matters that apply to the transaction.

Credential Enhancement. While not as important as in other disciplines, an economic development certification might be an advantage in the job market. Selected certificate programs include:

- International Economic Development Council—Certified Economic Developer (*www.iedconline.org*)
- National Development Council—Economic Development Finance Professional (EDFP) Certification Program (*www.nationaldevelopmentcouncil.org*)
- Center for Economic Development Education (*www.aiea.ualr.edu/econdev/certificateprogram/default.php*)
  - Advanced Certificate in Economic Development Research
  - Advanced Certificate in Business Retention and Expansion

For More Information

- Economic Development Directory (*www.ecodevdirectory.com*)
- International Economic Development Council (*www.iedconline.org*)
- See *www.corporatelocationdirectory.com/utilities* for a nationwide list of utilities that provide economic development services to companies.
- Government Accountability Office reports (*www.gao.gov*)
- Area Development Online (*www.areadevelopment.com*)
- LocationUSA.com (*www.locationusa.com*)

INTELLECTUAL ASSET MANAGEMENT

Introduction

Intellectual asset management (IAM) has emerged as one of the most important areas of business endeavor, thanks to increased global competition, the proliferation of knowledge- and technology-based businesses, the eternal quest for new revenue centers and ways to enhance the bottom line through exploitation of existing resources, and the fact that intangible assets now outnumber tangible assets in most companies (intangibles represent 78 percent of Fortune 500 companies' assets).

A recent example of IAM in action was the acquisition of a large portion of a North American beverage business by a British competitor. The British company discovered that the acquisition brought with it approximately 30,000 trademarks in various states of protection (with filings in more than 80 countries) and use. An IAM firm was engaged to sort through these trademarks and perform the necessary steps to protect and maximize their value, a years-long process.

What Is It?

IAM is the practice of transforming and leveraging intellectual property (IP) (such as patents, trademarks, and copyrights) and other intangible assets (such as trade secrets, brands, business processes, and employee know-how) into strategic corporate assets. IAM generates value by aligning the creation and use of intangible assets with core business strategies, enabling more effective technology licensing, and lowering IP creation and maintenance costs. In addition, IAM generates value by helping create new uses for IP and by enabling a company to create a better return on its R&D investments by more closely aligning its R&D resources with strategic business goals.

IAM consists of performing one or more of the following functions:

- Inventorying client IP assets
- Portfolio analysis (screening the IP portfolio for value opportunities)
  - Reviewing and clustering IP assets
  - Differentiating core assets from noncore assets
  - Differentiating revenue generators from purely defensive assets
- Assessing the status of protection of the IP assets
- Taking the necessary steps to protect IP assets
- Evaluating the commercial potential of IP assets
- Developing an IAM marketing strategy
- Marketing IP assets to potential licensees and others
- Reviewing, drafting, and negotiating licenses and other agreements
- Managing licensed assets
- Enforcement issues
- Developing an electronic IAM database
- Organizing paper files
- Advising senior management on technology licensing and IP issues

- Uncovering and countering IP infringements, counterfeiting, and piracy (a very important collateral benefit of IAM)

Who Does It?

IAM is spreading rapidly throughout the business and legal communities. Corporations, law firms, law firm consulting subsidiaries, colleges and universities, general management consulting firms, specialized consulting firms (that focus exclusively on IAM), and even government agencies have instituted IAM as a core component of their business. Clients of law firms, firm subsidiaries, and consulting firms are primarily corporations, universities, and other IP owners.

Corporations. IAM is big business. IBM, for example, earns close to $2 billion per year from licensing and marketing its IP. Other companies with highly developed IAM programs include Dow Chemical, Disney, Boeing, NEC, Kraft Foods, Procter & Gamble, AOL Time Warner, NASCAR and Calvin Klein. As you can see from this sampling, IAM impacts diverse industries.

Law Firms. Law firms that provide IAM services normally do so as part of their overall IP practice. A few, however, have separated out the IAM function and placed it in a subsidiary or have entered into a business relationship with an IAM consulting firm. See, for example, Maxiam LLC (Howrey & Simon).

Consulting Firms. This sector is comprised of the Big Four CPA firms (PricewaterhouseCoopers, KPMG, Ernst & Young, and Deloitte Touche), as well as management consulting firms (such as Accenture, Bearing Point, A.T. Kearney, Bain & Company, Booz Allen & Hamilton, Boston Consulting Group, the Corporate Executive Board, and McKinsey & Company) and consulting firms that specialize in IAM (such as UTEK, Consor, and PetrashWilliamson).

Colleges and Universities. Research institutions in particular are devoting increasing attention to IAM and technology commercialization. You can see the fruits of their IAM labors if you walk into any campus bookstore and see the books overwhelmed by the university-branded items for sale. A growing number of universities have established IAM/technology commercialization departments, which bring millions of dollars into college coffers each year. According to a 2007 survey by the Association of University Technology Managers (*www.autm.org*), 149 colleges and universities earned over $2 billion from technology licensing in 2007, more than a 60 percent increase over 2006.

Government. The U.S. government and its outside contractors run more than 700 federal laboratories, more than 260 of which have an IAM function, principally acting as technology transfer units. They are located all over the country and work in numerous science and technology disciplines. In addition, more than 30 U.S. government agency offices play a role in IAM, the principal ones being these:

- National Aeronautics and Space Administration (*www.nasa.gov*)
  - Office of General Counsel (OGC), Commercial and International Law Division; IP Law Division
  - Goddard Space Flight Center—Office of Patent Counsel, Technology Commercialization Office
  - Kennedy Space Center—Office of the Chief Counsel
  - NASA Glenn Research Center—Office of the Chief Counsel, IP Law Division
- U.S. Department of Health and Human Services (*www.hhs.gov*)
  - Agency for Health Care Research and Quality
  - National Institutes of Health—Office of Technology Transfer (and individual tech transfer offices)
- U.S. Department of Commerce (*www.commerce.gov*)
  - Office of the Chief Counsel for Technology
  - National Institute of Standards and Technology—Office of Technology Partnerships
  - National Oceanic and Atmospheric Administration, Office of Research and Technology Applications
  - U.S. Patent and Trademark Office—Office of International Relations
- U.S. Department of Energy (*www.energy.gov*)
  - OGC—Deputy General Counsel for Technology Transfer and Procurement

- – Office of Chief Counsel, Chicago Operations Office
- – Office of Chief Counsel, Oakland Operations Office
- U.S. Department of Defense (*www.defenselink.mil*)
  - – Army Research Laboratory, Office of Chief Counsel
  - – Office of Naval Research, Office of Counsel
- Smithsonian Institution (*www.si.edu*)
  - – Business Contracting Division
  - – National Museum of the American Indian
- U.S. Department of Transportation—OGC, DOT Patent Counsel (*www.dot.gov*)
- U.S. Postal Service Licensing Group (*www.usps.com*)
- National Science Foundation—OGC (*www.nsf.gov*)

Selected Trade and Professional Associations

- International Anti-Counterfeiting Coalition (*www.iacc.org*)
- Independent Film and Television Alliance (*www.ifta-online.org*)
- Association of American Publishers (*www.publishers.org*)
- Business Software Alliance (*www.bsa.org/GlobalHome.aspx*)
- Interactive Digital Software Association (*www.idsa.com*)
- Intellectual Property Owners Association (*www.ipo.org*)
- Motion Picture Association of America (*www.mpaa.org*)
- Recording Industry Association of America (*www.riaa.org*)
- Pharmaceutical Research and Manufacturers of America (*www.pharma.org*)
- National Cable Television Association (*www.ncta.com*)
- Food Marketing Institute (*www.fmi.org*)
- Electronic Industries Alliance (*www.eia.org*)

Selected International Organizations.

- World Intellectual Property Organization, Geneva, Switzerland (*www.wipo.org*)
- WTO (World Trade Organization) Secretariat Development Division, Geneva, Switzerland (*www.wto.org*)
- United Nations Industrial Development Organization, Vienna, Austria (*www.unido.org*)
- International Intellectual Property Law Institute (*www.iipi.org*)

What Does It Pay?

IAM compensation varies widely, but this has to be qualified by saying that it varies widely at the high end of typical compensation scales. Law firms and consulting firms pay their IAM practitioners well over $100,000. The Licensing Executives Society's annual compensation survey reflected the following salary figures. The median compensation package for corporate, government, and university IAM professionals was $157,500 in 2008. Those earning the most worked in the pharmaceutical industry (median compensation $180,000). Those earning the least worked for universities and government (median compensation $97,000). Median base salary was highest in the New York metropolitan area ($172,000) and lowest in the Midwest ($127,000).

Future Prospects

IAM and its close relation, technology commercialization and licensing, has become a very important source of new products and revenue and business growth for many companies and, thus, a major contributor to both the bottom line and shareholder value. The highly competitive 21st-century environment guarantees that IAM will continue to realize solid growth, perhaps even more so in economic downturns when companies feel added pressure to maximize revenue from existing assets.

Breaking In

IAM is a growing field for which an added credential can be very important, both for employability and to make the case for higher compensation. This is particularly the case for attorneys who have neither IP or licensing experience nor extensive IP education in law school.

Job Listings.
- Association of University Technology Managers (*www.autm.net*)
- Chronicle of Higher Education (*www.chronicle.com*)
- Higher Education Jobs (*www.higheredjobs.com*)
- Society of Competitive Intelligence Professionals (*www.scip.org*)
- American Intellectual Property Law Association (*www.aipla.org*)
- Licensing Executives Society (*www.usa-canada.les.org*)
- International Trademark Association (*www.inta.org*)

Graduate Programs
- Golden Gate University School of Law—LLM in Intellectual Property Law (*www.ggu.edu*)
- George Washington University Law School—LLM in Intellectual Property Law (*www.law.gwu.edu*)
- Suffolk University Law School—LLM in Global Law and Technology (*www.law.suffolk.edu*)
- Washington University School of Law—LLM in IP and Tech Law (*http://law.wustl.edu/LLMIP2*)
- Franklin Pierce Law Center (*www.piercelaw.edu/masters/llm.php*)
  - Master of Laws in Intellectual Property
  - Master of Laws in Commerce and Technology
  - Intellectual Property Diploma Certificate
- DePaul University College of Law (*www.law.depaul.edu*)
  - Certificate in Intellectual Property: Arts and Museum Law
  - Certificate in Intellectual Property: General
  - Certificate in Intellectual Property: Patents
- Licensing Executives Society (*www.licensingcertification.org*)
  - LES Professional Development Series
  - Certified Licensing Professional Program
- U.S. Department of Agriculture Graduate School—Technology Transfer Program (*www.grad.usda.gov*)
- University of California—Berkeley Extension—Certificate in Technology Transfer and Commercialization (*www.unex.berkeley.edu*)
- World Intellectual Property Organization—Seven different programs (*www.wipo.int*)

Selected Membership Organizations
- American Intellectual Property Law Association (*www.aipla.org*)
- American Bar Association: Section of Intellectual Property Law (*www.abanet.org/intelprop*)
- Licensing Executives Society (*www.usa-canada.les.org*)
- International Trademark Association (*www.inta.org*)
- Association of University Technology Managers (*www.autm.net*)
- Association of Patent Law Firms (*www.aplf.org*)

For More Information

- *Intellectual Asset Management* magazine (*www.iam-magazine.com*)
- *Managing Intellectual Property* magazine (*www.managingip.com*)
- *World Trade Executive* magazine (*www.wtexecutive.com*)
- Al-Ali, Nermien, *Strategic Intellectual Asset Management.* Franklin Pierce Law Center, Concord, NH. (*www.ipmall. fplc.edu/hosted_resources/Al-Ali/SIAM_files/frame.htm*)
- Technology Transfer Tactics (*www.technologytransfertactics.com*)
- Federal Laboratory Consortium for Technology Transfer (*www.federallabs.org*)
- National Technology Transfer Center (*www.nttc.edu*)
- Intellectual Property Rights Training Database (*www.training.ipr.gov*)
- Coalition for Intellectual Property Rights (*www.cipr.org*)

GOVERNMENT AFFAIRS

Introduction

During the glory days of government regulation, when legislators took their oversight responsibilities seriously and regulators regulated, the number of lobbyists and government affairs professionals in Washington, D.C. and the state capitals skyrocketed. Then, when deregulation was the mantra (approximately 1977–2009), the government affairs profession skyrocketed even more (from 1998–2008, when deregulation peaked, lobbying expenditures in Washington went up by 126 percent, and the number of lobbyists increased by 50 percent). Now that the pendulum has swung back in favor of regulation, we see the same pattern. Lobbyists and government affairs professionals are converging on seats of government like feeding-frenzied sharks after chum. The actual number of government affairs professionals nationwide is difficult to calculate. For Washington, an educated guess is to take the number of registered lobbyists (approximately 25,000) and triple it (75,000). If you throw a stick out of the window on K Street, it will likely bounce off five lobbyists before it hits the ground. There are approximately 40,000 registered lobbyists in state capitals and thousands more at the local level.

Government affairs is a multibillion-dollar industry in the United States. Virtually every industry maintains a presence in Washington, D.C.

and state capitals. Even the newest industries (e.g., the Custom Electric Bicycle Builders Association, Green Restaurant Association, at least six wind energy associations) realize from birth that they need to do this.

What Is It?

Government affairs encompasses more than going to Capitol Hill or Albany, Sacramento, Austin, Tallahassee, etc. to persuade legislators to pass or reject bills or to a federal or state agency to advocate for or against a proposed regulation. The profession values multidisciplinary skills and diverse talents, including legal, marketing, and management skills. Larger associations and other organizations practice division of labor with respect to their government affairs functions.

Typical government affairs responsibilities (using a company/association as a model) include the following:

- Overall management of government affairs activities, focusing on Congress, state legislatures, governors' offices, and other departments and agencies
- Representing the company before federal and state officials, legislatures, and industry/business organizations
- Managing the legislative agenda, including reviewing bills for potential impact on business, developing positions with internal or member business units and subject-matter experts, and communicating views to legislative committees and other officials
- Managing outside legal and lobbying resources, as well as contract (outside) lobbyists
- Organizing coalition activities with other companies and associations in the industry, and with consumer groups, to advance the company's or association's agenda
- Working with attorneys handling regulatory issues to gain political support
- Managing the political program, including use of corporate and political action committee (PAC) contributions
- Participating in federal and state administrative and regulatory proceedings
- Formulating policy positions on key issues

- Developing and implementing strategic plans on key policy positions
- Monitoring and analyzing key legislative and regulatory proposals that affect the industry and assessing the impact on the company or association members
- Reporting to company and association member executives on legislation and regulations
- Developing relationships with key regulators, legislators, and policy makers
- Positioning the company or association as a "thought leader" in industry policy
- Preparing policy briefings for association members, company and association executives, and company business units
- Representing the company at trade associations and industry coalitions
- Interacting with other companies/associations on key issues

Who Does It?

There are more than 100,000 trade and professional associations in the United States. Washington, D.C. is home to approximately 12,000 of them. Prominent examples include the American Petroleum Institute, National Association of Manufacturers, American Forest Products Association, American Psychological Association, and the Society of Human Resources Professionals. Only around 10 percent have their own legal counsel office (still a considerable number), but almost every one of them has a government relations office, usually populated by at least a few attorneys. More than 60 percent of these associations lobby Congress and/or agencies, says the American Society of Association Executives.

In addition, virtually all Fortune 500 corporations and many other companies have government relations representatives in Washington, usually attorneys. Similarly, states, municipalities, universities, and labor organizations make up a large and growing government affairs presence in the nation's capital.

That is not all. There are also several thousand advocacy organizations located or represented in Washington, plus the many lawyer-lobbyists who work in the legislative or government affairs practices of their law firms or for law firm subsidiaries.

Their reason for locating in Washington, D.C. is, of course, because Congress and the federal executive branch administrative and regulatory agencies are located there with a few exceptions (e.g., the Tennessee Valley Authority in Knoxville and the Railroad Retirement Board in Chicago). Washington is where the money is, and the government has plenary power to giveth and to taketh away.

Travel to many state capitals—especially those in the most populous states—and you will find a similar community of government relations and lobbying folks.

Association headquarters in particular can also be found in large numbers in other major cities: Chicago, New York, and Los Angeles are home to several thousand trade and professional associations. Moreover, thousands of government affairs positions are located at corporate headquarters, away from both Washington, D.C. and state capitals.

Small trade and professional associations that cannot afford to maintain a Washington, D.C. office often outsource their government affairs activities to association management firms—companies that provide Washington representation to multiple out-of-town associations. You can find a list of association management firms at *www.asaecenter.org*.

Law firms that have a government affairs practice or locate this function in a subsidiary should not be overlooked.

Also a number of management consulting firms either specialize in government relations consulting or have government relations practices.

While U.S. government departments and agencies are precluded from engaging in lobbying activities, as a line in the film *Casablanca* goes, don't be "shocked, shocked that gambling goes on at Rick's." Every U.S. government agency and many state counterparts have a legislative affairs office that does a good deal more than craft and submit their organization's legislative program once a year. Attorneys work in many of these offices.

Congress even lobbies itself, through its more than 200 Congressional Caucuses.

Lobbyists are required to register with the Clerk of the House and the Secretary of the Senate to lobby the U.S. government. They then must file semiannual reports detailing estimated money spent, broken down by client, as well as list the agencies and/or houses of Congress they lobbied. Individuals and organizations representing foreign interests in the United States must register with the Department of Justice under the Foreign Agents Registration Act (22 U.S.C. 611 et seq.).

States and many cities and counties have comparable registration requirements.

The following jobs, all of which either require or prefer a law degree, are representative of those found in a government affairs environment:

- Director of Government Affairs, Medtronic Inc., Washington, D.C.
- Corporate Counsel, Law and Government Affairs, Avaya Inc., Basking Ridge, New Jersey
- Manager, Government Relations and Legal Counsel, Flextronics, Delhi, India
- Government Affairs Counsel, American Family Insurance, Phoenix, Arizona
- Senior Government Affairs Manager, Verizon, Phoenix, Arizona; St. Paul, Minnesota; and Denver, Colorado
- Public Policy Counsel, Government Affairs Management, Microsoft, Redmond, Washington
- Legislative Counsel, Government Relations Team, eBay, San Jose, California
- Government Business Development Manager, IBM, San Jose, California
- Government Liaison, PJM Interconnection, Norristown, Pennsylvania
- Manager, Government Affairs Team, Sears, Roebuck & Co., Hoffman Estates, Illinois
- Public Affairs Government Relations Associate, W. L. Gore & Associates, Newark, Delaware
- Marketing Manager, Federal Government Segment, Thomson-West, Eagan, Minnesota

What Does It Pay?

Among government affairs professionals, lobbyists earn the most, with low- to mid-six-figure salaries being the norm. Nonlobbyists earn an average salary of around $100,000 in the Washington, D.C. area and somewhat less in state capitals and other cities, with those who work in larger jurisdictions earning more than those who work in less populous states and localities.

Government affairs professionals within the government are paid according to the same compensation scales that apply to most of their government colleagues.

Future Prospects

The introduction at the beginning of this section gives you a flavor of the likely future for government affairs professionals—very rosy, as far out as it is possible to predict.

We are at the beginning of an activist administration and Congress and can expect the flood of legislative and regulatory proposals emanating from Washington, D.C., to continue for quite some time. State and local governments are following suit in an attempt to grapple with massive policy issues and crises that have converged at the same time—two-and-a-half wars, struggling domestic and global economies, dying industries, climate change, energy transformation, healthcare reform, and others. All of this energizes the government affairs function and gives it greater prominence, while also creating numerous new job opportunities for attorneys.

Breaking In

Newly minted attorneys do not find nearly the same barriers to entry into government affairs, particularly in the association arena, that they encounter in the corporate world of the companies that trade associations represent. Experienced lawyers, primarily if they have relevant experience, also can move from practice into this realm without additional credentials.

One of the best ways of positioning yourself for a government affairs career is to go to work in one of the 25,000+ positions on Capitol Hill, in a state legislature on a legislator's personal staff, or on a committee staff. A client who was a senior associate at a prestigious national law firm just made such a move and is now working on the personal staff of a Congressperson, with an eye to making the necessary contacts to move up in the political/government affairs world. He views the salary decrease he has accepted as an investment in his future, more valuable than an LLM or other graduate degree.

Once you have this experience, you will be in an excellent position to transition into government affairs at a considerably higher salary than you earned in your legislative capacity.

Job Listings

- Association Jobs (*http://asaenet.jobcontrolcenter.com*)
- Association Jobs (*http://jobs.associationtrends.com*)
- House of Representatives Employment Information (*www.house.gov/cao-hr*)
- CQ House Action Reports (*http://moneyline.cq.com/corp/show.do?page=corp_hilljobs*)
- Senate Employment Bulletin (*www.senate.gov/visiting/resources/pdf/seb.pdf*)
- Senate Employment Website (*www.senate.gov/visiting/common/generic/placement_office.htm*)
- Lobbying Jobs (*www.lobbyingjobs.com*)

Enhancing Your Credentials. Several selected programs offer a government affairs credential:

- Georgetown University Government Affairs Institute—Certificate Program in Legislative Studies (*http://gai.georgetown.edu*)
- American Society of Association Executives—Certified Association Executive (*www.asaecenter.org*)
- Duke University—Nonprofit Management Certificate (*http://www.learnmore.duke.edu*)
- Arizona State University—Graduate Certificate Program in Nonprofit Leadership & Management (*www.asu.edu*)
- Northeastern University—Nonprofit Management Certificate (online option) (*www.spcs.neu.edu*)
- Brookings Institution—Certificate in Public Leadership (*www.brookings.edu/execed/certificateprograms.aspx*)
- Lobby School (*www.learn-to-lobby.com*)

Expanding Your Network

- American League of Lobbyists (*www.alldc.org*)
- Women in Government Relations Incorporated (*www.wgr.org*)

- State Government Affairs Council (*www.sgac.org*)
- Federal Bar Association (*www.fedbar.org*)

For More Information

- *Roll Call* newspaper (*www.rollcall.com*)
- *The Hill* newspaper (*www.thehill.com*)
- *Association Trends* newspaper (*www.associationtrends.com*)
- Government Affairs Yellow Book (*www.leadershipdirectories.com*)
- Association Yellow Book (*www.leadershipdirectories.com*)
- Lobbyist Databases (*www.opensecrets.org/lobbyists; http://sopr. senate.gov*)
- Lobbyist Finder (*www.lobbyistfinder.com*)
- Lobbyists.Info (*www.lobbyists.info*)
- Top Lobbying Firms (*www.publicintegrity.org*)
- State Lobbying (*www.publicintegrity.org/hiredguns/information.aspx*)
- Registered Foreign Agents (*www.usdoj.gov/criminal/fara*)
- Foreign Representatives Yellow Book (*www.leadershipdirectories.com*)

THE ACADEMIC SECTOR

Introduction

When I suggest that clients consider an education position, most respond that they either (1) are not qualified to teach in a law school because they did not attend a top-tier law school or were not "law review" or (2) don't know of any legal teaching opportunities other than at law schools. I always point out that law school teaching is just one of many legal opportunities—not only teaching but also a variety of nonteaching positions—in the academic sector.

The nation's 4,000+ colleges and universities provide a diverse and expanding environment for lawyers, thanks to two parallel trends that have heavily influenced campus legal hiring and staff development over the last 20 years:

1. The establishment of in-house counsel offices and the bringing on campus of much legal work that used to be farmed out to law firms. Today, only a handful of colleges

and universities (two-year schools included) do not have in-house counsel offices.

2. The realization that, due to the increasing complexity of campus life, many legal and law-related staff functions require more specialized attention than they could receive from overburdened general counsel offices. This has resulted in the separating out of certain highly specialized legal/law-related activities from the general counsel's office (see below).

Increasingly, colleges "legalize" their decision making. Traditionally, the courts have deferred to faculty and academic administrators with respect to the issues listed below. However, that principle is eroding rapidly. Matters previously confined to the academy have now become subjects of public scrutiny.

Academic institutions have become embroiled in a growing number of disputes over such matters as the following:

- Termination of probationary faculty
- Tenure codes
- Discrimination (race, gender, age, disability, veteran status, sexual orientation, etc.)
- Sexual harassment
- Hiring procedures
- Intellectual property rights
- Professional misconduct
- Falsification of data
- Attribution of credit and authorship
- Plagiarism
- Student-advisor relations
- Student rights
- Admissions
- Grades
- Graduation requirements
- Discipline
- Labor relations

In addition, legal issues on campus have pervaded numerous campus activities, such as these:

- Operating summer camps
- Regulating alcohol and drugs on campus
- Union organizing of faculty and teaching assistants

- Employment law for faculty and academic administrators
- Financial Modernization Act of 1999 Safeguarding Rules
- Safety security searches
- Room assignments/changes
- Substance-free housing
- Reductions-in-force—faculty and staff
- Impact of HIPAA on employment decisions
- Copyrights—library, art museum, publications
- Campus violence
- Liability for on-campus crime
- College athletics and risk management
- Immigration issues since 9/11
- The status of *in loco parentis*
- Suicidal students
- Study abroad—risk management
- Email and Internet—acceptable uses
- Intellectual property in the digital/electronic environment
- Family and Medical Leave Act
- Workers' compensation
- Wage and hour issues

- Distance education
- Investigators on campus—USA Patriot Act
- Student workers—students or employees or both?
- Student aid administration
- Title IX
- Transgender students
- Academic advising and the duty to advise
- Academic freedom
- Revocation of admission
- Degree revocation
- Performance evaluations
- Student privacy; parents' rights
- College catalogs and contract commitments
- Extracurricular activities and institutional liability
- Hate speech on campus
- Fundraising: Tainted gifts, reneging donors, and donor control postgifting
- Student discipline and off-campus misconduct
- Academic fraud and scientific misconduct
- Practicums, internships, service learning, and institutional liability
- Student publications: Libel and potential institutional liability
- Fiduciary duties of university trustees

Moreover, federal and state government legal oversight now reaches much more deeply into academic institutions than ever. Colleges have had to establish extensive compliance programs in response to a barrage of government laws and regulations covering areas such as healthcare, fundraising, student loans, foreign students, disabled students, and records management.

Campuses are one of the last bastions of labor organizing, and collective bargaining agreements typically bring with them their own array of dispute resolution mechanisms.

There is also a growing trend toward hiring in-house counsel by local school districts. The United States has more than 13,500 school districts (California alone has more than 1,000). In addition, a number of law firms specialize in school district representation.

What Is It?

Teaching law is not restricted to law schools. Interest in law among students at all higher education levels is avid and growing. There are now many opportunities—and different venues—for aspiring law teachers. Attorneys teach law courses in undergraduate institutions, graduate departments, paralegal schools, foreign universities, governments, and corporations.

Law School. Traditional law teaching positions are growing slowly. U.S. law schools are a mature industry, and few additional ones come online in any given year. The competition for law school teaching positions is intense. Thousands of highly qualified attorneys with stellar academic and practice backgrounds compete fiercely for the few hundred such positions that open up each year. A typical successful competitor's résumé would manifest a top-tier law school, law review, Order of the Coif, a federal appellate judicial clerkship, and/or some experience with a large, national law firm.

The growth in *nontraditional* teaching positions in law schools, however, is quite strong and is open to less than "dream" résumés. Law schools realize that they have to offer a more diverse curriculum and prepare their students better for the harsher, more competitive practice world of the 21st century. Consequently, they now pay more attention to basic legal skills (research, analysis, and writing) and offer more clinics and special programs.

In addition to tenure-track-positions (assistant, associate, and full professors), law schools hire non-tenure track teachers under titles such as instructor, lecturer, academic support instructor, clinical program director, legal research and writing program instructor, adjunct professor, and others. Beyond the tenure-track titles, there is no uniformity among law schools.

Undergraduate and Graduate Programs. This is where most teaching opportunities for lawyers exist. One of the most interesting recent developments has been the formalization of "pre-law" studies into an actual undergraduate major, most commonly called Legal Studies. Hundreds of undergraduate institutions now offer a Legal Studies or comparable major. Legal studies program instructors are usually attorneys.

There is also a strong market for attorneys in other, more traditional undergraduate and graduate departments, such as business, accounting, criminal justice and law enforcement, real estate, insurance, and international affairs, among others.

The following list is representative of undergraduate, graduate, and professional schools, departments, and programs employing JDs as teachers:

- Accounting
- Anthropology
- Business
- Criminal Justice
- Journalism
- Economics
- Forensic Science
- History
- Industrial and Labor Relations
- International Studies
- Legal Studies
- Library Science
- Medical Schools
- Political Science
- Psychology
- Public Affairs
- Public Health
- Real Estate
- Social Work
- Sociology

Paralegal Programs. The rapid expansion of paralegal certificate programs also means more teaching positions for lawyers. Attorneys from a practice background predominate in paralegal program faculties.

Teaching Law Abroad. English has become the *lingua franca* of international business. This has given rise to a proliferation of law and law-related course and degree offerings in English by foreign academic institutions. There has been a corresponding increase in demand by these institutions for U.S.-educated individuals as teachers.

Legal Opportunities in Education Administration. Colleges and universities also provide a richly diverse and expanding *nonteaching* environment for lawyers. Attorneys are becoming ubiquitous on campus. They work in campus General Counsel offices, of course, on a range of issues comparable in most respects to those in a corporate in-house counsel office. They are also found in other staff offices, such as those that deal with the following matters, among others:

- Equal employment opportunity and affirmative action
- Risk management
- Technology transfer and licensing
- Contract management
- Ethics
- Campus judicial affairs
- Environmental matters
- Legislative and regulatory affairs compliance
- Government affairs
- Sponsored research and industry alliances
- International student affairs
- Disabled student affairs
- Real estate

The most often advertised legal and law-related campus job opportunities are found in the following areas:

- University legal counsel
- Affirmative action/EEO
- Assistant to the president/chancellor
- Business affairs
- Ombudsman
- Contracts, procurement, grants
- Diversity management
- Employee relations
- Environmental affairs
- Human resources
- Judicial affairs
- Intellectual property manager
- Law library
- Law school academic support

- Law school career services
- Law school development/ fundraising/institutional advancement
- Law school admissions/ financial aid
- Law school alumni affairs
- Law school communications
- Law school marketing
- Law school student affairs
- Law school publications
- Law school registrar
- Mediation services
- Paralegal program administration
- Planned/deferred giving
- Real estate
- Risk management
- Sexual harassment/ sexual assault counseling
- Sponsored research
- Technology commercial- ization/licensing

Note: Campus job titles vary in the extreme from one institution to another. It is always important to read the fine print to determine what a particular job title really means in terms of the duties and responsibilities of the position.

Legal Positions in the K–12 Academic Sector. School attorneys (whether school district in-house counsel employees or outside [law firm] attorneys) fill the role of corporate counsel. They advise school boards and administrations on the full panoply of issues that any corporate counsel must handle, as well as constitutional and other issues, such as the following:

- Equal educational opportunity
- Separation of church and state
- Student free speech
- Teaching evolution and/or "intelligent design"
- Individualized Education Plans for disabled students
- Student dress codes
- Open meeting laws
- Disabled student partici- pation in sports
- Textbook selection controversies
- No Child Left Behind Act (Pub.L. 107-110) requirements
- School vouchers
- School violence

Who Does It?

There are currently 200 American Bar Association-approved (ABA) law schools in United States, supplemented by 39 non-ABA-approved U.S. law schools.

Virtually every U.S. college and university offers at least one undergraduate or graduate law or law-related program. Many offer multiple programs.

The ABA has approved 260 paralegal programs. There are also a large number of non-ABA approved paralegal programs, as well as online programs.

Most law-teaching opportunities outside the United States are found in the English-speaking common law countries (Canada, the United Kingdom, Australia, and New Zealand), countries where English is a primary second language (India, South Africa, other former and present Commonwealth nations), and in countries that are—or aspire to be—international business centers (e.g., Belgium, the Netherlands). There are also programs that teach in English in the Caribbean, Scandinavia, Continental Europe, the Middle East, Asia, Africa, and even Fiji. More than 180 institutions offer such programs.

What Does It Pay?

Law professors in ABA-approved law schools are among the best-paid teachers in academe.

Ranges for 2007–2008 salaries were as follows:

Title	Salary Range ($)
[1]Assistant Professor	48,849–142,500
[1]Associate Professor	67,000–148,000
[1]Professor	104,800–206,000
[2]Legal Writing Program Director	95,631 (average salary)
[2]Legal Writing Program Asst. Dir.	82,152 (average salary)
[2]Legal Writing Instructor	57,420–63,313
[3]Clinical Attorney/Instructor	34,000–57,000
[3]Lecturer	36,000–80,000

Notes:
[1]Survey by the Society of American Law Teachers
[2]Survey by the Legal Writing Institute
[3]AttorneyJobs.com salary figures (from active database and archives)

In addition, a majority of law schools offer their writing program faculty summer research grants averaging around $7,700.

Compensation varies widely among undergraduate, graduate, and professional institutions. Typical ranges are $24,000–$84,000 for instructors, $32,000–$76,000 for lecturers, $38,000–$160,000 for assistant professors, and $50,000–$185,000 for full professors. These variances are the result of factors such as geographic location, size of the institution, whether the institution is private or public, and other factors.

Positions at ABA-approved paralegal programs, which are frequently associated with four-year colleges and universities, generally pay better than those at non-ABA programs. Salaries at ABA-approved institutions range from $40,000 to $88,000.

Foreign academic institutions have historically compensated faculty at levels below those of their American counterparts. However, much depends on the exchange rate between the local currency and the U.S. dollar. Consequently, some institutions, because they pay their faculty in euros or local currencies, now exceed U.S. academic pay scales.

Compensation for campus professional staff positions varies widely by institution and position. As a rough rule of thumb, positions that earn revenue for the institution—such as in Planned Giving, Technology Transfer, Business Affairs, or Sponsored Research—tend to pay better than positions for which it is difficult to measure revenue earned or revenue saved.

School district compensation is largely dependent on the size of the jurisdiction and, if relevant, the salary scale for government employees. Law firms that represent school districts generally pay better than public sector positions, with large law firms paying the best.

Future Prospects

In August 2008, with little fanfare, President George W. Bush signed the Higher Education Opportunity Act (Pub.L. 110-315) (HEOA). Despite the fact that you can safely bet your subprime, interest-only, variable-rate mortgage that neither the president nor any member of Congress actually read this foot-high monster, it contains sweeping new regulatory mandates. The Act requires that colleges and universities report to the federal government on at least 300 new topics, including tuition and fee information, tuition cost reduction initiatives, textbook

prices by course, transfer-of-credit policies, file sharing, meningitis outbreaks, missing persons, fire safety, voter registration, drug and alcohol
violations, fatalities and student sanctions, and technology disposal,
among others.

Another name for HEOA might be "The Attorney Higher Ed Employment Act of 2008."

HEOA is part of an ongoing trend, now 40 years old and counting,
of imposing increased regulatory burdens on academic institutions. This
trend is sure to continue, especially given President Obama's ambitious
education reform plans.

While law school teaching opportunities will not grow very much,
for the reasons outlined earlier in this section, undergraduate legal studies and other law-related disciplines and their graduate counterparts
will grow significantly as life becomes more, not less, complex and law
extends its tentacles into additional areas of human endeavor.

Education reform is also likely to invigorate increased attorney and
law-related job opportunities at the K–12 level and in federal and state
education agencies.

Breaking In

Every fall, the Association of American Law Schools (AALS) (*www.aals.
org*) sponsors a Faculty Recruitment Conference in Washington, D.C.
In a typical year, it receives more than 3,000 résumés from would-be
law professors who compete to interview with participating schools. The
AALS also runs a Faculty Appointments Register where candidates for
teaching positions can post their qualifications, which are then shared
with law schools. In addition, the AALS advertises faculty positions in its
quarterly *Placement Bulletin* (a subscription publication).

Non-tenure-track positions are easier to obtain and, depending on
the institution's standards for promotion and tenure, may become or
lead to tenure-track opportunities. Most writing program faculty are on
short-term contracts of one, two or three years' duration.

The qualifications for many undergraduate and graduate law teaching positions are not as rigorous as they are for traditional law school
teaching positions. A large number of professors and instructors at this
level come directly from practice backgrounds with varying levels of
experience.

Professional staff (nonteaching) positions generally do not require any particular set of qualifications. Rather, each campus hiring office devises its own criteria, usually ad hoc, depending on the nature of the specific position offered.

Networking Organizations.
- Education Law Association (*http://educationlaw.org*)
- Association of University Technology Managers (*www.autm.org*)
- National Association of College and University Attorneys (*www.nacua.org*)
- National Council of University Research Administrators (*www.ncura.edu*)
- University Risk Management & Insurance Association (*www.urmia.org*)
- Society of American Law Teachers (*www.saltlaw.org*)
- Council of School Attorneys (*www.nsba.org/SecondaryMenu/ COSA.aspx*)

For More Information

Law School Teaching
- Chronicle of Higher Education (*www.chronicle.com*)
- Higher Education Jobs (*www.higheredjobs.com*)
- Academic360 (*www.academic360.com*)
- The Adjunct Advocate (*www.adjunctnation.com*)
- Society of American Law Teachers (*www.saltlaw.org*)
- Journal of Legal Education (*www.law.georgetown.edu/jle*)
- Inside Higher Ed (*http://insidehighered.com*)
- Legal Writing Institute (*www.lwionline.org*)

Teaching in Undergraduate and Graduate Programs
- Academy of Legal Studies in Business (International) (*www.alsb.org*)
- *Chronicle of Higher Education* (*www.chronicle.com*)
- Higher Education Jobs (*www.higheredjobs.com*)
- Academic360 (*www.academic360.com*)
- The Adjunct Advocate (*www.adjunctnation.com*)

- Inside Higher Ed (*http://insidehighered.com*)
- National Minority Faculty Identification Program (*www.southwestern.edu/natfacid/*)

Paralegal Teaching

- *Chronicle of Higher Education* (*www.chronicle.com*)
- Higher Education Jobs (*www.higheredjobs.com*)
- Academic360 (*www.academic360.com*)
- The Adjunct Advocate (*www.adjunctnation.com*)
- National Federation of Paralegal Associations (*www. paralegals.org*)
- National Association of Legal Assistants (*www.nala.org*)
- American Alliance of Paralegals (*www.aafpe.org*)
- American Bar Association Standing Committee on Paralegals (*www.abanet.org/legalservices/paralegals*)
- International Paralegal Management Association (*www.paralegalmanagement.org*)
- American Association for Paralegal Education (*www.aafpe.org*)
- Directory of Paralegal Schools in the United States (*www.paralegalschools.com*)

Information Sources for Law Teaching Opportunities Abroad

- *Chronicle of Higher Education* (*www.chronicle.com*)
- *Times Higher Education Supplement* (*www.timeshighereducation.co.uk*)

Selected Information Resources—Academic Professional Staff Positions

- Academic360.com (*www.academic360.com*)
- The Adjunct Advocate (*www.adjunctnation.com*)
- American Association of State Colleges and Universities (*www.aascu.org*)
- American Association of University Professors (*www.aaup.org*)
- Association for Student Judicial Affairs (*www.asjaonline.org*)
- Association of American Colleges and Universities (*www.aacu.org*)
- Association of American Law Schools (*www.aals.org*)
- Association of University Technology Managers (*www.autm.net*)
- Campus ADR.org (*www.campus-adr.org*)

- *Chronicle of Higher Education* (*www.chronicle.com*)
- College and University Professional Association for Human Resources (*www.cupahr.org*)
- Council of School Attorneys (*www.nsba.org/MainMenu/ SchoolLaw.aspx*)
- Higher Education Jobs (*www.higheredjobs.com*)
- Inside Higher Ed (*www.insidehighered.com*)

Sources of K–12 School Law Information
- National School Boards Association (*www.nsba.org*)
- National Center for Education Statistics (*www.nces.ed.gov*)

Additional Law Teaching Information Sources
- Anthony, Rebecca and Gerald Roe, *The Curriculum Vitae Handbook: How to Present and Promote Your Academic Career.* San Francisco: Rudi, 1998.
- Caplan, Paula J., *Lifting A Ton of Feathers: A Woman's Guide to Surviving in the Academic World.* Toronto: University of Toronto Press, 1993.
- Collins, Lynn H., Joan C. Chrisler, and Kathryn Quina, *Career Strategies for Women in Academe: Arming Athena.* Thousand Oaks, CA: Sage, 1998.
- Jacobs Kronefeld, Jennie and Marcia Lynn Whicker, *Getting an Academic Job: Strategies for Success.* Thousand Oaks, CA: Sage, 1997.
- Sowers-Hoag, Karen M., and Dianne F. Harrison, *Finding an Academic Job.* Thousand Oaks, CA: Sage, 1998.
- Vick, Julia M. and Jennifer S. Furlong, *The Academic Job Search Handbook* (4th ed.). Philadelphia: University of Pennsylvania Press, 2008.
- National Association of College and University Attorneys (*www.nacua.org*)
- National Association of College and University Business Officers (*www.nacubo.org*)
- Ombuds Directory (*http://ombudsdirectory.com*)
- University Ombuds Office Links (*www2.ku.edu/~ombuds/ other.html*)

- University Risk Management and Insurance Association (*www.urmia.org*)

ALTERNATIVE DISPUTE RESOLUTION

Introduction

ADR has become an omnipresent means of resolving disputes of every type. It is now a fixture in American society. ADR providers have gone through an industry shakeout after which only the legitimate and committed ones survived. The concept of a cheaper, less contentious, and more efficient dispute resolution process as an alternative to expensive, protracted, and highly contentious court proceedings has woven its way successfully throughout the country and has been incorporated into the daily doings of many industries, courts, government agencies, collective bargaining agreements, etc.

Attorneys are ideally positioned to offer ADR services. Most states do not regulate ADR providers in any significant way and do not preclude attorneys from adding an ADR provider component to their services. Many legitimate institutions offer ADR training and certification programs, often lasting a week and frequently offered online at reasonable prices, so costs of entry are low. Volunteer opportunities in which an attorney can gain ADR experience abound, too. That experience can position the ADR provider to compete for lucrative contracts offered by government and the private sector.

ADR has proven its worth and is now such an accepted and essential component of lawyering that major law firms often label their litigation practices "Dispute Resolution."

What Is It?

ADR is an umbrella term used to describe a variety of problem-solving processes that are used in lieu of litigation or administrative adjudication to resolve issues in controversy. These processes include, but are not limited to, settlement negotiations, conciliation, facilitation, mediation, fact-finding, neutral evaluation, ombuds, settlement conferences, mini trials, summary jury trials, binding arbitration, private judges, or hybrid processes that combine two or more of these techniques.

ADR is an alternative to litigation that allows the parties to use a resolution method that best suits their needs. It saves money, time, and stress on the parties and their representatives and results in increased party satisfaction.

ADR was first used as an alternative to trials, but appellate ADR programs are also available in more than one-half of the states. Parties may choose ADR to resolve an issue before filing a court case, but most cases are referred to ADR by the courts. Because of that, the final ADR resolution is often presented to a judge for approval or for enforcement.

Many courts have court-connected ADR programs for small-claims, civil, family, juvenile, probate, and restorative justice matters and even certain criminal matters.

ADR can be used in almost any type of case. Once a claim is filed in court, the parties are subject to the restrictions placed on ADR by the court in which the claim is filed.

Who Does It?

Everybody.

Disputants may use a private ADR program to resolve their dispute before filing a court claim.

When courts refer cases to ADR, they make referrals to a roster from which an ADR provider is selected, a private ADR program, or a particular ADR provider. Some courts have ADR coordinators who help parties select a suitable program or provider. Providers may be in-house court employees, volunteers, or private providers (paid through a grant or contract).

ADR is mandatory in certain cases in some states and can vary from court to court and judge to judge.

According to the National Center for State Courts, there are now more than 1,200 court-connected ADR programs at the state and local levels. Court-connected ADR has spread throughout the country over the past few decades. Every state has some type of court-connected ADR at some level. However, such programs are rarely statewide, found primarily in cities and metropolitan areas.

Referral methods for court-connected ADR vary by jurisdiction and case type and largely depend on the ADR resources available within a geographic location.

The Administrative Dispute Resolution Act of 1990 (ADRA) (Pub.L. 101-552) required each federal agency to adopt a policy on ADR use. In 1996, ADRA was re-enacted as the Administrative Dispute Resolution Act of 1996 (Pub.L. 104-320).

ADR has caught on internationally, too. The following selected international organizations have adopted ADR:

- International Chamber of Commerce (*www.iccwbo.org*)
- International Centre for Settlement of Investment Disputes (*http://icsid.worldbank.org/ICSID*)
- American Arbitration Association (*www.adr.org*)
- London Court of International Arbitration (*www.lcia-arbitration.com*)
- Permanent Court of Arbitration in The Hague (*www.pca-cpa.org*)
- China International Economic and Trade Arbitration Commission (*www.cietac.org.cn/index_english.asp*)
- Chamber of Commerce and Industry of Geneva (*www.ccig.ch/pages/Arbitrage_international.asp*)
- Ad hoc arbitrations, including proceedings under UNCITRAL (UN Commission on International Trade Law) (*www.uncitral.org*)

ADR Roster Referral Programs for Outside Contractors. In addition to employment dispute roster referral programs cited in the section on employment law (above), a number of organizations have comparable programs dealing with other topical area disputes. A selection follows:

- *U.S. Department of Agriculture (USDA) ADR Program* (*www.usda. gov/cprc*). While most of the conflicts are workplace disputes, USDA also has an occasional need for ADR contractors for other subject matter disputes.
- *U.S. Department of Energy Mediation Program* (*www.energy.gov*). Most mediations concern workplace disputes, but ADR is utilized for other disputes as well. The headquarters mediation program manager assigns mediators throughout the country. Mediation services RFPs are not generally advertised because they fall below the public announcement

threshold, so you need to contact the Energy Department's
Office of Dispute Resolution to receive notice.

- *Federal Deposit Insurance Corporation (FDIC) (www.fdic.gov).*
  Cases include creditor claims, real estate disputes, commercial matters, and professional liability cases. The FDIC also
  uses ADR techniques in labor-management matters.
- *U.S. Environmental Protection Agency (EPA) Conflict Prevention
  & Resolution Services (www.epa.gov).* ADR providers must have
  experience in environmental dispute resolution.
- *U.S. Institute for Environmental Conflict Resolution (http://ecr.
  gov/Resources/Roster/Roster.aspx).* Roster members are all
  impartial third-party practitioners (e.g., professional facilitators and mediators) experienced with environmental,
  natural resource, and public lands issues, including matters
  related to energy, transportation, and land use.
- *American Arbitration Association (AAA) (www.adr.org).* The
  AAA maintains rosters of both mediators and arbitrators on
  a chapter-by-chapter basis nationwide. Focus areas within
  which both types of ADR providers operate include these:
  - Commercial
  - Construction
  - Consumer
  - Domain names
  - e-Commerce
  - Elections
  - Energy
  - Healthcare
  - Insurance
  - International
  - Labor
  - Mass claims
  - Reinsurance
  - Securities
- *Association for Conflict Resolution (ACR) (www.acresolution.org).*
  To be listed on the ACR's mediator register, you must be
  an advanced practitioner member of the ACR Family Law
  Section.
- *American Health Lawyers Association (AHLA) (www.healthlawyers.
  org).* Applications to become a listed mediator/arbitrator are
  available online.
- *Financial Industry Regulatory Agency (FINRA) (www.finra.org).*
  The FINRA Dispute Resolution Arbitrator Program requires
  five or more years of business or professional experience.
  You can download the Arbitrator Application Kit from the

website. The FINRA Dispute Resolution staff conducts a preliminary review of your application before forwarding it to a subcommittee of the National Arbitration and Mediation Committee for final approval. The screening process generally takes 60 days. Before you serve as a FINRA arbitrator, you will be required to complete a mandatory basic arbitrator training.

- *Transportation Lawyers Association* (*www.translaw.org*). The Association maintains a roster of transportation ADR professionals.

What Does It Pay?

ADR compensation ranges widely, depending on the nature of the dispute, the contracting organization, the parties to the dispute, and other factors.

A rough standard for U.S. government compensation of outside (contract) ADR providers (usually mediators) is $300 per hour. Certain neutrals, primarily those engaged for complex cases (such as acquisition and contract controversies), can charge from $1,000 to $9,000 per ADR service.

Government (including court system) ADR personnel are paid at standard government pay scales (see *www.opm.gov* for federal General Schedule pay rates).

Future Prospects

Although widespread, ADR still has a lot of room to grow. In many states, court-connected ADR flourishes in some counties and cities but has not yet spread throughout the entire state. At the administrative adjudication level in the federal and many state governments, ADR is still in a very early stage of development. Given that the federal government alone has more than 130 administrative forums where disputes are heard, there is a great deal of potential for ADR.

Colleges and universities have greatly increased their own ADR programs through the medium of the campus judicial officer or office, as well as by the appointment of ombudsmen. These ADR techniques have served academic institutions very well as deflection mechanisms, keeping disputes out of courtrooms. Judicial officers primarily handle student matters. However, the utility of this approach has prompted some institutions to include grievances, complaints, and disputes involving other university constituencies.

Increasingly, ADR clauses are being written into every conceivable kind of contract. From a personal standpoint, I never negotiated an agreement on behalf of my company without insisting on the inclusion of an ADR provision.

ADR has reached a "tipping point" and is expanding rapidly. It is unaffected by economic fluctuations because it is a money saver for the parties involved, as well as governments.

Breaking In

ADR provider qualifications vary widely from method to method and state to state. Contact the state or federal court ADR office for the jurisdiction in which you are interested for information regarding required provider qualifications or certifications.

One advantage of an ADR practice is that a great deal of experience can be gained by participating in volunteer programs, which then positions you to apply for inclusion on court and other ADR rosters. Another advantage is that, with few exceptions, an ADR practice can be combined with a law practice.

Training and Credentialing. ADR training and credentialing programs abound. Selected programs include the following:

- American Bar Association Section on Dispute Resolution— ADR Training Providers by State (*www.abanet.org/dispute/ adr_training.html*)
- American Arbitration Association Programs (*www.adr.org*)
- Straus Institute for Dispute Resolution—Certificate in Dispute Resolution (*http://law.pepperdine.edu/straus/ lawyers_judges*)
- Association for Conflict Resolution—Family Mediation Training Programs (*www.acrnet.org*)
- Mountain States Employers' Council—Mediating Workplace Disputes (*www.msec.org*)

- Center for Legal Studies—Alternative Dispute Resolution Certificate (online option) (*www.legalstudies.com*)
- International Association of Facilitators—Certified Professional Facilitator (*http://iaf-world.org*)
- New York University—Certificate in Conflict and Dispute Resolution (*www.nyu.edu*)
- Marquette University—Graduate Certificate in Dispute Resolution (*www.marquette.edu*)
- Hamline University School of Law (*www.hamline.edu/law*)
  - Certificate in Dispute Resolution
  - Certificate in Global Arbitration Law and Practice
- World Trade Organization (*www.wto.org*)
  - Dispute Settlement System Training Module
  - General Agreement on Trade in Services

Networking Organizations
- Professional Mediation Association (*www.promediation.com*)
- Academy of Family Mediators (*www.mediators.org*)
- National Association for Community Mediation (*www.nafcm.org*)
- International Association of Facilitators (*http://iaf-world.org*)
- World Mediation Forum (*www.worldmediationforum.org*)

For More Information
- State and Local Bar Association Dispute Resolution Summary Profiles; American Bar Association Section of Dispute Resolution (*www.abanet.org/statelocal/profiles.html*)
- CPR International Institute for Conflict Prevention & Resolution (*www.cpradr.org*)
- National Center for State Courts (*www.ncsconline.org*)
- Campus Conflict Resolution Resources (*www.campus-adr.org*)
- Center for Appropriate Dispute Resolution in Special Education (*www.directionservice.org/cadre*)
- The Minitrial: An Alternative to a Lengthy Lawsuit (*www.mediationnow.com/communal/Articles/robertsmith/article3.htm*)

- *Early Neutral Evaluation: Getting An Expert's Assessment—Practical Guidelines and Steps for Getting Started.* American Arbitration Association (2005) (*www.adr.org/si.asp?id=4443*)
- *ADR and the Law* (22nd ed.) American Arbitration Association (2008) (*www.adr.org*)
- Folberg, Jay et al. *Resolving Disputes: Theory, Practice, and Law.* New York: Aspen, 2005.
- *Report on Mediator Credentialing and Quality Assurance.* Task Force on Credentialing, ABA Section of Dispute Resolution (October 2002) (*www.abanet.org/dispute*)
- Interagency Alternative Dispute Resolution Working Group (*www.usdoj.gov/adr*)
- *ADR and Settlement in the Federal District Courts.* Federal Judicial Center. (1996) (*www.fjc.gov/public/pdf.nsf/lookup/adrsrcbk.pdf/$File/adrsrcbk.pdf*)
- Mediation & Conference Programs in the Federal Courts of Appeals. Federal Judicial Center (*http://www.fjc.gov/public/pdf.nsf/lookup/mediconf.pdf/$File/mediconf.pdf*)
- *Nationwide Survey on Mediator Qualifications: State Statutes and Court Rules.* Ohio Commission on Dispute Resolution & Conflict Management (2001) (*http://disputeresolution.ohio.gov*)
- *Resources for Facilitators.* Free Management Library (*www.managementhelp.org/grp_skll/resource.htm*)
- United States Ombudsman Association (*www.usombudsman.org*)
- Judicial Settlement Conferences. Oregon State Bar (*www.osbar.org/public/legalinfo/1220.htm*)
- Bateman III, Thomas H., *The Summary Jury Trial: An Introduction.* (*www.2ndcircuit.leon.fl.us/Resources/summary_trial.pdf*)

Part III

Job-Hunting Tactics for Tough Times

Chapter 6

Moving Forward

OVERCOMING "RECESSION DEPRESSION"

Sure, losing your legal job is tough. Maybe even unfair. But if you stew or obsess about it, that vibe will be apparent to everyone in a position to help you: references, networking contacts, and interviewers. They may empathize. They may feel sorry for you. More likely, they will think: "Better you than me."

So the best advice is: Get over it. The sooner the better.

CREDENTIAL ENHANCEMENT 101

Each practice area section in this book contains recommendations about enhancing your credentials to position yourself better for job-search success. However, there are credentials, and then there are *credentials*. The advice that follows is designed to suggest how to differentiate between the two.

An LLM can be useful, but getting it is also time consuming and expensive (some LLM programs charge more than $50,000 per year just for tuition). A far less expensive, faster alternative is a graduate certificate program. Certificate programs are proliferating, and some are offered online. They are generally very inexpensive, often costing $1,000 or less.

Before you write the check for any program, perform a thorough "due diligence" investigation of the program's value to you. The suggestions below (which apply to any credential enhancement offering in any practice area) should help you select a credentialing program:

- *Expand your survey of credentialing programs to include law-related ones.* Depending upon your background and interests and the employment market, you may be better off obtaining a *law-related* graduate degree or professional certificate rather than an LLM or law certificate.
- *Talk to individuals who have already earned the degree or certificate.* They are the best judges of how the credential advanced their careers. Here are some key questions to ask them:
  - Did the credential make a difference to their careers?
  - How difficult was it to find suitable employment after completing the program?
  - How much help did they receive from the granting institution's career office?
  - Would they select the program again?
- *Talk to employers of individuals who have the degree or certificate.* Ask them these questions:
  - Do they value the degree or certificate?
  - If so, how does it contribute to their organization?
  - Do they believe the credentialing program in question is truly a career booster?
  - What is their opinion of the reputation of the school (or certificate-granting organization) among professionals in the field? Is it top rated, mediocre, or a joke?
- *Talk to current students.* Ask them:
  - Do they think the program is worth the time, effort, money, and career interruption?

- What do they intend to do with their degree or
    certificate?
- *Talk to the career placement professionals and program directors
  at the sponsoring school or organization.* Ask them:
    - Where can you expect to work once you have successfully
      completed the program?
    - What is their track record when it comes to placing
      program graduates?
    - What career paths will be open to you as a result of the
      credential?
    - To give specific examples of what they can do for you
      during and after the program.

If the career or program officials stonewall you or become defensive,
or if their answers are otherwise unsatisfactory, say "Thank you," pick up
your check, and walk away.

MAXIMIZING AND MOTIVATING YOUR CONTACTS

Why Network?

Networking means communicating with people about what you are doing
and where you want to go in your career. Networking means telling others
your story, asking them for advice and suggestions, and developing new
contacts beyond your core group.

Your professional and personal contacts can provide a rich source of
job leads and potential employment opportunities. For this reason, networking is one of your most valuable and important job-search tools.

Although a popular myth has it that "over 80 percent of all jobs are
not advertised," a statement that is insupportable in the extreme, it is a
fact that many professional jobs are filled by means other than by publication of a job ad. Moreover, even if a job opportunity is publicized,
competing for it with the advice and assistance of an intermediary could
give you a decided edge.

The only way to find out about these unadvertised positions is through
networking with a group of contacts who, because they either work for
the prospective employer or are themselves well connected to people who

work for an employing organization, can alert you to job opportunities that might otherwise pass you by and, by virtue of their entrée into the employing organization, can serve as endorsers of your candidacy and/or conduits of your résumé directly to the people who count.

Who Constitutes Your Network?

Former President Bill Clinton may be the best networker in history. He began as a teenager compiling notecards with the names, addresses, phone numbers, and personal and family information about everyone he met. By the time he ran for president, he had 17,000 file cards. His intention was to develop a list of contacts and contributors who could help him achieve his prodigious ambition. It worked.

I do not expect you to be as obsessive-compulsive as Bill Clinton. However, at a minimum, your network should consist of the following individuals:

- Friends
- Relatives
- Friends of friends
- Friends of relatives
- Neighbors
- Friends of neighbors
- Fellow academic alumni
- College and law school professors
- Current classmates
- Workplace alumni
- Colleagues at work
- Other professional colleagues
- Job interviewers
- Political contacts
- Former employers
- Members of clubs and organizations that you have joined (such as bar associations, community and cultural groups, church/synagogue/mosque, PTAs, athletic teams, and volunteer groups)
- Others (e.g., vendors, tradespeople, etc.)

Don't limit your list to only those people who might help you *directly*. Speculate also on how different individuals might be able to help you *indirectly*. The last bullet point, above, can be very important for this purpose. One of my clients got an interview through his postal carrier, another through her beautician.

Information for Your Networking Contacts

To get the most from your networking contacts, you need to provide them with enough good information about you so that they can channel their thinking according to *your* career aspirations. The more quality information you supply, the more impressed, energized, and effective your contacts will be.

Specific matters your contacts should know about you and your job campaign include the following:

- *Your confidentiality requirements.* The need to protect the clandestine nature of your job search, if that is an issue. This is particularly important in smaller markets.
- *Your employment history.* Where you worked, why you made your job moves, your areas of expertise and interest, and the quality of your experience.
- *Your ideal next career/job.* What you want to do and why and where you think that ideal could be realized. If your ultimate goal might seem unrealistic given your background, advise your contact that you are seeking a "transitional" position that will move you toward your goal.
- *Any geographic preferences and constraints.* Be as specific as you can.
- *The compensation you seek.* Be real. Cite a range rather than a specific number, mindful that the low number is probably what your contact will relay to prospective employers.
- *Any employer constraints.* For example, "I don't want to work for a tobacco company."
- *Your job-hunting activities to date, if any.* Indicating a well-thought-out plan and presentation impresses the contact and will spur him or her on to greater efforts.
- *Selected other contacts in your network.* If you cite too many people, your contact may feel that you are conducting networking "overkill" and conclude that he or she does not have to exert much effort on your behalf. Or your contact may learn that you have invoked the assistance of his or her worst enemy.

- *Your résumé(s).* If your contact may be of assistance in more than one area of interest, provide alternate versions of your résumé and explain the purpose of each version.
- *A writing sample.* If you are seeking a position where your writing ability will be important, provide a strong writing sample that can (1) impress your contact and (2) be passed on to his or her contacts or to prospective employers.
- *Your job/career "roadmap."*

Your Job/Career Roadmap

The roadmap is a document that you provide your contacts so that they can better serve you in (1) contemplating where you could work given your background and aspirations and (2) responding quickly and intelligently to your request for "intermediation," because the roadmap will minimize their need to think about where you might fit. Key elements of the roadmap include the following:

- Examples of specific positions that interest you
- Why it is logical for you to be interested in such positions (experience and/or education)
- Examples of specific employers where such positions are found
- Examples of where you might fit in an employing organization

The roadmap is critical for another reason: *It greatly eases the discomfort of networking.* It will give you confidence when approaching the contact. You won't feel embarrassed asking for help, and the contact will see immediately that you are a person of forethought and consideration for his or her time pressures, as well as someone with exceptional organizational skills.

Chapter 7

The Strongest Résumé

THIS SECTION HIGHLIGHTS SOME of the essential things you need to think about when you prepare your résumé in tough economic times. This does not mean that these issues are not important when times are good, only that they loom even larger when jobs are scarce and you need to make a powerful impression on a prospective employer quickly.

Universalizing your experience—speaking the employer's language—is something that will be immediately noticed by its absence, which in turn will likely mean immediate rejection. Employers flooded by résumés do not have time to translate your language into theirs.

Neglecting to mitigate the obvious weaknesses that will appear in your résumé gives an employer another opportunity for quickly dispensing with your candidacy. You need to spend much more quality time on your weaknesses than on your strengths. The latter will not require nearly as much effort.

Once you have persuaded an employer to give your résumé a serious look, you need to make sure you stand out from the crowd. Employers, once they have waded through the applications and put them aside, remember those that differentiated themselves from the competition.

FROM OBSCURITY TO CLARITY: UNIVERSALIZING YOUR EXPERIENCE

If you present a prospective employer with a résumé containing language alien to his or her experience, you will not be seriously considered for the position. Buzzwords, jargon, and other language unique to your particular industry, employer, or occupation is off-putting to anyone who does not share your background.

The following *before* and *after* examples are taken directly from two versions of a résumé. In the first version, the candidate initially used the most "inside" of insider language conceivable to describe his work experience—a nightmare for any employer forced to read such obscure gobble-dygook and a virtual guarantee of rejection for any legal position.

The second version is the actual clean-up I performed on the first version. The new approach universalized the candidate's experience and made it comprehensible to prospective employers.

Before: Experience Portion of Résumé Using Insider Jargon

Drafted DOD rules and regs on DOA, DON, USAF, and USMC's (and USCG in time of war) DOPMA and ROPMA staffing requirements and obligations in the event of a 50 U.S.C. 447, as amended (Act of 14 June 1947, ch. 6, §17(a)91)(ii), 49 Stat. 1685) mobilization; liaised with HASC, SASC, DMDC, DMA, DNA, UUHS, JCS, and other DOD components, and with Unified and Specified Commands on pending legislation and regulatory proposals; advised ASD (ISA), PDASD (Antiterrorism), and DASD (RA) on personnel and national security law issues; and coordinated legislative development of legislative program for GC office.

**After: Same Experience
Expressed in Universal Language**

- Drafted comprehensive regulations governing military personnel matters.

- Coordinated and explained pending legislation and proposed regulations to congressional committees and Department of Defense components.

- Advised senior management on employment, international, counterterrorism, and national security law.

- Participated in the development and review of the annual departmental legislative program.

It is critical that you excise insider language from your résumé and other application documents so that everyone who reads them can understand them without strain. Forcing an employer or a contact to scratch his or her head in befuddlement is a losing strategy. This is especially important in applying for law-related positions and those outside your immediate practice area. Remember, the first person to see your résumé may not know a thing about law or your particular practice area(s).

COMMON RÉSUMÉ WEAKNESSES . . .
AND THEIR ANTIDOTES

Employers tend to zero in on what they perceive to be the weak points in your résumé. This can happen at two critical decision points in the hiring process: Initially, during the evaluation of résumés; and subsequently, during job interviews.

Employer reactions to résumé weaknesses typically take one or more of the following forms:

- Outright rejection of your candidacy upon reading the résumé
- Total obsession with the perceived résumé weakness, to the exclusion of your positive selling points and gems that you have addressed elsewhere in the document
- Seeking an explanation for a weakness in your cover letter

- Seeking an explanation for a weakness you showed during your job interview

Consequently, you have to be prepared to counter your weaknesses through extenuation and mitigation and by employing certain résumé techniques that de-emphasize problem spots or make them more difficult to pinpoint (without, of course, engaging in a cover-up).

You can address some weaknesses directly in the body of the résumé, others in your cover letter, and most at the interview, provided that the weaknesses do not foreclose that opportunity.

When preparing for a job interview, it is essential that you prepare more thoroughly for "weakness" questions than for the "home run" questions you know you can knock out of the park. Unfortunately, most job seekers do just the opposite, honing their responses to the feel-good questions while ignoring those that will make them squirm, because they know how difficult and discomfiting these are. You must avoid the natural tendency to stay within your comfort zone.

The most common résumé weaknesses and examples of some possible cures follow. You should, of course, use only those strategic answers that apply to your situation, and you should always be truthful.

- *Academic underperformance.* You worked your way through school to support yourself/your family and were unable to devote as much time to study as your nonworking colleagues.
- *Employment Gaps.* You had to suspend your career to care for a sick relative, raise children, travel around the world, work in a political campaign, or relocate for family reasons.
- *Current unemployment:*
  - *If you were laid off:* Your practice area dried up due to the economy.
  - *If you were fired:* Make sure that what you tell the interviewer is consistent with what he or she will hear from your prior employer. You may want to discuss this with your prior employer and agree on what will be said.
  - *If you have been unemployed for a long period of time:* Your résumé will look much better if you fill in the gap with

something, such as a volunteer activity, a credential
enhancement, language study, etc.

- *History of job-hopping.* Reasons for leaving jobs might include
  that your firm went belly-up or that specific practice areas
  suffered a decline in business. Consider leaving very short-
  term jobs off your résumé. State your dates of employment
  in years only, not months and years. For example:

Before

Associate, *Barracuda & Serpent,* Redding, CA
December 2008–Present
Associate, *Serendipity & Chance,* Eureka, CA
December 2007–January 2008

After

Associate, *Barracuda & Serpent,* Redding, CA
2008–Present
Associate, *Serendipity & Chance,* Eureka, CA
2007–2008

- *Checkered work history/unremarkable career progression.* Get it out
  of the way fast in your cover letter or during your interview
  and counter with the substantive expertise and skill sets that
  you developed along the way.
- *Undistinguished job titles.* Talk to your prior employer(s) about
  what *else* you might label yourself with their approval, e.g.,
  paralegal → law clerk or legal researcher or legal analyst;
  alternative dispute resolution specialist → mediator or
  ADR manager.
- *Too much "seasoning."* If it is possible that an employer might
  consider you to be too old, include strenuous outside activities, such as sports, on your résumé. Point out how your
  seasoning would benefit an employer (e.g., through mentoring less experienced attorneys or through bringing your
  extensive knowledge to bear). Don't waste your time applying to places where age will probably be an issue. Don't omit
  dates of education on your résumé, a sure sign that you are

hiding your age; rather, put education at the end of the
document.

- **Lack of a life outside of work:** Employers today want to
  see that their employees have a life outside of work, if only
  because it indicates some business/client development
  potential. Join something; volunteer; cite some activities
  on your résumé.

DISTINGUISHING YOUR RÉSUMÉ FROM THE COMPETITION

Making An Immediate Impact

The attorney job market is almost always a buyer's market. Consequently,
legal employers are typically inundated with résumés. If you want your
résumé to attract positive attention, you need to know one very important
item and to do another.

You need to know how a typical employer reads a résumé. An employer's initial read is almost always a quick scan, lasting 20–30 seconds. In
that time, the employer cannot possibly see and absorb much more than
the top half of the first page of the résumé, if that much.

The purpose of this scan is to winnow the pile of résumés down to
those few survivors worth closer scrutiny in a moment of quiet contempla-
tion, say at home in the den with Mozart in the background and a drink
in hand. Because you want your résumé to be one of the survivors, you
need to say the most important things about yourself right up front.

Begin your résumé with a *profile* **or** *summary of qualifications* **immediately after your name, address, etc.** This section should be no more than
two or three sentences (not necessarily complete sentences) that quickly
grab attention and alert the employer to the most important information
about you, information that might otherwise be buried so far down that
the initial scan will never reveal it.

Here are two examples:

> *Successful securities and commercial litigator in state and federal
> courts. Handle securities arbitration before FINRA, NYSE, &
> AAA. Additional background in corporate transactions and
> financing. Law review. Yale BA; Harvard JD.*

Experienced editor, writer, and legal advisor at a 28,000-member nonprofit corporation. Highly skilled in drafting and editing legislation. Proficient in Spanish.

Liberating Your Experience

Another way for your résumé to make an impact is to liberate yourself from the traditional reverse chronological approach to describing your prior experience. Instead, list your *employment history* immediately after the *profile* (to disabuse the employer promptly of any suspicion that you might be trying to hide a questionable employment history by putting it at the end); then, under the heading *experience,* describe your background using boldface headings to highlight your different areas of expertise. This technique gives the quick-scanning employer an instant snapshot of what you bring to the table, and it has the collateral benefit of giving you the flexibility to move your expertise around for greatest impact in response to different job opportunities without the need to consider when you did something. This approach is also good for attorneys with a prior nonlegal background, where the combination of experience might be an advantage. For example:

EMPLOYMENT HISTORY

Senior Attorney—Federal Deposit Insurance Corporation, Dallas, TX (2004–Present)

Associate, French Kline & Smith, Dallas, TX (2001–2004)

Staff Attorney—PepsiCo Inc. (Frito-Lay Inc.), Dallas, TX (1999–2001)

Staff Attorney—Block Drug Company Inc., Jersey City, NJ (1996–1999)

Managing Pharmacist—Hampton Pharmacy Corporation, Brooklyn, NY (1990–1996)

LEGAL EXPERIENCE

Real Estate Sales/Commercial Lending

- Handled multimillion-dollar transactions for major developer.
- Successfully closed more than 30 project financings.

Real Estate Leasing/Dispute Prevention
- Developed standard-form commercial lease subsequently adopted nationwide.
- Negotiated numerous large-tenant, long-term office space leases.

Litigation/Litigation Management
- Managed all aspects of outside counsel/litigation management for two companies.
- Partnered with outside counsel to devise litigation strategies.

MANAGEMENT EXPERIENCE

Project Management
- Supervised all aspects of several major domestic and international development projects.

Personnel Management
- Hired, managed, and terminated attorneys, paralegals, and support staff for large law department.
- Supervised several cross-disciplinary teams involved in acquisitions and divestitures.

Elaborating In an Addendum

Congratulations. You survived the elimination round. But putting some distance between you and your remaining competition is not over.

A résumé addendum, labeled "Significant Highlights" or something similar, is your opportunity to escape the cryptic constraints of your résumé and show your prospective employer how your brain functions. I have yet to encounter an employer who thinks that a résumé addendum violates any unwritten rule about résumé length. An addendum is your chance to shine, to be a *storyteller,* and to set yourself apart from the competition. The following example is one that one of my clients used successfully to move from government to the private sector.

SIGNIFICANT HIGHLIGHTS
Executive Summary

This example describes my approach to handling major issues I faced as an FDIC attorney. It describes how I handled a difficult issue that arose in the context of resolving numerous failed banks.

Establishing a National Environmental Program

Problem

As a result of the 2008–2009 financial crisis, I was tasked with establishing and leading several major new programs during a time of rapidly changing law and business operations at the FDIC. The FDIC was faced with numerous bank failures and large volumes of assets—primarily real estate assets—from failed banks to aggregate, evaluate, and sell. We needed to resolve failed banks with minimum disruption to the banking system and to millions of depositors, while maximizing asset sale revenues in order to repay the Bank Insurance Fund.

I was assigned supervision of environmental legal services nationwide. I had to develop an environmental program and quickly provide essential legal services at the same time that the FDIC was hiring hundreds of new staff and establishing new field offices around the country.

Analysis

It became quickly apparent that environmental issues had to be factored into the disposition of tens of billions of dollars of real estate assets assumed by the FDIC from failed institutions and that this had to be accomplished rapidly. If not, the FDIC risked the likelihood of having to defend hundreds of lawsuits, as well as potential liability for hugely expensive environmental cleanups.

Proposed Solution

I devised a nationwide program that included a proposed budget, a manpower requirements estimate, a strategy for incorporating environmental considerations into real estate dispositions, a template for analyzing environmental risks associated with real estate assets, and an implementation timeline.

Implementation

My success in persuading the FDIC of the importance and urgency of environmental laws and issues—and in proposing a systemic program to manage them—is reflected by the fact that the FDIC established environmental policies and procedures nationwide and by the fact that the FDIC hired environmental attorneys and program specialists in all of its field offices.

Results

The program I designed worked so well that the FDIC has not been successfully challenged regarding any environmental matters it inherited in taking over failed banks. I received an FDIC Meritorious Service Award—the highest honor the agency confers—along with a substantial cash bonus.

Chapter 8

Winning the Interview

DISSECTING A JOB ADVERTISEMENT

A well-written job advertisement tells you a lot about how you need to respond to it. You maximize your opportunity if you take apart the job ad, breaking it down into its component parts and analyzing your qualifications vis-à-vis each component. The purpose of this exercise is twofold: (1) to help you determine if you should apply for the position and (2) to help target your application so that you will be responsive to the job ad and, thus, better able to compete for the position. Here is an example:

> **Position:** Corporate Associate, Smith & Jones LLP, Los Angeles, CA.
>
> Seeking an associate with 3–5 years of experience; strong corporate background including public M&A and private equity experience. Demonstrated experience in M&A

transactions, private equity investments, 1934 Act reporting and Sarbanes-Oxley essential. Candidates should have excellent writing, negotiating, and research abilities, top academic credentials, a willingness to assume responsibility, demonstrated leadership qualities, and interest in sharing those talents through mentoring and training junior lawyers. Large law firm experience preferred.

Required Qualifications	My Qualifications
1. 3–5 years of experience	1. 2.5 years of experience
2. Strong corporate background	2. Yes—assigned to Corporate practice group in current firm.
Public M&A transactions	Yes—participated in several transactions $1.5–$40+ million.
Private equity investments	Yes—part of team structuring one deal.
1934 Act reporting	Limited exposure
Sarbanes-Oxley	Yes—advise clients' Audit Committees on filing requirements.
3. Excellent writing ability	3. Two annual firm evaluations cited me for my writing ability.
4. Excellent negotiating ability	4. Participated in five successful transactions.
5. Excellent research ability	5. Called upon by partners to research issues in preparation of presentations to clients and professional audiences.
6. Top academic credentials	6. Top 25% of law school graduating class.

7. Willingness to assume responsibility	7. Seek out new and diverse assignments.
8. Demonstrated leadership qualities	8. Chair of PTA Safety Committee; organized fund-raiser for local charity.
9. Interest in mentoring and training junior lawyers	9. As 3L, trained 2Ls in Legal Aid Clinic in intake procedures and trial techniques.

Preferred or Desired Qualifications	My Qualifications
Large law firm experience	Currently work for a 30-attorney firm with a diverse, sophisticated corporate and litigation practice.

AVOIDING THE GATEKEEPERS

Overcoming the Electronic Submission Conundrum

Employers increasingly require that résumés and, of course, online job applications be submitted electronically. My clients find this method to be close to 100 percent nonproductive. The electronic documents go straight into a black hole, and that seems to be the end of it.

The best way to avoid your application entering the Witness Protection Program is to submit *two* applications: one that you dutifully submit following the electronic submission instructions and a second that you send directly—via email or regular mail—to the decision maker (or someone close to him or her if you cannot discover the identity of "The Decider"). Your transmittal email or letter that accompanies the second copy should state that you (1) submitted your application electronically per instructions but (2) wanted to make sure that The Decider had the opportunity to see your qualifications directly.

Getting Lost in the Ether ... and Getting Found

An antitrust attorney at a U.S. government agency's Office of Competition Policy wished to move into private practice and applied for an antitrust position with a large law firm. He submitted his résumé electronically, and it went into a database.

The firm's hiring partner asked her secretary to extract résumés that met the qualifications listed in the job ad. She used the term *antitrust* as one of her search criteria. The government lawyer's résumé did not make it beyond the database "event horizon."

Why not? Because the word *antitrust* was not in his résumé! The closest word to it was *competition*. A great candidate got lost in the ether, and a great opportunity was never realized.

If you know or believe that your résumé or application is going into a database for later extraction, make sure that every possible keyword that could be used to pull it out is in there.

PREVAILING AT THE INTERVIEW

Giving Interviewers What They Want

Following are the most important goals you need to achieve at a job interview:

1. *Establish why you are the best candidate.* You do this by getting across the *key points about yourself*—which means you have to decide beforehand what these are. They will not necessarily be exactly the same for each opportunity. However, you cannot go wrong if you prepare to speak about the following:

   Your "Tangibles"
   • Your ability to do the job
   • Your intelligence
   • Your verbal ability
   • Your listening skills
   • Your significant professional accomplishments
   • Your persuasive ability
   • Your other strengths
   • Your genuine interest in working there

Your "Intangibles"
- Your self-confidence
- Your "normalcy"
- Your leadership qualities
- Your problem-solving skills
- Your team-player attitude
- Your initiative
- Your organizational skills
- Your temperament
- Your energy level and enthusiasm
- Your "fit" (your alignment with the organization and the interviewer)
- Your "likeability"

2. *Determine the next step in the recruiting process.*

3. *Leave the interviewer(s) wanting more.*

Handling the Interview Question From Hell

You have to be prepared for this question. If you can answer it, the rest is easy:

Q: "Why do you want to leave your current job?"

or, if you are currently out of work:

Q: "Why did you leave your last job?"

Much less stigma is attached to job loss today than it was ten years ago, particularly during the Great Recession when you have a lot of company. Potential employers tend to be more sympathetic and receptive to candidates who have experienced a period of unemployment.

If you lost your job, the fact that you are being interviewed at all is a very positive sign. One of the most important variables in successfully addressing either a resignation or a termination is *your demeanor when responding to this question.* If you come across as nervous or discomfited, your response may not strike the interviewer as credible, which will likely mean the end of any chance of a job offer. Similarly, if you manifest anger about a job loss or a "doom-and-gloom" attitude, you can likely kiss the job goodbye. Negativity is very easy to spot. It comes across like nothing else. Nobody likes to contemplate being around a negative person. Remember, you are speaking to an *employer,* someone more likely to identify with your former *employer* than with you. Don't waste your time seeking understanding. Move on.

If you are voluntarily leaving—or have already left—your job, this question will not pose a problem. You can respond with the unvarnished truth, something on the order of

- *"I have gone as far as I can at _____ and am now seeking new challenges,"* or
- *"I advanced as far as I could at _____ and now wish to pursue an opportunity where I can grow with an organization."*

If your departure is—or was—compelled by economic circumstances beyond your control, your response might be any of the following:

- *"The company was acquired, and the acquiring company is eliminating our legal staff."*
- *"The company has decided to outsource a significant portion of its legal work, and several positions are being eliminated."*
- *"The firm lost a large client and has to cut back on personnel."*
- *"The firm lost its private equity practice group to another firm and was forced to eliminate positions."*
- *"The firm went out of business."*

If you were fired for cause, in retaliation for blowing the whistle on someone or on some questionable conduct, due to a personality conflict with a colleague or supervisor, or for some other reason (you may not even know the reason), the answer becomes more difficult. You have to decide how much you are going to reveal, mindful that the reasons behind your termination may be revealed in the event the prospective employer contacts your prior employer, and that the story the latter tells will definitely be from his or her slant.

The bottom line is: *Your response will be controlled by what your former employer would say about you* if contacted by your prospective employer. Thus, the most important piece of business you can conduct before, during, or even after a firing is to *determine what your employer would say about your reasons for leaving the organization.* Ideally, you and your former employer would agree to say something positive that will not kill your opportunity.

Law firms and many corporations are especially anxious about keeping a lid on employee terminations and often enter into written settlement/release agreements with their employees. If you find yourself in this position, make sure the documented agreement contains specific language covering this point. If it does not, then you must speak to your employer and attempt to get him or her to agree on what you will both say about your departure.

An important collateral point is that law firms are especially sensitive when it comes to admitting they have cut back on attorney personnel due to economic circumstances. A recent example (2008) is a Wall Street firm that abruptly terminated numerous attorneys and then insisted to the media that the economy had nothing to do with the job cuts. Sure.

A fallback position, in the event your former employer balks at saying anything other than that you were fired, is to attempt to persuade him or her to say that *it is the organization's policy not to provide references but only to confirm the term of employment.* This is increasingly common, particularly in the legal industry, because attorneys are so sensitive to potential litigation arising out of either a negative or even a (false) positive endorsement. Consequently, many legal employers have decided to say nothing other than "Yes, she or he worked here from _____ until _____."

Whatever your reason for leaving, craft a succinct statement of the circumstances of your departure, *practice* saying it aloud, and make it sound as *unpracticed* as you can. This will help organize your thoughts about a situation that is often very emotional and help you present yourself in the best possible light.

Leveling the Interview Playing Field

Virtually every job interview comes to a stage where the interviewer asks the candidate if he or she has any questions. The absolutely incorrect, toxic, job opportunity-killing response is something like: "No, I think you have adequately answered all of my questions."

There are two reasons for posing good questions at the interview. First, you may get answers to your most pressing questions about the organization and the position—part of your "due diligence" investigation of your prospective employer. Second, this is an opportunity to shine, to cement the interviewer's impression of you as a thoughtful, articulate individual with insight and foresight and to imprint yourself favorably in the mind of the employer before you leave the interview room.

The questions that follow are general in nature. Certain questions, of course, will not be germane to or appropriate for certain employers. These will be obvious from the context of the interview and the position for which you are applying. For example, you would not ask a government agency interviewer "How does the legal department contribute to increasing shareholder value?" while this would be a perfectly appropriate question if you are interviewing for an in-house position in a corporation.

Specific questions geared to the particular position, employer, or industry you will need to devise for yourself, depending upon the results of your pre-interview research.

Select around five good questions to ask. There is usually not enough time to ask more than that.

Note: Do not ask any questions that are answered by the job ad, or that you should know by virtue of any other information you received from the employer, including information the interviewer just gave you during the interview. For example, do not—as one of my clients did—ask the interviewer "Why is this position open?" if the job ad said "This is a new position."

"Why is this position open?" Why ask this question? To determine why there is a vacancy. The response may give you pause when considering a job offer (e.g., "The incumbent left after two months," or "We had to let her go because . . ."). Conversely, the reason given may give you cause for optimism about the position (e.g., "Ms. Doe was asked by the president to serve as deputy assistant secretary of energy. She felt that she could not pass up the opportunity.").

"Which practice areas are growing, and which are declining?" Why ask this question? One of my clients began her debriefing about her interview for an associate position with a major law firm by saying, "The interviewer told me that I was the only candidate who had ever asked this question." She was offered the position.

This question may do more for you than any other you can ask. It accomplishes five key objectives favorable to your candidacy:

1. It goes a long way toward equalizing the interview power equation, leveling the interview playing field and helping to make you feel more comfortable.
2. It demonstrates your keen business sense and foresight.
3. It sets a powerful tone for the rest of the interview.
4. It answers a very important question that should be foremost in your mind.
5. It "imprints" you on the interviewer, making you memorable once you depart and during the hiring decision process.

"How does the legal department contribute to increasing shareholder value?" Why ask this question? This great question for corporate employers shows that you are bottom-line business oriented and understand, in a sophisticated way, the legal department's role. Like the previous question, it is rarely posed to interviewers and distinguishes you from other candidates.

"What do you look for in a prospective employee?" Why ask this question? The response will give you an indication of the qualities and traits you will want to emphasize before the interview concludes. If the interviewer says, for example, that he or she is seeking someone with strong organizational skills, you can make sure that you inject examples of how you manifest such skills.

"What are the likely challenges and difficulties that you foresee I might have to confront?" Why ask this question? The answers may alert you to issues you may need to consider when determining whether or not to accept an offer. If the interviewer tells you that everyone on the staff has to pitch in and do fundraising when grants and donations to the nonprofit decline, you may hesitate to take the position, having reasonably concluded that something that might be distasteful to you actually occurs from time to time and could threaten your job security.

"What is a typical day like for someone in this position?" Why ask this question? "Day in the Life" stories show the type of matters you'll work on and the amount of responsibility you'll get. Listen for descriptions of colleague, client, and staff interactions as well. If the response is something like: "There is no such thing as a typical day," follow up by asking what will be on the interviewer's to do list today. If the further response is: "I am interviewing candidates all day today," ask what will be on his or her desk when he or she returns to a normal schedule.

"How is performance evaluated?" Why ask this question? You need to know how you are performing as soon as possible in advance of your scheduled review. Early notice will enable you to fix any problems and avoid surprises. You also need to know, in advance of accepting a position, that your employer both communicates expectations and provides formal evaluations on a regular basis.

"For what activities do you engage outside counsel?" Why ask this question? If you contemplate going to work for a corporation, you need to know which matters are handled in-house and which are farmed out so that you can recognize when to call in outside counsel.

"Please describe your training program." Why ask this question? Formal training programs are best. They include specific, measurable goals and assessments that can help you achieve them. Anything less might arrest your professional development and make career advancement dicier.

"Do you have (and if so, would you please describe) a mentoring program?" Why ask this question? This is a follow-up question to the preceding question. A good mentor can be an invaluable part of the learning process. What is the firm's approach to mentoring? The more formal and structured the mentoring program, the better.

"What is the profile of a successful aspirant for promotion?" Why ask this question? The response will enable you to model yourself after the ideal candidate for promotion.

"What are the short- and long-term goals of the organization?" Why ask this question? Every business should have a plan for growth that its employees understand and buy into.

"What is your staff turnover?" Why ask this question? Naturally, you want to work for an organization that has low staff turnover, an indicator of stability and job satisfaction. *Caveat:* In certain organizations and practice areas, low staff turnover may be a negative. For example, if you go to work for an equine law boutique firm, you may find that there are not many positions available outside of this narrow practice area and highly concentrated industry.

"Who are your organization's internal clients?" Why ask this question? If the response is preceded by a lengthy pause, then you are probably hearing that the legal office does not think of itself as having internal clients (good legal offices *do* think in those terms). Do not, of course, pose this question to a law firm interviewer, unless you are seeking a support position, such as general counsel (a growing number of law firms now have them), professional development, knowledge management, marketing, etc.

"What best demonstrates the organization's strengths?" Why ask this question? Listen closely for information about organizational values, culture, and priorities, in addition to information about specific matters handled by the firm. If the response includes information from outside the interviewer's own practice milieu, that will speak volumes about interrelationships, firm cohesiveness, cross-selling, etc.

Follow up: Ask more about what the organization does best (and worst) to learn where your talents might contribute the most and how they might be valued. Will you be able to work on interesting cases?

"Did you achieve your office goals during the past fiscal year?" Why ask this question? Both the content and the tone of this response can be revealing. Do not settle for a simple "Yes, we did," answer. Probe enough so that you pierce the organizational veil and get some details.

"Can you give me an example of how your office has had to adapt to unanticipated change?" Why ask this question? The response will give you an insight into the organization's agility and ability to react to changing events and circumstances.

"How would you describe the organization's personality?" Why ask this question? The response can provide insight into whether your personality and the organization's align, and it goes toward answering one of your most important unstated questions: "Will I be comfortable here?"

If you cannot get good answers to your key questions, consider posing those questions to other attorneys or executives in the employer's organization. Also consider running any responses you receive by junior-level employees for confirmation and/or a different perspective.

Telephone Interview Tips

Telephone interviews are becoming more popular with employers, primarily as a means to prescreen job applicants. In rare cases, the telephone interview is the only interview.

Telephone interviews have a different feel than in-person interviews and have to be approached from a different vantage point. In many ways, it is easier to "blow" a telephone interview than the face-to-face variety.

Here are a few simple suggestions for handling a telephone interview, which will make the experience much more productive for both you and your prospective employer.

Visualize a face-to-face interview. Telephone interviewees tend to come off sounding unenthusiastic. Because neither party can see or react to the other party's nonverbal cues or body language, you consciously have to *sound interested and enthusiastic* (without going over the top) on the phone. This might be particularly daunting if you naturally speak in a monotone.

Don't ramble. It is easy to fall into this trap because you cannot see and interpret the visual cut-off signals from the interviewer. The best way to ensure that you do not wander into a monologue is to *take off your watch and keep it in front of you* so that you can see how long you have been talking. Keep your responses short and crisp—90 seconds max.

Have your résumé in front of you. If questions arise regarding your work history, your résumé should be able to answer most of them. Be careful not to read the interviewer your résumé verbatim. If your résumé does not outline, step by step, what you do at work, prepare a list of such steps, in sequence, so that you can paint a strong visual image for the interviewer. Moreover, if you work in an esoteric area not well understood or easily grasped by outsiders, put your activities into a framework and language that they will understand.

Have your cover letter in front of you. The interviewer may ask you questions generated by your cover letter. Since job hunting usually means sending out multiple applications, make sure you have handy a copy of the specific cover letter that you sent the employer.

Have the job ad in front of you. This will enable you to emphasize your background and capabilities that conform to what the employer specified in the job ad. In addition, it can serve as the stimulus for good questions you can pose to the interviewer.

Prepare to deal with the employer's relocation concerns. Many telephone interviews arise, in part, because good candidates reside out of the employer's geographic area. Be prepared to indicate (1) your intention to move to the employer's location, (2) any ties you might have to that location, (3) the steps you have taken or will take to meet any local bar requirements, (4) your willingness to travel to the employer for a face-to-face interview, and (5) your acknowledgment that you will be responsible for interview travel expenses and relocation costs (provided you have determined beforehand that the employer does not usually cover those costs).

REFERENCE MANAGEMENT THAT MAKES A DIFFERENCE

Sometimes prospective employers request a list of references at the time you submit your résumé and other application materials. Sometimes you will provide your references only after you have had an interview. Either way, a good, compelling reference list should contain the following elements: (1) name, title, address, and phone number of your reference; (2) a précis of your relationship to the reference (i.e., why this person is your professional reference); (3) ideally, something that you did or accomplished vis-à-vis the reference that shows you in a positive light; and (4) how and when it is appropriate to contact your reference.

This kind of reference list can give your candidacy a big boost because it underscores your thoroughness and your organizational skills, as well as your superb anticipation of just what an employer needs to know to check your references. In addition, if you are able to include something that you did vis-à-vis the reference, you also gain an opportunity to have some positive control over the conference between the employer and your reference. For example:

Professor Cant Do Teach

Cheshire YMCA Night School of Law
141 Volunteer Fire Lane
Cheshire, NY 14321
(C): (585) 555-5789

Professor Teach was my thesis advisor for my honors paper entitled: "Peggy Lee *v.* Brenda Lee: Fever? ... I'm Sorry!" *21 Faded Diva Law Journal* 268 (2008).

Contact Information: Professor Teach can be contacted between 10:00 AM and 2:00 PM at the listed phone number.

Epilogue

MY INTENTION IN WRITING the *Lawyer's Guide to Finding Success in Any Job Market* is to expand your horizons when it comes to the many excellent legal career options that provide both a bright future and considerable staying power, regardless of the economic outlook. This book provides you with the best tried-and-true advice that has helped many of my most successful legal career transition counseling clients achieve their career goals and realize job security, success, and satisfaction.

In addition, my clients virtually always report back that this kind of legal career advice boosted their self-confidence and energized their job searches and career transitions. It is my hope that the *Lawyer's Guide to Finding Success in Any Job Market* will do the same for you.

The practice areas identified in this book are not static. They are incredibly dynamic, and that dynamism means that there will likely be even more opportunties for lawyers in these practice areas as time goes on. Financial regulatory reform, healthcare reform, the pursuit of energy independence, vigorous new education compliance, re-energized food and drug regulation and enforcement, and the relentless advance of nontraditional family arrangements are just a few of the rapidly moving areas of legal and societal concern that are constantly generating new jobs, new careers, and new opportunities.

The *Lawyer's Guide to Finding Success in Any Job Market* provides you with a platform. It is now up to you to step up and pursue these opportunities, keep up with the trends that might indicate new or changing opportunities, and connect the dots to realize them.

Index